P9-CBY-098

ENCOUNTERING THE WEST

Professor Lamin Sanneh was educated with chiefs' sons in the Gambia and subsequently went to the United States on a U.S. government scholarship to read history. After graduating he spent several years studying classical Arabic and Islam, and working with the churches in Africa and with international organizations concerned with Christian–Muslim relations. He was a professor at Harvard University for eight years before moving to Yale University in 1989 as the D. Willis James Professor of Missions and World Christianity and concurrently as Professor of History at Yale College. He is the Chairman of Yale's Council on African Studies. He is an editor-at-large of the ecumenical weekly, *The Christian Century*, and serves on the editorial board of several academic journals. He is the author of over a hundred articles on religious and historical subjects, and of several books, including *West African Christianity: The Religious Impact* (1983) and *Translating the Message: The Missionary Impact on Culture*, now in its fourth printing. He was made Commandeur de l'Ordre National du Lion, Senegal's highest national honour.

He and his wife, a native of South Africa, are the parents of two musical children.

'An interpretation of Christian history full of profundity and insight. It will shatter many commonplace assumptions about the Christian encounter with Africa; and it points tellingly from the experience of that encounter to some often neglected characteristics of the Christian faith itself.' ANDREW F. WALLS
Director, Centre for the Study of Christianity in the Non-Western World, University of Edinburgh

'It is rare that a work can change one's mind on a major issue. This fine and persuasive work does exactly that.' DAVID TRACY
Distinguished Service Professor, University of Chicago

Also available in
the World Christian Theology Series

Christian Systematic Theology
in a World Context
Ninian Smart and Steven Konstantine

Series Editor: Revd Dr Frank Whaling

Encountering The West

Christianity and the Global Cultural Process: The African Dimension

LAMIN SANNEH

Maryknoll, New York 10545

The Catholic Foreign Mission Society of America (Maryknoll) recruits and trains people for overseas missionary service. Through Orbis Books, Maryknoll aims to foster the international dialogue that is essential to mission. The books published, however, reflect the opinions of their authors and are not meant to represent the official position of the society.

Published in the USA and Canada
by Orbis Books
Maryknoll, New York 10545

First published in Great Britain in 1993 by Marshall Pickering

Printed and bound in Great Britain by Hartnolls Limited, Bodmin, Cornwall

---

ORBIS/ISBN 0–88344–929–3 Cloth
ORBIS/ISBN 0–88344–934–X Paper

Cataloging-in-Publication-Data for this book
is available from the Library of Congress.

The Problem Defined:

'The medieval Christian, taught by the Bible, saw as the end to which all history moves, the second coming of Christ, the judgment of living and dead, and the holy city in which all that is pure and true in the public and private life of nations is gathered up in eternal perfection. This vision of the end is, of course, part and parcel of the teleological view of creation and history, which has the will and purpose of God at its centre. The eighteenth century transferred the holy city from another world to this . . . The eighteenth century witnessed the birth of the doctrine of progress, a doctrine that was to rule – with fateful consequences –well into the twentieth century . . . we shall not be wrong, I think, if we take the abandonment of teleology as the key to the understanding of nature for our primary clue to understanding the whole of the vast changes in the human situation . . . this is what underlies that decisive feature of our culture that can be described both as the division of human life into public and private, and as the separation of fact and value.'
Lesslie Newbigin, *Foolishness to the Greeks*, 28, 34.

Contents

Acknowledgements

This book consists of essays written on the general theme of religion and culture from the comparative perspectives of Africa and the West, and of the Muslim world and the Christian Church. All the essays hang on the idea of religion both as compatible with culture and as a critique of cultural idolatry, with the worldwide Christian expansion providing a fresh perspective on the course and development of Christianity in history.

A work of this nature and scope must necessarily intrude on the time and expertise of many people, as this has, and, consequently, my indebtedness to all these is, in the venerable phrase, self-evident. A number of such obvious individuals I have indicated in the sources and footnotes, but I must bring forward the names of scholars from whose work and personal interest I have profited immensely. These include my friends and former colleagues at Harvard Divinity School: John Carman, Harvey Cox, Diana Eck, Paul Hanson, William Hutchison, Gordon Kaufman, Jon Levenson, Wilfred Smith, now retired, and the former Dean, George Rupp; my colleagues at Yale: George Lindbeck, Nicholas Wolterstorff, Tom Ogletree, John Middleton, Bill Foltz and David Apter. In the same vein I wish to mention Max Stackhouse, Patrick Ryan, John Hick, Andrew Walls, David Dalby, Adrian Hastings, Richard Gray, John Hargreaves, Humphrey Fisher, Meg Guider, John Mbiti, Mercy Oduyoye, John Taylor, Lewis Rambo and Bill Burrows. Special commendation needs to go to Kathy Palen, my student assistant at Yale Divinity School, for help with the bibliography. I remember with deep appreciation the kindness and friendship of Benno Schmidt, Jr, who as President of Yale welcomed me at Yale and generously supported my professional work, of which this is one tangible result.

I am pleased to acknowledge the help of the Pew Charitable Trusts through the Evangelical Scholarship Initiative for a grant that allowed me to take time off to produce this work as part of a larger piece on conversion in Africa. Portions of this material I prepared and delivered as the Currie Lectures at the Austin Presbyterian Theological Seminary, and I am grateful to the president, Jack Stotts, and his colleagues for the invitation. I am also grateful to Kirkley Sands of the Templeton Theological Seminary, Nassau, Bahamas, for the gracious invitation to deliver the lectures from which parts of this book are drawn, and to the Templeton Foundation for sponsoring the visit.

David Barrett's pioneering statistical work has been crucial for the kind of analysis and interpretation I have done in several parts of this book, and I record my thanks to him, but he and all the others bear no responsibility for errors, defects, judgments, obscurities and idiosyncrasies that may or do remain in the book.

As usual my family deserves recognizing for putting up with the absent-mindedness, unpredictability, thoughtlessness, self-absorption, absenteeism and other hazards and pitfalls of authorship, and for their indulging me in a habit in which pecuniary gain, if it ever existed, has long ceased to be a convincing or adequate justification for neglect.

Lesslie Newbigin's shadow falls over much of the ground covered in this book, and in numerous places he is also explicitly quoted in support of substantial views and ideas I have come to hold myself. This was not obvious at first, since Newbigin and I begin our inquiries from rather different positions, he as a leading figure in the modern ecumenical movement, and I as a professional academic with interests in comparative religion. But there it is. We join at the point where cultural secularism claims an Enlightenment immunity and pretends to the prerogatives of absolute truth, suspending faith of the religious kind only to replace it with faith of the henotheist variety. However, a bowdlerized faith may be telltale evidence of the hankering of the religiously impaired, and should, in consequence, elicit hunger for its healthy original. When Newbigin has spoken to this hunger, I find myself in substantial agreement with him.

I am also grateful to valued colleagues and friends in the Gospel and Culture movement in Britain and North America whose companionship has afforded a uniquely rich and congenial environment for the sort of critical reflection that has shaped this book and spurred its development. I remember with gratitude the life and work of Tom Beetham, an architect of the new Africa, and among its most sensitive and consistent interpreters to the West. His death in London in December 1992, while on his way from an ecumenical meeting is appropriately characteristic of the modern pluralist cause he had served so long and so generously. It is hard, with his example, to think how the future could compare or compete with the past, all the more reason for safeguarding and transmitting the heritage.

A confession: I am aware that religious and cultural pluralism is in many places under tremendous strain, if not under open attack and in retreat. Lebanon, where I was a student in the late 1960s, comes readily to mind. Similar forces have been at work in Northern Ireland, India, the Sudan, Nigeria, the countries of the former Eastern Europe, not to say anything of the strife-torn cities and the restive college campuses of the United States. What purchase, then, for pluralism?

Clearly, whatever the solutions to current conflicts, in so far as they impinge on culture, and whatever the legacy of mistrust, it is unlikely that uniformity and conformity will work, so that some version of humanity's pluralist heritage will have to be the context for any meaningful and lasting peace and goodwill. Responsibility for such a new world order rests in large measure on the heritage that the Church represents as a force in the rise of the West, and whose cumulative wisdom is today critical both as a deterrent to the purveyors of violence and intolerance and as an incentive to peacemakers and community builders. It is not futile, therefore, to persevere with a religious account of the righteousness, justice and fulfilment after which we all hunger as human beings without regard to race, colour, class, creed or national origin.

Introduction

Setting the Context

The subject of this book is the encounter of Africans and others with the modern West, in particular the West as the bearer simultaneously of religion and an intellectual tradition critical of religion.[1] The deeper logical inconsistency between the claim that culture is independent of Christianity on the one hand, and, on the other, that the religion is reducible to its cultural forms, is connected to an unexamined assumption about the intrinsic innocence of indigenous cultures whose primitive purity has been contaminated by imperialist missions. With indigenous societies culture contact is viewed as detrimental, while in the West such contact is proof of religion as a cultural flag of convenience. In either case Christianity is brought within range of a double-barrelled attack: its extension in mission is a cultural phenomenon, while in its Western origins the religion is an idealized myth which evaporates once it is demythologized.

We need to transcend this approach to the subject in order to deal with the phenomenon of world Christianity and with the extraordinary movements of cultural renewal taking place under its shadow. It would not be possible or desirable in these circumstances to uncouple religion from culture. On the contrary, Christianity has entered a renewed destiny with its affirmation of cultural particularity, and vice versa. Thus, in so far as modern Africans have become Christian, they have done so

1. *The Christian Century* reported that the Library of Congress and the Book-of-the-Month Club found in a survey they conducted that the two most influential books in people's lives were the Bible and, what had been until then been completely unknown to me, Ayn Rand's *Atlas Shrugged*, 'a novel that – like most of her writings – glorifies extreme individualism, scorns altruism, and promotes what Rand calls "rational self-interest".' *Christian Century*, January 29, 1992, p. 85. The juxtaposition of the two books shows how squint-eyed society is.

with a Christianity mediated to them by the West, but in so far as Christianity has successfully penetrated African societies, this is largely because it has been assimilated into the local idiom, without, however, the local idiom being unaffected or Christianity itself being immune to the intellectual critique of the Western tradition. In the event, the central question for us is how the religion coalesced with local cultures to become the vehicle of indigenous idioms and aesthetic forms, and how those idioms and forms were transformed. Western writers have tended to polarize the issue between a Christianity that is opposed to culture and a Christianity that is culturally determined, a misconceived dialectic that pursues religion and culture into non-Western societies, and with it a self-perpetuating controversy. One such controversy is that converts have ipso facto capitulated to Western cultural imperialism, and that their sins have been visited on their children who are condemned to an ambiguous identity, being born, as it were, with a foreign foot in their native mouth. Converts may, for that reason, be considered cultural orphans and traitors at the same time.

This view of the matter postulates violence and alienation as the only forms culture contact can take, with domination and submission the only language Christianity knows, or is capable of knowing, as the price of its European captivity. It is not surprising that critics propose as remedy dropping Christianity and promoting in its place local cultures, or those elements in cultures that would resist Christianization.

I shall attempt to resolve this dichotomy between religion and culture, not by repeating various and different forms of standard arguments, but by confronting the view that in Africa, Christianity could not be shaken out of its Western cultural forms. In this respect I shall pursue the historical roots of the religion-versus-culture controversy in Western intellectual thought and consider whether and how the mother tongue projects of Scriptural translation encouraged local people to embrace the new religion while also embracing their own cultures. It seems to be the case that the assurances that converts received from mother tongue literacy introduced a fundamental qualification into the schemes of Western cultural and intellectual domination and the forced sequestration of local populations. That some missionaries wanted to dismantle the older indigenous cultural dispensation, to subvert the native genius, is without question, but employing mother tongues in their Scriptural translation is a tacit surrender to indigenous primacy, and complicates the arguments of Western cultural superiority. Had it wanted to, the West could have demonstrated its undisputed superiority over African culture, and chosen to do so on any number of fronts, including its possession of an infallible intellectual canon, in, say, Plato, Virgil, Michelangelo, Galileo, Aquinas, Cervantes, Shakespeare, Milton, Goethe, Descartes and Kant, and required Africans to learn these masters in the original. Indeed, in those instances where the French, the Portuguese and the Spanish followed a policy of 'assimilation', Africans, or an amenable selection of them, were required to conform to such a cultural template. Even as late as 1960, a French missionary in Africa was claiming for European culture a unique, normative status, saying it possessed the 'high degree of perfection which the entire world recognizes'.[2]

However, for many other missionaries the Bible was the greatest authority, and they believed that it should for that reason become the living truth for the people to whom they brought the message. So they set out to translate it into the mother tongue. In doing so missionaries gave local people a standard by which to question claims of Western cultural superiority, and it does not matter whether that was the result of a conscious decision by the missionaries or the perception of Africans as receivers and adapters. Whatever linguistic distortions, compromises, egregious inventions and other forms of invasive interference missionaries may have introduced, the shift into the vernacular paradigm in the long run, if not immediately, would excite local ambition and fuel national feeling. In this respect the Scriptures are unlike Plato or Milton, for they are preserved in a community of memory and observance, so that in their translated form they continue to speak authoritatively to transmitter and recipient alike. It is not simply what the translator or, for that matter, what the recipient says that makes the Bible what it is, but what both of them hear – and do not hear – in the Bible that gives the book its

2. Cited in Richard Gray, *Black Christians and White Missionaries*, New Haven: Yale University Press, 1990, 62.

special, peculiar power and status. It would do violence to everything involved in possessing and transmitting the Scriptures to treat them as a random gallery of texts that missionaries could plunder for their own illegitimate purposes, let alone see them as a vehicle of cultural malice and racial cynicism. In some examples we shall be considering, missionaries were convinced that vernacular translation would minimize, even prevent, continued Western cultural and political domination and the subverting of other peoples. Even those missionaries who held to a Book-centred view of religion, their making the Bible available in the mother tongue upgrades the language and the people whose it is. Such vernacular sanctioning sometimes runs foul of colonial authorities, as happened, for example, in many parts of French and Portuguese Africa, where the relevant colonial power acted to disenfranchise the mother tongue. Even today a stigma continues to attach to the vernacular in those societies where it was suppressed, and it seems odd to claim, as some have, that adoption and suppression are two sides of the same coin.

There is, I shall argue, a vital compatibility between mother tongue cultures and Christianity, however limited or distorted may have been missionary calculations of that compatibility. I have no intention of doing a whitewash of missionaries. On the contrary, almost every educated person is aware of the dark side of the record, so that no one, however partisan, can be oblivious to what went wrong, or is believed to have gone wrong, with the whole enterprise. For what it is worth, there are probably vastly many more people who believe in the worst motives of missions than those who think missions did no wrong, and it is probably accurate to say that most people today belong to one or other of those two categories: missions as cultural imperialism, or missions as God's favourite design. Yet what is really historically interesting about missions has little to do with either of those opposing positions, but rather with the unintentional and unpremeditated consequences of practice and conduct. The linguistic projects of mother tongue development belong preeminently to this unrehearsed side of missionary history, and exploring them should reveal meaningful vistas into indigenous reserves of culture and religion. We will not get to that level if we restrict our view to the handy rhetoric of caricature or hagiography.

Since my intention is to go beyond the academic and the popular status quo, I have given less weight even to missionary preaching and other forms of missionary self-representation than to the internal forces thus activated as part and parcel of promoting mother tongue literacy. By their root conviction that the gospel is transmissible in the mother tongue, I suggest, missionaries opened the way for the local idiom to gain the ascendancy over assertions of foreign superiority. To tell the story of Christianity under those circumstances demands that we become attuned to the internal religious dynamics of cross-cultural mission. It would involve also our downplaying the Western metropolitan emphasis and keeping close counsel with the people on the ground.

A story originating in a different part of the world tells how missionaries were preceded in the Pacific Islands by European sailors who sought to take advantage of the inhabitants' keen desire for contact, especially trade, with the West. The sailors exploited this desire. They pretended to perform a ritual of Christian baptism, promising the people the new religion, or its pirated form, would bring prosperity with it, and extorted property from the people for providing healing and prayers. The sailors were scarcely literate, singing sea shanties as hymns and clutching any book as the Bible. The example spread to numerous islands where the pretence threatened to be taken for real, to the alarm of missionaries who came later. One of these missionaries, John Williams, scandalized by the threat of Christianity turning into a cargo cult, asked one of the sailors whether the people understood him. The sailor replied frankly, 'No, but they says they knows it does 'em good.'[3] Williams's question about the people understanding what was told to them had a double edge, on the one hand, in exposing the fraud that was being committed against the people, and on the other, in identifying the form in which Christianity would reach the people. A gap as wide as the

3. John Williams, *A Narrative of Missionary Enterprises in the South Sea Islands*, New York: D. Appleton & Co, 1838, 383. Williams added with respect to the sailors: 'I remonstrated with them upon the fearful wickedness of their conduct; and they promised that they would not again pursue such a course.' Stevenson also says the islanders were taken advantage of by colonial officials for whom he had little liking. *Vailima Letters*, 78f, 90.

Pacific separates Williams's mission from the exploitative schemes of the sailors whose devious methods kept the 'natives' down. What makes one group of Westerners opt for one approach rather than another rests on the nature of religious commitment which requires, among other things, that people should understand in their own tongue. The early missionaries in the Pacific Islands, as in Africa, fought hard to shield local people from traders who came determined to strike rich by hook or by crook, and one weapon such missionaries introduced was mother tongue literacy and all that goes with it.[4] Robert Louis Stevenson, who settled in Samoa, thought the missionary translations of both the Bible and indigenous literature constituted a cultural resource of unequalled merit. Here is his testimony:

> Well, after this excursion into tongues that have never been alive – though I assure you we have one capital book in the language, a book of fables by an old missionary of the unpromising name of Pratt, which is simply the best and the most literary version of the fables known to me. I suppose I should except La Fontaine, but L.F. takes a long time; these are brief as the books of our childhood, full of wit and literary colour; and O, Colvin, what a tongue it would be to write, if one only knew it . . . Its curse in common use is an incredible left-handed wordiness, but in the hands of a man like Pratt it is succinct as Latin,

4. G. S. Parsonson has spoken about the 'literate revolution' in the Pacific Islands in terms of Christian literacy as a cultural precursor. Independent of Christianity, the islanders had developed a taste for literacy, and when literacy came along with Christianity, they embraced both, though religion mattered less. Thus did Parsonson view Christianity as a cultural anticlimax, making little distinction between literacy in English and that in the vernacular. By contrast, a significant number of missionaries made that crucial distinction. Thus did Hiram Bingham (1789–1869), a missionary to Hawaii, incline against introducing English literacy in spite of the great demand for it. About two years after arriving in the islands, Bingham in 1822 spoke about his opposition to teaching the young people English, 'a language unintelligible to their parents; and the mass of the community around them . . . and a perseverance in such an attempt would have given over the adult and aged population to incurable ignorance and degradation.' Cited in Parsonson, 'The Literate Revolution in Polynesia', *Journal of Pacific History*, vol. 2, 1967, 39–57, 52.

> compact of long rolling polysyllables and little and often pithy particles, and for beauty of sound a dream.[5]

Missionaries were not altogether unaware of the novelty and wider significance of the linguistic activities that commanded so much of their thought, time, talents and resources, and one of them, Richard H. Dana, Jr, in a piece in the *New York Tribune* in 1860, reflected as follows:

> It is no small thing to say of the Missionaries of the American Board, that in less than forty years they have taught this whole people to read and write, to cipher and to sew. They have given them an alphabet, grammar, and dictionary; preserved their language from extinction; given it a literature, and translated into it the Bible and works of devotion, science and entertainment, etc., etc.[6]

A relevant issue about the mother tongue projects of mission is how generalized abstractions about culture and language gave way to details of specificity and concrete experience. The 'one' God of missionary doctrine turns out to have 'many' names and symbols of local provenance. Culture in this scheme was not a dangling modifier but the subject of inalienable possession for religion. More than just cannon fodder for general rational principles and categories, culture in hitherto illiterate societies is the very stuff in which we encounter thought 'immersed in matter and clothed in innumerable circumstances'. In promoting mother tongue translations, then, missionaries and their converts moved beyond universal abstractions in which cultures are nothing but mimetic contrivances, and beyond the reductionism which makes cultural symbols identical in a unilinear sense with the conceptions we formulate for them.[7] Instead vernacular translation

5. Robert Louis Stevenson, *The Works of Robert Louis Stevenson: The Vailima Letters*, Edinburgh: Longmans, Green & Co., 1897, p. 46. For similar comments of Stevenson on the Bible, see H. J. Moors, *With Stevenson in Samoa*, London, N.D., 69.

6. The *New York Tribune*, June 5, 1860. Cited in *Missionary Album: Portraits and Biographical Sketches of the American Protestant Missionaries to the Hawaiian Islands*, Honolulu: Hawaiian Mission Children's Society, Sequicentennial Edition, 1969, 17.

7. John Stuart Mill (1806–1873) argues that 'the grand mistake that has been the bane of philosophy from its very beginning to this day: the persuasion, that every thought in the mind, must be a copy of some archetype out of the mind;

assumed the truth of contingency, an assumption that allowed people to regard thought not as a by-product of natural contingency, nor, by the same token, as an idealized principle as *Allmacht der Gedanken*, thought as almighty. Thus did missionaries discard the premise of philosophical idealism and its contending corollary of scientific positivism without necessarily knowing they were doing so.

The Rationale

In the rise of modern consciousness in the West, especially since the European Reformation, culture has assumed an important place in intellectual circles, so much so that when the West extended its domination over much of the world it has been assumed that Western culture and customs had accompanied the political and religious expansion. Notions of Western cultural superiority found a congenial niche in the Christian missionary enterprise where spiritual values were assumed to enshrine concrete Western cultural forms, so that the heathen who took the religious bait would in fact be taking it from the cultural hook. Indeed, in numerous cases, culture and religion, as sanitation and salvation, were for many missionaries one and the same thing. There was no better harbinger of the new creation than silent plumbing, no brighter hope than electricity and no higher symbol of a redeemed humanity than the modern biomedical system. It was easy for cultural sensibility to assume religious significance, and vice versa, contrary to what cultural critics assumed about the separability of culture and religion. Small wonder, then, that in the field many missionaries felt as scandalized when their cultural sensibilities were offended as they did with any religious offence. By the same token, when the same missionaries would come upon evidence of genuine religious knowledge among non-Western peoples, they would flag it as worthless, or else as fraudulent, continuing to make cultural

---

that whenever two or more ideas are united by association in our thoughts, the correspondent sensations or objects must be united in nature.' J. S. Mill, *Essays on Philosophy and the Classics*, p. 227n. However, Mill's philosophical interest, being rooted in the Enlightenment, leads him away from epistemological realism to the efficacy of universal theories. See pp. 288ff, 367.

differences the litmus test. In that form, missionaries might have conformed to the type described by Thomas Hardy of setting out to graft technical (cultural) belief onto actual (religious) scepticism.[8]

All this makes it understandable, though not entirely justified, that missionaries should be accused of cultural insensitivity, and of being unable or unwilling to separate the religion of the Bible from its Western cultural encapsulation. This cultural failure of the missionary was used by the critics to demonstrate another kind of failure, namely, the allegedly hypocritical religious motives of mission which persisted under a cultural guise. As a consequence, the moral ideals of missionaries were construed as cultural bad faith, and their humanitarian projects condemned as a machinery of alienation and domination. Religion and culture were, according to this understanding, illicit bedfellows, with cultural triumphalism parading under religious cover. Given the long history of tension and distrust between religious believers and cultural champions, the history of Christian mission in the context of Western colonialism provided a bonanza for critics, with bulky and inept missionary apologetics often furnishing conclusive proof from the horse's mouth, so to speak. It relieved critics of the need for solid and specific groundwork and instead gave them so-called hard historical evidence with which to bring down the enterprise. It is as such that a whole academic industry was able to thrive from the use of missionary sources, an irony whereby we establish our scholarly bona fides by impugning the motives of missionaries. Thus anthropologists, philosophers, historians and others began to question whether normative claims for Western culture, and the corollary of moral condemnation of non-Western cultures, are valid by any objective criteria, and to insist on the plurality of relative cultural traditions in the interests of intercultural equality, harmony, tolerance and mutual respect. The assumption in this line of reasoning is that missionaries rejected equality with other cultures and belittled them as a prerequisite for introducing Christianity. I would not contend with this charge except to say that in the linguistic field missionary intentions were peripheral to the on-site factors of mother tongue interest and

8. Thomas Hardy, *Tess of the D'Urbervilles*, London: Tiger Books International, 1958, 126.

understanding. The contention of critics that Christianity and Western culture are inseparable turns out to have the positive analogue in the mission field of mother tongues as the natural habitat of the Gospel. Religion and culture here are complementary.

Be that as it may, in the three formative stages of culture consciousness in the West, namely, the Enlightenment, the Romantic and the Modern, the cultural project was often conceived as an alternative to religion, and the programme of ethical renewal so offered was perceived as superseding religious injunctions. Because relevant Western writers have pushed this notion of culture as implicit religion, and have subordinated the ethical domain to existential affirmation and individual fulfilment, I have had to bring the cultural theme forward into the centre of my own examination of the subject. I felt I could approach the subject in one of two ways: either to allow myself to be bound by nationalist scruples and launch a tirade against all the obscurantist and repressive forces that hinder the mature flowering of the culture of oppressed peoples, and in so doing target religion as chief offender, or, conversely, to view religion in its vernacular idiom as the ally of weak, oppressed cultures. In that case we would have to press the view of the worth of cultures in terms of that concrete religious possibility, suggesting that theology has a great deal to do with culture consciousness, that cultural descriptions are driven not just by the raw facts of perception and enumeration but by normative principles of qualitative evaluation and insight, and that, furthermore, such qualitative insights have been in our case grounded in the specific mother tongue projects of mission.[9]

This book is, in addition, something of a personal intellectual testament, one individual who was educated on four continents and who carries within him some of the formative strands of several distinct cultural traditions: the African, the Islamic, the Christian and the modern West. Often these four strands are unalterably intertwined, and when one strand is drawn out to

9. In his *Religious System of the AmaZulu*, the missionary, Canon Henry Callaway, for example, translates 'ancestors' as *amadhlosi*, the messengers of God, uMvelinqangi. Then these messengers became *amatongo*, lizards, who were obedient to God. Thus did local categories become adopted for Christian ones.

provide a perspective, the others resonate in sympathy, and their combined synthesis becomes the unspoken rationale for whatever merit there is in a multicultural vocation such as mine.

I do not for one moment think that such multiculturalism is unique to one individual, and must, indeed, represent an increasingly common phenomenon in the thrust towards global mutuality. One of its consequences for me is that I find the notion of cultural purity, and the attendant exclusiveness, unsatisfactory and untrue to life, whether it is the exclusion of the religious from the secular, or the identification of the two, precisely the reason why I felt discomfited with the bifocal treatment of culture as implicit religion or as antireligion. Tillich has rightly observed that religion, even in the way he defined it, and the secular 'are in the same predicament. [Consequently] Neither of them should be separated from the other, and both should realize that their very existence as separated is an emergency, that both of them are rooted in religion in the larger sense of the word, in the experience of ultimate concern.'[10] However, to amend C. S. Lewis's comments in *A Grief Observed* (1961), we might say that, whether it is hidden or flaunted, there is a sword drawn between moral truth and culture until, as Newbigin expresses it, Christ disarms culture by reconciling it to the truth, i.e., culture made discarnate, deabsolutized, in the incarnate logos, and thus transformed from being our idol or enemy to being our rightful possession. Since I personally belong to several cultures at once, I gladly and eagerly support the view that multiple cultural boundaries may coexist harmoniously and fruitfully. As such, cultural boundaries are not exclusive or immutable. In that light I cannot see myself a hostage to those border patrols whose occupational hazard is to see any intercultural traffic as incriminating evidence of unfaithfulness. Human life in the small individual slice that is mine happens to have subsisted on a great diversity of sources, and I happily and gratefully acknowledge my plural indebtedness.

That is the origin of such interest as I possess to make the cultural project a legitimate field for sustained intellectual enquiry across cultural traditions. I would wish to avoid the

10. Paul Tillich, *Theology of Culture*, New York 1959: Oxford Galaxy Book, repr. 1968, p. 9.

ideologically motivated agendas so characteristic of the left- and right-wing dichotomy which rightly senses something profoundly wrong with cultural exclusivism. Cultural inclusiveness on my reading, is, I believe, indispensable to the human enterprise as we know it, and we should do all that is necessary to encourage and foster it. On the other hand, we need to recognize that without interpersonal ethics such inclusiveness may become a cover for cultural captivity and the antireligious ethos it fosters. Yet the cultural commissar is no more attractive than his or her religious opposite number. This does not imply religion is itself blameless, but that past excesses do not in themselves invalidate religion, and that the answer to such excesses is to repossess the religious subject in its multicultural dimensions rather than abandoning it to commissars and zealots. I have attempted in the following pages to demonstrate through religious enquiry the wider and deeper ethical foundations of multiculturalism, to bring within range of religious interest materials from both the Western and non-Western traditions, and to encourage us to open our hearts and minds to what God might be saying to us in the world of cultural diversity and pluralism. I wish here to urge, by whatever persuasive powers I happen to possess, a less parochial and more open-minded understanding of what might be involved in Christianity and the global cultural process.

Definition and Scope

Culture as generally used has to do with the customary beliefs, social forms and material traits of a racial, religious or social group. Lesslie Newbigin adds a new dimension to the definition when he says culture is the sum total of ways of living 'developed by a group of human beings and handed on from generation to generation'. He continues: 'Central to culture is language. The language of a people provides the means by which they express their way of perceiving things and of coping with them . . . And one must also include in culture . . . religion.' (*Foolishness to the Greeks*, 3).

In his influential essay, *Culture and Anarchy*, Matthew Arnold (1822–88) includes in the definition of culture not merely the scientific passion for pure knowledge, but the moral and social passion for doing good in order 'to make reason and the will of God prevail!'[11] He continues:

> And religion, the greatest and most important of the efforts by which the human race has manifested its impulse to perfect itself – religion, that voice of the deepest human experience – does not only enjoin and sanction the aim which is the great aim of culture, the aim of setting ourselves to ascertain what perfection is and to make it prevail; but also, in determining generally in what human perfection consists, religion comes to a conclusion identical with that which culture – culture seeking the determination of this question through all the voices of human experience which have been heard upon it, of art, science, poetry, philosophy, history, as well as of religion, in order to give a greater fullness and certainty to its solution – likewise reaches. Religion says: *The kingdom of God is within you*; and culture, in like manner, places human perfection in an **internal** condition, in the growth and predominance of our humanity proper, as distinguished from our animality . . . Not a having and a resting, but a growing and a becoming, is the character of perfection as culture conceives it; and here, too, it coincides with religion.'[12]

Connected with these understandings, I employ culture in this book with particular regard to language and religion and explore within that framework the intellectual and moral foundations of culture.

Given both Newbigin's and Arnold's definition of the term, no philosophy of culture can ignore entirely or for ever the issue of moral commitment, and in dealing with that one has to move, however deftly or reluctantly, from demonstrable propositions to matters that correspond to actual experience. Thus affirmations of the kind I deal with in this book rest on a 'hypothetical emancipation from that which is merely culturally conditioned'

11. Matthew Arnold, 1869, 'Culture and Anarchy', in *Selected Prose*, ed. P. J. Keating, London: Penguin Classics, 1987, 205.
12. Arnold, *Selected Prose*, 207–8. Emphasis in original.

in order 'to acquire free insight into what is valid, stemming from the a priori of reason. Such an insight will be initially attainable only by recourse to the peculiar sense of the evidence (*Evidenzgefühl*) that is the psychological concomitant of all intuitive penetrations into the realm of the valid that may finally be attained. This sense is admittedly subject to error and is threatened by relativism due to its dependence (*Haftung*) upon extremely varied types of knowledge. Practically, all one can do is to make clear to oneself, on the basis of serious comparison, deliberation, and absorption, the common thrust of these values, to enter into their thrust, and to think of particular values as approximations to an objective whose general direction is known, even though the ultimate goal is not known. It is an act of the will – not an arbitrary whim but a fully considered decision – that dares to believe that the right path has been found. This act is indirectly confirmed by the possibility it affords of interpreting life by reference to this objective.' (E. Troeltsch, *Religion in History*, 37f.) So wrote Ernst Troeltsch, and with the import of his words I associate myself.

1

Religion and the Cultural Project: An Examination of Thought and Action

Introduction

While we may claim that in the process of transmitting the message of the Bible through the mother tongue modern Christianity has played a pivotal role in the emerging importance of cultures in the non-Western world, in general the Western conception of culture has promoted critical distrust of religion. Consequently when we try to examine the fruitful convergence of religion and culture outside the West, we hit the rock of stumbling in the West where culture has been a hostile contender with Christianity. In the West the secular disaffection with religion expresses itself in cultural attitudes, and this creates problems for our understanding of religion elsewhere given its proximity to culture there.

It was as a rival contender with religious faith that I first made my formal acquaintance with culture, and, in its extreme form, such contention was pretty close to cultural fundamentalism which is nearly as implacable as its religious analogue, in part because the cultural critic evokes and begets his or her religious foe, and in part because cultural moralization hardens in its own defence. However, the proximity of culture to the religious subject demands some kind of harmonious synthesis, though I did not know at the time how or where I might find that. It was a condition that affected my generation of American undergraduates who had been exposed to the 'cultural relativism' of Ruth Benedict's *Patterns of Culture*. For many of us, culture was the grand strategy by which to bring down Christianity, or at least the Christianity we associate with missionary ambition so oblivious were we to the 'tacit language' of cultural and religious communication. It did not occur to us to ask whether the cultural contention against Christianity and the a priori rejection of reciprocity between cultures had any merit in it, so potent was the ferment that galvanized the ranks. In that setting, evidence, or a semblance of it, could prove but one thing, the question in doubt being the scale of religious mischief.

For a long time all of us thus affected found ourselves pre-empted by the reigning shibboleths, our straightforward lines of enquiry and understanding broken by high-profile ideological stakes: on the left were ranged single-minded reductionists and on the right the avatars of cultural elitism. Both flanks laid on us a duty we could not fully carry out, of responding consistently to lunges from the left against moral universalism, and from the right which insisted on religious uniqueness, and with that catch-22 we felt ourselves religiously annd culturally disenfranchized. I recall my professor of French, a self-avowed child of the French Enlightenment, tweaking my nose because I represented for him what he called 'religious mystification in an age of reason'. He loved driving, he said, and it was not, he challenged, divine power that made his motor car perform but premium grade capitalist gasoline. Because he had the upper hand, my choice in class was to submit or else have him flunk me – but on what grounds? That is hard to say, yet at what point do the upholders of the cultural project threaten to become the inquisitors of a narrow creed?

I believe the cultural project does not, indeed cannot, avoid moral judgment simply by claiming a limited, relative ground for itself. The historian who claims impartiality must still illuminate the field by letting his or her light shine on the righteous and unrighteous alike rather than by persisting in denying the distinction altogether, or, a variation of the same, by exchanging appreciation for other cultures with scepticism and repudiation of one's own. Thus it is difficult to see how a cultural project, defined in hard agnostic terms, can help but duplicate the parodies it noisily identified in religion, or how it can survive the habit formed in denying one's heritage. A cultural project that set itself the task of fighting religion as antirational would, all things being equal, find it hard not to express the shadow image of what it opposes. Voltaire (1694–1778), for instance, exploits historical examples to attack religion, but distorts, through his peculiar telescoping of history, pre-sixteenth-century Christianity. Thus did Collingwood point out gaps in Voltaire's historical method[1] and its cramping effect on his view of religion, saying Voltaire founded a historical school that took little interest in the remoter past, or, we might add, in non-Western societies, which left its mark on both Kant (1724–1804) and Hume (1711–1776), as it did on the pop avatars of the 1960s and their perfunctory view of culture history. For them knowledge was like a biological organism, a complex pattern and combination of feelings rooted in sensation and emotion,[2] feelings that by their nature are specifically conditioned by Western culture. There was little incentive to look beyond the West for contrasting idioms. Our teachers were firmly locked into the prevailing cultural attitudes, and I recall, for example, how in my philosophy classes there was little willingness to hear counterarguments to current views on material and psychological determinism. In that sense Aristotle was psychologized and operationalized to produce a mechanical autonomous system. His structure of 'four' causes was collapsed and his teleology hobbled. We found it easy to dismiss any notion of moral purpose and the need for interpersonal ethics. I do not personally remember any of our professors teaching us about truth, trust, duty and service to others. We were taught that we made ourselves as we acted, or did not act, in pursuit of expressive goals, and could otherwise live or vegetate without profit to anyone else. However, in our hearts we knew better.

Many of my college superiors were comfortable with the knowledge that they had figured out the world, that not much of surprise remained within the realm of possibility to upset their equilibrium, and that a warm, genial rationality in which human beings found their own answers to life's questions would become the universal condition for all people. The liberal arts curriculum, adjusted if need be here and there to accommodate new knowledge, was the fundamental catechism for this enlightened

1. R. G. Collingwood, *An Essay on Metaphysics*, Oxford: Oxford University Press, reprinted Lanham, Md.: University Press of America, 1972, 246–47. See also J. B. Bury, *A History of Freedom of Thought*, New York: Henry Holt & Co., 1913, 153ff. This is an old classic, a spirited anti-Christian polemic.

2. ibid. 113. In this view theoretical reason is a pattern of sensations, practical reason that of appetite or self-interest.

dispensation. Essentially, the basic forms and conditions of human fulfilment have been put in place, a human fulfilment in which religion was accounted for and superseded. Individual contentment had replaced all inherited tradition and systems, and the rule was to claim such contentment as the goal of all effort in order to go beyond norms of conformity and community obligation. Living in that world as children of a different culture, my friends and I had no idea what had hit us, except that we felt on the defensive, constrained to move deferentially in the intimidating shadow of those who knew better. Despite it all, we persisted for a sign.

I now find to my relief that we do not have to capitulate to material or psychological determinism to affirm the cultural project, especially in its global setting. That is my intention here, and, in doing that, I follow in the footsteps of writers like Ernst Troeltsch and Lesslie Newbigin. In the first part, I want to assess the religious interest in culture and the forms in which culture was used to harbour and propagate antireligious sentiments. In the second stage of the analysis, I want to restate the theological initiative for elucidating the cultural process. The full development of some of these views will emerge in subsequent chapters.

The Cultural Critique

In their very different ways, Sir James Frazer (1854–1941) and Lévy-Bruhl (1857–1939)[3] agree that superstition and prelogical thinking, what Lévy-Bruhl controversially calls 'mystical collective representations of society', characterize the worldview of tribal peoples and constitute their religion, the views of these scholars being typical of the current that has carried the spurt of evolutionary thinking into the battle against religion. That was the context in which progress was conceived as a staged development from magic to religion to science. Frazer put it tersely with the statement that religion is 'the despair of magic and merely succeeds it in time'. Magic was conceived as the crude, primitive form

3. For an assessment of these writers, see Sir Edward Evans-Pritchard, *A History of Anthropological Thought*, ed. André Singer, New York: Basic Books, 1981, and Evans-Pritchard, *Theories of Primitive Religion*, Oxford: Clarendon Press, 1965.

religion took in prescientific societies whose primitive mentality, Lévy-Bruhl argued, interposed a collective subjective mystical layer on all sense perceptions. Another modern writer speaks of magic as nothing but 'mysticism in the fetters of fixed idea'.[4] We may thus take Frazer and Lévy-Bruhl as representative of those who believe natural causation to be the root of reality and the grounds for objective knowledge, and it is not incidental for them that religion, in promoting the idea of the supernatural and transcendent, contradicts this truth at its long deserved peril.

Yet we may quibble with this view on two grounds. First, our evolutionary notions result in a demotion, stereotype, or at any rate a denial that the past played any meaningful role in shaping our views today. Second, we may encourage by our attitudes an ideological wilfulness in restricting the word 'magical' to the negative side of the disparity between obscurantism and progress, slavery and freedom, or absolutist and relativist, and thus ignoring what the word may have meant to those who used it.

Magic in the Renaissance

These two caveats of stereotype and ideology are supported by evidence. To the writers of the Renaissance, for example, it is true that magic and science stood at nearly opposite ends of the spectrum, but it was never remotely their intention to equate magic with obscurantism and science with progress, the one with slavery and the other with freedom in the manner we have done today. Rather the reverse. For them, magic stood for freedom and progress while science represented fatalism and absolute dogma.[5] Even when he meant to be damning, Pliny wrote that magic 'embraces the three acts that most rule the human mind, medicine, religion and mathematics – a triple chain that enslaves mankind.'[6] If the Renaissance thinkers had no one else as their inspiration, they would still be keen to recruit magic for their

4. John Oman, *The Natural and the Supernatural*, Cambridge: Cambridge University Press, 1931, 384.
5. For an exhaustive historical treatment of the subject, see Keith Thomas, *Religion and the Decline of Magic*, New York: Charles Scribner's Sons, 1971.
6. Cited in T. R. Glover, *The Conflict of Religions in the Early Roman Empire*, London: Methuen, 3rd edition, 1909, 18. Reprinted New York: Cooper Square Publishers, 1975.

enterprise in pursuit of a humane, compassionate world order, a sentiment expressed by Prospero in Shakespeare's *The Tempest*. Although he lived in a cave on an isolated island, Prospero had turned one of his apartments into a study where he kept books 'which chiefly treated of magic, a study at that time much affected by all learned men; and the knowledge of this art he found very useful to him . . .'[7] For that age, science, given its unbending, immutable laws and principles of causation, actually enslaved human beings with the fetters of natural causation. On the other hand, as Francis Bacon put it, when magic was shorn of 'centaurs and chimeras', it would bring us to the position where, in Dürer's words, 'men can do if they will'. Bacon elaborated on this, saying he understood magic 'in general as the science which applies the knowledge of hidden forms to the production of wonderful operations'.[8] Thus magic became identified with freedom and science with determinism. And determinism in the age of the Enlightenment was fixed in frigid cosmic space, with human destiny left at the behest of blinking stars and gyrating planets, beyond the reach or influence of people. This view found its way into theology, with Ficino, for example, arguing that planetary bodies exert an influence on human beings: they affect 'the soul, and move it through that [human] spirit which the Physicians often call the bond of the soul and body',[9] and others finding support in the works of Thomas Aquinas who taught that God rules in everything through the stars, though free will might be exempt from this astral determinism.[10] In science, especially the form assimilated in 'bad' astrology, our fate hangs on non-sentient, invisible and invincible forces whose natural impact on our minds is to reduce us to futility. The mind is thus reduced to the category of a physical organ, its hidden form an argument for reducing it to a subunit of natural contingency.[11]

7. Charles and Mary Lamb, N.D., *Tales From Shakespeare*, New York: Grosset & Dunlap.

8. Cited in W. P. D. Wightman, *Science in a Renaissance Society*, London: Hutchinson University Library, 1972, 142–43.

9. D. P. Walker, *Spiritual and Demonic Magic: From Ficino to Campanella*, London: The Warburg Institute, University of London, 1958, 48.

10. ibid., 57, 214ff.

11. For aspects of the subject see Gilbert Ryle, *The Concept of Mind*, London, 1949, reprinted Penguin Books, 1990.

However, this was an intolerable situation for all concerned. For many such people, including thinkers like Del Rio and Telesio, scientific culture needed to be rescued from blind conformity and made amenable to human experience and instrumentality. That human beings could participate meaningfully in the cumulative construction of the universe was the overriding proof and burden of magic as Renaissance science understood it, since progress as 'cumulative construction' is an issue of moral teleology, not simply a mechanistic or logistical matter. It was under the influence of 'magic' that 'the scientists and inventors of the seventeenth century reveal a breath-taking faith in the potentialities of human ingenuity.'[12] In its creative stage 'magic' was prominent by its use, not its abuse. Therefore the scientists and others saw in the cycle of calculation, enumeration, measurement, observation and description what a critic called the ideological penumbra of 'the magic of numbers, the fetish of quantification, the self-defeating quest for certainty in matters sublunary',[13] room for moral purpose and human partnership.

At its simplest, writers believed that the new science should be a servant not master of humans. Bacon therefore urged that the new knowledge be sought for the power it puts into our hands rather than as an end in itself. It should be, in his words, 'a spouse for fruit', not a 'curtesan (sic.) for pleasure'.[14]

This resolve of writers to place human beings at the forefront of affairs produced an intellectual breakthrough in the contemporary conception of 'man'. Medieval Christian theology has viewed the human being as a composite creature, an *animal rationale*, in whose power it lay to be governed by reason or animality. Such a choice, however, was circumscribed by limits set by God: we could become saints but not angels, brutes but not beasts. In other words, the boundary between the moral order and the natural world was strictly drawn whatever the latitude available to us as

12. Keith Thomas, *Religion*, 1971, 662.

13. Roy Porter, 'What Price Gadgetry?' review article, *New York Times Book Review*, 10 May, 1992, 20.

14. Cited in C. S. Lewis, 'New Learning and New Ignorance', *Oxford History of English Literature: English Literature in the Sixteenth Century*, London and New York: Oxford University Press, 1954, 14.

moral agents. It was this distinction that defined the medieval notion of culture. It was to suffer a massive retrenchment in the shift now afoot.

The new view departed from the old in a radical way. Pico della Mirandola (1463–1494), a Renaissance scientist who defended magic, said that the human being has no specific nature but creates this by his or her own acts. He put the following words into God's mouth:

> To thee, O Adam, We have giuen no certain habitation or countenance of thine owne neither anie peculiar office, so that what habitation or countenance or office soeuer thou dost choose for thyselfe, the same thou shalt enjoye and posses at thine owne proper will and election – We haue made thee neither a thing celestial nor a thing terrestrial, neither mortal nor immortal, so that being thine owne fashioner and artificer of thyselfe, thou maist make thyselfe after what likenes thou dost most affecte.[15]

Another writer of the period places 'man' in this indeterminate position, throwing off the earlier certainty of the old limits and its theological anchor. This writer says:

> man containeth in himself the stars and the heauen, they lie hidden in his minde . . . if we rightly knew our owne spirite no thing at all would be impossible to vs on earth.[16]

Bacon's buoyant confidence is driven by this sense of new possibilities open to human beings as human beings rather than as natural adjuncts, a confidence upheld by the idea of a purposeful creation and our moral stewardship for it. True knowledge, he says, is a 'rich storehouse for the glory of the Creator and the relief of man's estate.' He continues, 'Let no man . . . think or maintain that a man can search too far or be too well studied in the book of God's word, or in the book of God's works, divinity or (natural) philosophy; but rather let men

15. Cited in Lewis, 'New Learning', 13.

16. ibid., 14. The words are those of Paracelsus. See also Hugh Trevor-Roper, *Renaissance Essays*, Chicago: University of Chicago Press, 'The Paracelsian Movement', 149–99, 1985, esp. 156ff.

endeavour an endless progression in both: only let men beware that they apply both to charity, and not to swelling; to use and not to ostentation . . .'[17] Faith and science for him were allies, though he cautioned it would be unwise 'to mingle or confound these learnings together'. Yet neither did he intend to oppose them to each other, for God's designs, he felt, may be discovered in nature by a knowledge of the 'chain of causes' which 'cannot by any force be loosed or broken nor can nature be commanded except by being obeyed.'

However, if we have not learnt the habit of obedience from God, then we are not likely to obtain it from nature, which then leaves us in a merely exploitative relation to it. In a work published in 1603 called *The Masculine Birth of Time*, subtitled 'The Great Instauration of the Dominion of Man over the Universe', Bacon appended a petitionary prayer in which he prayed that 'our human interests may not stand in the way of the divine, nor from the unlocking of the paths of sense . . .'[18]

Given all this, our attitude today of binding magic to religion and bringing them in their shared defect to the butchering block of science is too abrupt a break from the motives of Renaissance authors for whom the objective chain of natural causation does not bind more securely on the basis that a subjective religious chain of disrepute be first unscrambled, however dialectically satisfying that may be.

In the classical Enlightenment definition of culture, then, this theme of confidence in a purposeful creation and its corollary of human instrumentality and moral agency forms an animating and coherent principle of the cultural project. As such, the life of the mind plays a preponderant and central role. As a consequence, the door was open to the triumph of human self-

17. Wightman, *Science in a Renaissance Society*, 159. In the *New Atlantis* Bacon wrote: 'The end of our foundation is the knowledge of causes and the secret motions of things and the enlarging of the bounds of human empire, to the effecting of all things possible.' See also Sir P. Medawar, 'On the Effecting of all Things Possible', *Listener*, 1969, lxxxii.

18. Cited in Eugene M. Klaaren, *Religious Origins of Modern Science: Belief in Creation in Seventeenth Century Thought*, Lanham, Md.: University Press of America, 1985, 92–3. Also Trevor-Roper, 'Three Foreigners' in *Religion, The Reformation and Social Change*, London: Macmillan, and *Essays*, 1967, 186f.

sufficiency and to the cultivation of inner autonomy and intellectual harmony as superior, or at any rate as prior to the practical efforts of production and industry. This view came into ascendency in the Enlightenment and has its roots in classical Greek sources. As we shall see at the end of the present chapter, Aristotle, for one, promotes the virtue of 'moderation' as an expression of contemplative mental exercise. (*Nicomachean Ethics*, x. 7). The two fundamental principles of culture in terms of this intellectual legacy were considered to be, on the one hand, the idea of humanity and, on the other, of progress or teleology as in Aristotle, in contrast to the activist and exploitative employment of human powers. Bacon, who might be considered the founder of culture in the modern sense, writes in his *Advancement of Learning* (1605) that the day on which God rested at creation was deemed more blessed than the other six on which he laboured, while from the records of antiquity we learn that founders of states were but demigods and inventors among the gods themselves. It was Socrates, Aristotle and Cicero that antiquity praised and honoured rather than Xenophon, Alexander and Caesar. For Bacon, the life of contemplation was far superior to the life of conquest, which makes culture a matter of culture consciousness and thus of progress towards humanistic consciousness. It is an idea permeating all modern theories of culture.

It is to Bacon that we owe, if not the exact formulation, then the justification for the modern threefold conception of culture in terms of the Enlightenment, Romanticism and Realism. Spinoza might be regarded as representative of the Enlightenment view of culture when he declared that the highest motive in being human is the rational and the disinterested love of God, an idea so forceful that it persisted in Romanticism under the *culte du moi* doctrine of Maurice Barrès.

Enlightenment and Romantic Views

A later extreme Enlightenment trend saw culture as one in which all valid intellectual projects are facets of Bacon's perfect 'globe of knowledge', a rigid formalism that encouraged blind rationalism or else a static natural religion in which the leading figures were

Hobbes in naturalistic ethics, Locke in natural reason and Grotius in natural rights. Consequently, a reaction ensued with the Counterenlightenment whose leaders felt called upon to repudiate the static tendencies of their forerunners and to retrieve the issue of culture consciousness as a problem for their own age. The rigid conceptualism of Enlightenment thought about culture received some softening with the appropriation of aesthetics. Thus the idealization of beauty was added to the exaltation of reason to make room for sentiment, the 'nostalgia' theme in Benjamin Britten, or 'innocence' in Sir Michael Tippett. Nevertheless, aesthetic appreciation began itself to freeze cultural forms as writers looked to what might be characteristic norms or general types, all of this somewhat removed from the subjective, intuitive capacity. Lessing (1780) gave this rationalistic aspect a strong emphasis, as did Winckelmann, who expressed it well thus, 'beauty should be like the purest water, which, the less taste it has, is regarded as the most healthful because it is free from foreign elements.'[19]

With Kant we reach an important turning point between the Enlightenment view of culture and the Romantic. In his *Critique of Pure Reason* (1781), Kant gives philosophical reasons for abandoning the classical Enlightenment account of culture. He wrote that 'Metaphysics is the completion of the whole culture of reason.' Yet it was in his *Critique of Judgement* (1790)[20] that Kant propounded a new aesthetic theory on beauty and taste to the effect that aesthetic appreciation is based on 'that which pleases universally without requiring a concept' (77ff), a proposition that understands culture to be nothing but the intellectual life in imaginative free play. At one stroke Kant removed culture from any transcendent religious norms,[21] and, equally moment-

19. Winckelmann, *Werke*, Dresden, 1808–25, bk. iv, chap. ii, #23.
20. tr. J. H. Bernard, New York: Hafner Press, Macmillan, 1951.
21. George Steiner assesses Kant's long-range impact in this area as decisive. He says: 'The logical and psychological location by Kant of fundamental perceptions within human reason, Kant's conviction that the "thing in itself", the ultimate reality-substance "out there" could not be analytically defined or demonstrated, let alone articulated, laid the ground for solipsism and doubt. A dislocation of language from reality, of designation from perception, is alien to Kant's idealism of common sense; but it is an implicit potential.' Steiner, *Real Presences: The Leslie Stephen Memorial Lecture*, Cambridge: Cambridge

ously, like Hegel, Kant sundered culture from all local, mother tongue moorings,[22] though it turns out he established for culture its own system of transcendentalism, a transcendentalism that was to have an enormous impact on the romantic school of philosophy and poetry, as well as on the sort of distinction of culture as theoretical, practical and aesthetic (moral, physical and aesthetical) that Schiller (1793) introduced.

Schiller was occupied by two main ideals, namely, the ideal of humanity as ethical and the fact of human beings as creatures of sense. Schiller uses aesthetics to mediate between the extremes of sense impression and ethical idealism, although in fact Schiller moderates, if he does not abandon, his confidence in culture as understood by the Enlightenment by turning to nature for final vindication. Feelings and sentiments grounded in nature acquired in Schiller's scheme a status higher than culture as something constructed. Thus Schiller praised naiveté as the mark of natural genius, a view that allowed him to classify literary and poetic genius according to how the subject of human alienation from nature is treated. 'The poet,' he declared, 'either *is* nature or he *seeks* her. One makes a naive poet, the other a sentimental one.' (*Über naive und sentimentalische Dichtung*, 1796). Naive poets apprehend the truth of nature immediately, while sentimental ones pick their way by hints and clues that are for the moment unbundled. Virtue for Schiller resides in nature, while culture is tainted with evil.

The combined effect of such disparate ideas as identity, transcendentalism, passion, irony, naiveté, idealism, freedom, aesthetic autonomy and progress was to open the way for the

---

University Press, 1986, 2. Cf. Geoffrey H. Hartman, 'Art and Consensus in the Era of Progressive Politics', *The Yale Review*, vol. 80, no. 4, October, 1992, 50–61.

22. A modern philosopher traces a similar epistemology to Hegel, saying Kierkegaard, for example, found the root of the problem 'in the philosophy of Hegel, according to which the historical particulars became subsumed under the generalizing abstractions of reason . . . Particularity was lost in abstraction, the individual person in the mass society.' Hegel was himself rooted in the Enlightenment which in turn rested on the terms of Greek rationalism that the Enlightenment developed in its own peculiar way. Colin Gunton, 'Knowledge and culture: towards an epistemology of the concrete', in Hugh Montefiore, ed. *The Gospel and Contemporary Culture*, London: Mowbray, 1992, 84–102, 84.

next paradigmatic shift to natural realism, precisely the view Maurice Barrès formulated with his *culte du moi* doctrine, an idea that Nietzsche for one carried to rhapsodic heights with his dethronement of spirit and truth and their replacement with the culture of egoistic nihilism and activism. In this new realism, writers were quick to notice the appealing distinction drawn by Schopenhauer between will and intellect, or will and spirit,[23] and these writers went on to draw together the great Romantic urge and classical views of culture and put them through the crucible of passion as the source and shaper of values. As one character explains in Goethe's *Torquato Tasso* (1789), 'Talent is formed in solitude, character in the stream of the world' (Act I, scene ii). Wagner expressed a kindred idea in a letter to August Rockel in 1854 about his opera *Siegfried* thus: 'The progress of the whole drama shows the necessity of recognizing and submitting to the change, the diversity, the multiplicity, the eternal novelty, of the Real. Wotan rises to the tragic height of willing his own downfall. This is all we have to learn from the history of Man – to will the necessary and ourselves to bring it to pass.'[24] With that act Wotan becomes the unacknowledged patron saint of the super egoist. With Wagner, Nietzsche and others like them, the modern West turned its back on the Apollonian assurances of tradition and launched precariously into the Dionysiac culture of will and defiance. This is the culture also of Max Stirner, Zola, Ibsen, Turgenev and, in the United States, of Emerson (1803–1882) and Poe (1809–1849), among others. (Max Stirner, *The Ego and His Own*, 1845; Turgenev, *Fathers and Sons*, 1862; Ibsen's writings, in particular *Brand*, 1866, *Peer Gynt*, 1867 and *Emperor and Galilean*, 1873, and Edvard Grieg's musical settings of some of Ibsen's works; Emerson, *The American Scholar*, 1837).

In their own ways, Poe and Ibsen harp on a common cultural theme, that having to do with the morbid and mysterious and the sense of conflict or alienation. Their works represent an attempt to objectify in a fresh medium the depths of the human soul, a culture-consciousness of the decadent and vicious in human life.

23. Arthur Schopenhauer, *The World as Will and Representation*, 2 vols., tr. E. F. J. Payne, New York: Dover, 1958, repr. 1969, #25.
24. Cited in C. S. Lewis, 'The Funeral of a Great Myth', *Christian Reflections*, 94.

Nevertheless, in seeking to express the shadow side of culture, both Poe and Ibsen have also introduced a critical note, with culture being assessed not in the 'naive' and transcendental terms of the Romantics, but in the hard, despairing mood of the post-Realists. It is to Matthew Arnold, however, we must look for the constructive completion of this cultural criticism. Arnold once described himself as 'a man without a philosophy', but we must not take him at his word. The issue that theologians have learnt to deal with as law and grace was familiar to Arnold as 'Hebraism' and Protestantism, though Arnold seems to have shifted the burden of proof from 'Hebraism' which he describes as constituting 'conduct' which is 'three-fourths of human life', while Protestantism sat flat-footed between 'Hellenism' and the culture of lax morals. Without being unkind, we may say that Arnold shared the flaw he thus diagnosed, for sometimes he praised Hellenism as the highest spiritual development of the West and at other times claimed this spiritual ideal was premature, leaving the way clear for 'Hebraism' to rule the world. It is, consequently, a hard choice he places before us and himself, either to embrace the ideal, and thus risk exchanging naiveté for realism, or else endorse 'Hebraism' and the rules of conduct it makes available, but then forgo what he calls the 'sweetness and light' of Hellenism. That might explain why in his *Culture and Anarchy* (1869) Arnold adopted a double tone of, on the one hand, being egoistic and nihilistic, and on the other, being progressive in the bourgeois sense of the term. The 'man without a philosophy' had in fact found two, and the cultural prophets of our own age should sincerely claim Arnold as the prophet of indulgence and defiance, of spontaneity and criticism, as the figure that tried, sometimes successfully, to give contemporary 'sweetness and light' an elitist moral framework. He himself admitted his method to be of a free Socratism noted for its 'disinterested play of consciousness', as he calls it (chap. 4).[25]

On the conceptual side, Arnold identified four levels in culture: 1 as an internal condition peculiar to humanity rather than being a mark of animals, 2 as a process of growing and becoming

25. For an appraisal of Arnold, see Lytton Strachey, *Eminent Victorians*, 1918, New York: Modern Library.

rather than a finished achievement, 3 as a feature of humanity rather than of particular individuals within it, and 4 as a development embracing the whole of human life rather than only one part of it, such as the religious, though here Arnold sees a role for the church as a 'clerisy' that acts as a cultural preservative. It is this progressive general theme that qualified Arnold's nihilism and egoism and introduces for modern popular culture, and its consumer and entertainment ethos, a self-critical note.

For these thinkers the problem of culture is a problem chiefly of interior cultivation and contemplative discipline with the accent on deliberate powers of concentration and consciousness. It is a project for the emancipation of the human spirit from the oppressive and rigid Christian intellectual formalism of the scholastics. In the eighteenth and nineteenth centuries, perhaps, writers could speak sanguinely about mansions of splendour waiting to be refurbished within an autonomous immanentist edifice, but ever since Freud (1856–1939) we have become less assured. Freud began a revolution to topple the imposing structures of reality with claims for the power of fantasy and 'elaboration'. Consequently we inherited from him the irony that subjective projection is the truth normally at work combined with the view that such projection is a calculated distortion. Reality is an illusion, though illusion is not reality, and neither is it, on the earlier premise, illusory. Nothing better dramatizes the irony of modern cultural attitudes. Freud himself talks about waking wish fulfilments as the stuff of artistic creation, so that the artist achieves in the world of pretence and make-believe what has eluded him or her in the real world: 'honour, power, riches, fame and the love of women.'[26] It is a devasting *coup de maître* for Freud to put us in a state of mind in which we concede the potency of the imperious id to such an extent that we abandon trust in the very structured channels, such as intellect, art and tradition,[27] in which the id pours out its subterranean secrets.

26. Sigmund Freud, *Introductory Lectures on Psychoanalysis*, tr. Joan Rivière, London, 4th. ed., 1933, 314.

27. 'The Freudian view and use of human speech, of written texts . . . radically dislocates and undermines the old stabilities of language. The common sense . . . of our spoken or written words, the visible orderings and values of our syntax, are shown to be a masking surface.' Steiner, *Real Presences*, 3–4.

The two great ideas of Freud in this matter, that behind cultural images there lies erotic thought, and that images function as disguise, thanks to consciousness, may have gratification as their object, but result in making coping strategy our only recourse. Denied or suppressed pleasures that are conveyed under elaborate facades must seek their revenge through forms of self-deception, and that is scarcely the source of great creativity.[28]

The conscious and unconscious intellectual life that Freud has done so much to try to bring down from its pedestal suffered a setback as a consequence, not just in its overt forms and conventions but in its hidden, tacit dimension. Yet language in all its infinite subtlety as well as elaborate design and form remains indispensable for culture, even the culture that Freud would probe and dissolve. There would, in any case, still be the culture of deconstruction and of deconstructionists whose regime, while liberating us from old conformities and conventions, might tie us to new orthodoxies of distrust and alienation. The new underclass would be those defined (and disarmed) by the exegesis of naming, tagged in spite of themselves. Structures created on such a basis would perpetuate ancient antagonisms with new cleavages, indicating how new cultural projects leave us with old questions and old suspicions. We continue to face the question, for example, of how we adjudicate ultimate issues of justice and truth with the relative tools of deconstruction, how to move from identifying aesthetic themes of sense and sensibility to adjudicating principles and norms of equity and service to each other.

28. Freud wrote about the phenomenon of religion, for example, in such pessimistic terms. His thesis is that religion is a continuation of an infantile prototype. He continues: 'man's self-regard, seriously menaced, calls for consolation; life and the universe must be robbed of their terrors; moreover his curiosity, moved, it is true, by the strongest practical interest, demands an answer . . . This situation is not new. For once before one has found oneself in a similar state of helplessness: as a small child, in relation to one's parents.' *The Future of an Illusion*, tr. & ed. James Strachey, New York: W. W. Norton, 1961, 1975, 16–17. Freud and Jung had lectured to American audiences as early as 1909, but it was only in the 1920s that Freud's ideas took hold in a soil anthropology and popular science had prepared with views about men and women 'being merely animals of a rather intricate variety, and that moral codes had no universal validity and were often based on curious superstitions.' Frederick Lewis Allen, 1931, *Only Yesterday*, repr. New York: Bantam Books, 1959, 69.

Such ultimate and normative criteria require a reappraisal of the autonomous claims for culture and require a synthesis that would take out of the equation the old battlelines between contingency and teleology, between the imperatives of moral reasoning and the episodic facts of the cultural and contemplative life. Goethe's solution in *Faust* to claim 'activity' as a function of 'nostalgia', and therefore as a principle of consciousness, returns to the problem by a different route, extrapolating from a mode of necessary cultural activity remedies for a transcendent moral condition. In the final analysis, the Goethean project depends for its success on the passionate egoist joining forces with the thinking egoist: '*Verweile doch, du bist so schön.*' All of which recalls Plato in *The Republic* considering poetry and drama as parasitic and consequently banishing them from the state.

The 'culture problem' is not simply a matter of arguing for what is necessary and useful, but of conceiving the human enterprise in such terms as are compatible with our overwhelming sense of moral truth. Therefore, we may ask: can the human instrument, without a sense of transcendence, achieve a fulfilment that is different from murky self-centredness? What is to prevent intellectual egoism from becoming a creed for self-centredness? What is to distinguish nihilism and egoism, for instance, from dogmatic subjectivism or liberal fantasy? What moral imperatives can check these unwholesome tendencies of life and thought? How do we intellectually and institutionally cater for this moral view of life? Does obedience in 'nature', to employ Bacon's terms, presume its analogue in a higher obedience? Is culture-consciousness complete without the prior consciousness rooted in God, a consciousness that brings the creative impulse into manifest harmony with its divine prevenience?

We cannot, I think, be satisfied with a merely mechanistic and materialist notion of culture. A purely mechanistic or instrumental view of culture, that is, a concern only with culture as a subject of organization and administration, brings us inescapably to the problem of culture as a contest of national wills and individual endowment, with culture theory serving to promote a sentiment of cultural destiny and imperial grandeur. This has obvious implications for the cultures of weaker nations, not to say anything of the disadvantaged classes in the West itself. The problem is actually made even more acute if we idealize language and empty it of all content, such as we find in Winckelmann's statement that culture, like beauty, 'should be like the purest water, which, the less taste it has, is regarded as the most healthful because it is free from foreign elements.' This sort of abstraction is what provoked John Ruskin (1819–1900) to complain of modern art as 'the graceful emptiness of representation' in regard to which religious subjects are exploited 'for the display of transparent shadows, skilful tints, and scientific foreshortenings . . . and academical discrimination.'[29] When culture has been thus dissolved and distilled into Kantian ideals of 'universal pleasure', it leaves in place an elite corps of cultural arbiters whose sensibilities determine the course of evolutionary development from primitive forms to abstract conceptions. Yet no abstract refined formulation should make us forget the stage when the noble character of common speech falls on our ears with the fresh spontaneity of lived experience, unmediated by formal categories. Such was the complaint of Troeltsch when he wrote, with Kant not far from his mind,

> . . . as far as this creative life is concerned, it is impossible, at least *a posteriori*, to strip away the particularity of a given phenomenon and then distill from the remainder a concealed but operative universal. The impossibility of proceeding in this way is shown by the fact that the idea of a universal, wherever it arises, is itself brought into being in terms of particular historical conditions. It can arise only by effecting what becomes a historically necessary departure from the living content that dominated whatever form preceded it, and it always takes shape in relation to definite intellectual and ethical influences of a given situation and moment.[30]

In that connection, a study of Elizabethan life found that the ordinary, humbler folk possessed the creative spark that fired the wider cultural impulse, so that 'the art of the higher regions of

29. John Ruskin, *The Art Criticism of John Ruskin*, ed. & abridged, Robert L. Herbert, New York: Da Capo Press, 1964, 260.
30. Troeltsch, *The Absoluteness of Christianity*, 1971, 64.

society was most strongly influenced by the vigour in the cultural activities of the common people in their popular pageants, folk songs and dances.'[31] It is one reason why it could be said of the art of John Bunyan that it 'reeks heavily of the soil, and is not ashamed of its origins',[32] because, as C. S. Lewis puts it, Bunyan's 'homely immediacy' may be attributed to 'a perfect natural ear, a great sensibility for the idiom and cadence of popular speech, a long experience in addressing unlettered audiences.'[33]

The circularity of thought involved with the abstraction of culture, with using a specific idiom to advocate an abstract universal idea, would render the whole cultural project doubtful unless we allowed the specificity of idiom as 'foreign elements' a role in culture-consciousness. For then, Western formulations themselves, 'foreign' by the standards of others, would acquire a validity on the basis of their own cultural specificity. That is why, to amend John Keats, certain kinds of philosophy, in stripping culture so completely, would also clip the wings of angels, for even refined imagination requires to be clothed in the language and circumstance of historical conditionality. A universal language, in that case, may not dispense with the innumerable rules and forms and characteristics that constitute the bones and sinews of cultural particularity. Similarly, we do not get universal culture merely by abolishing, or merging, the tones and sounds bequeathed to us by the uncountable vessels and arteries of custom, convention and rules of observance. Stripped of those means and circumstances, culture has little solidity, though it may be a category of intellectual abstraction, what Butler called 'the entertainment of the mind' (*Sermons*, xv.).

Modern Attitudes

It is, as I said at the beginning, perhaps inevitable that the upholders of a materialist doctrine of culture should fall into a

31. Ernest H. Meyer, *Elizabethan Chamber Music: the History of a Great Art from the Middle Ages to Purcell*, London: Lawrence & Wishart, 1946.
32. R. H. Tawney, *The Radical Tradition: Twelve Essays on Politics, Education & Literature*, London: Penguin Books, 1966, 208.
33. C. S. Lewis, 'The Vision of John Bunyan', in Lewis's *Selected Literary Essays*, Cambridge: Cambridge University Press, 1979, 146–53.

narrow ideological trap, preaching freedom, progress and reason with the commitment fired by opposition to religion. This problem became ever more pressing in the 1930s and 1940s. Thus we find Joseph Stalin, not in other ways a salutary figure, expressing a sentiment that lies at the heart of the Western experience. He made the cultural project a matter for instrumental control, with the nation as its embodiment. In that connection he said that a nation 'is a historically evolved, stable community of language, territory, economic life, and psychological makeup manifested in a common culture.' A modern commentator remarked: 'Put a centralized government on top of that, allow for neutralized monarchs to remain in place where the populace retains a lingering respect for royalty, and you have the kind of modern country with which we are all familiar.'[34] But national loyalty begs the moral question: is the nation final arbiter of our moral responsibility? The nation as moral agent might produce the sort of sentiment that led a British army officer then fighting the Nazis to say to a German anti-Nazi victim of Hitler after the victim fled to Britain: 'I can respect no man who has no loyalty to his country, especially the country of his birth.'[35]

Mussolini made an even bolder and more direct claim when he taunted Christians with observing that the religion would have remained what he termed 'a wretched little oriental sect' in an undistinguished corner of the world had not the Italian cultural genius 'salvaged' it from an almost certain demise and raised it above the floodmark.[36] It was thus that Italy's chief city, Rome, carved its name on the Church that became a worldwide body. More than a whiff of such sentiments exists within the Church itself. On the occasion of Mussolini's invasion of Ethiopia in October 1935, the Bishop of Cremona consecrated the regimental flags and declared: 'The blessing of God be upon these soldiers who, on African soil, will conquer new and fertile lands for the

34. David Lawday, 1991, 'My Country, Right . . . or What?' *The Atlantic*, vol. 268, no. 1, 22.
35. (Peter and Leni Gillman, *Collar the Lot!*, London, 1980, p. 230, cited by Adrian Hastings in *English Christianity*, 1987, p. 374.)
36. Cited in Arnold J. Toynbee, *Christianity among the Religions of the World*, New York: Charles Scribner's Sons, 1957, 92–3.

Italian genius, thereby bringing to them Roman and Christian culture.'[37] Similarly, Cardinal Schuster of Milan hailed the Italian army for being destined to achieve 'the triumph of the Cross . . . opening the gates of Abyssinia to the Catholic faith and civilization.'[38]

The views of Stalin and Mussolini in this and other matters are, of course, extreme, but they represent a phenomenon which in its moderate forms has characterized the spread and expansion of Christianity, for on the face of it the Enlightenment national state and the Christian cultural assimilation are undeniable facts however lamentable in either case some aspects may be. What is different now is that both Stalin and Mussolini are feeding off the long-standing legacy of the cultural project as an anti-Christian project, and in riding the crest of cultural triumphalism, they articulate a corresponding radical emasculation of religion. From now on, if not before, whenever we see or hear of Western cultural contact with non-Western societies, we can only assume violence and imperialism as the basis and logic of the encounter, precisely the view Joseph Conrad expressed in *The Heart of Darkness*, and it takes little imagination to understand how Western Christian missions filled this role, an issue I shall take up in subsequent parts of this book. Stalin and Mussolini, however, had their allies where it counted, in the political project of the architects of wartime Europe. The new masters of the scene followed a theory of culture that rests on the split-level foundation of biology and force. The first provides the natural advantage of racial superiority while the second provides the instrument of its effectiveness. Thus could Alfred Rosenberg, the theorist of National Socialism, argue in favour of Aryan cultural superiority, because for him 'culture is determined mostly by biology, so that one ethnic group's acceptance of another's cultural legacy [i.e., northern Europe's adoption of a Jewish-influenced Christianity] is unnatural and takes place

37. Cited in Adrian Hastings, *A History of English Christianity: 1920– 1985*, London & Glasgow: Collins Fount Paperbacks, 1987, 314.

38. ibid. Soon after the war was concluded the pope promptly sent as his Apostolic representative a notorious Fascist, and replaced with Italians all non-Italian Catholic missionaries in the country, not excepting a French bishop who had spent fifty years in the country.

only because of violence . . . If the cultural system is already implicit in the biological self [i.e., the body], then any large-scale cultural shift, such as the Christianization of northern Europe, must be altogether owing to domination and in no sense the result of the greater persuasiveness of the new order . . .'[39] Rosenberg's method of seeking cultural ascendancy over what he considered the Jewish conspiracy drove him to repudiate the Jewish connections of the New Testament with his wholesale condemnation of the doctrines of humility, self-denial and peacefulness as Jewish distortions of the genius of Christianity. The cultural values Rosenberg wished to promote are determined by blood and affinity, although it is evident biological ideas alone are too haphazard not to require even a warped moral web to unify them. 'Unless,' as Lewis says, 'the measuring rod is independent of the things measured, we can do no measuring',[40] including the pernicious enumeration of racial advantages.

The movement that began with the courageous and joyful celebration of the emancipation of the human spirit saw itself as opposed to Christianity, though its faith and vision derived from the religion. However, in trying to outrival Christianity, this immense cultural movement became a distorted replica of its religious foe and degenerated into a partisan crusade centred on race and nation. In the first place, intercultural contact was reduced to nothing more than a biologically conceived self-interest, with force, or at any rate the means for success, the ruling principle in human relations. The problem of excess of culture thus turned on Dionysiac dichotomies in culture. In the second, science and technology, stripped of all moral stewardship, produced or promoted vested interests and the instruments for protecting them that vied with Baconian and Kantian assurances. Both the destructive and the diversionary entertainment culture of modern science and industry encouraged the ascendancy of will over intellect, making acquisitive desires and goals more than adequate substitutes for intellectual pleasure, and, indeed,

39. Jon D. Levenson, 'The God of Abraham and the Enemies of "Eurocentrism"', *First Things*, October,1991, 15–1, 17.
40. C. S. Lewis, *Christian Reflections*, Grand Rapids, Michigan: Wm. B. Eerdmans Publishing Co., 1967, 73. However, see Mill, *Essays*, 419ff.

bringing the progress – and decline – of humanity within the general scope of industrial competence. For the great Kantian dictum, 'Know thyself', military industrial culture, the technopolis, substituted, 'Make thyself', a shift threatening to swamp us with effluents of rampant consumerism.

Thus the problem persists: our commitment to the cultural project as such is too deeply intertwined with our original affinity with the ultimate moral order to leave us entirely unaffected with regard to spiritual values. On the positive side, this cultural movement has produced imperishable testaments of human creativity, scientific exploration, personal courage and the discourse of rational argument, though on the negative side it has brought the human spirit into unspeakable agony and moral confusion. The costs of this negative side have now threatened to undo the positive benefits unless we reject the ideology of cultural innocence and human autonomy. So long as culture continues to make a bid for the ground properly occupied by religion, so long will we continue to have an alienating hostility embedded in the cultural project, all of which points to an acute crisis in the nature of values and truth. Freud's observation is relevant here, namely that cultural ideals, and what is achieved by them, incite cultural superiority. 'In this way,' Freud claims, 'cultural ideals become a source of discord and enmity between different cultural units, as can be seen most clearly in the case of nations.'[41] A triumphant culture, we know only too well, is by no stretch of the imagination synonymous with moral rectitude,[42] nor, for example, is the historical failure of vanquished populations evidence simply of their moral inferiority. Many cultures have triumphed both as ideas and movements that have also wrought great misery in the world

41. Freud, *The Future of an Illusion*, 1975, 13.
42. John Carey has written about the unwarranted sense of moral superiority that characterized, for example, the British and Irish intellectual class whose views on cultural breeding targeted the lower social classes as fit for extermination. John Carey, *The Intellectuals and the Masses: Pride and Prejudice among the Literary Intelligentsia, 1880–1938*, London: Faber, 1992. Paul Johnson remarked in his review, 'Faithful Christians and orthodox Jews are about the only groups who can be relied on to provide tough opposition' to such ideas. Paul Johnson, 'Eliminate the negative . . .', *The Sunday Times Book Review*, 12 July, 1992.

and many other cultures have been trampled upon whose fate, in continuing to go unchallenged, has diminished our capacity for truth.

There is, in fact, no neutral ground in culture, for every inch is contested, say, between egoism and dogmatism, between possessing and betraying, but in any case held sub judice to interests and suppositions that are themselves forms of commitment. Cultural forms often assume qualitative values and description turns into evaluation, with the rules of prescription and preference controlling the perception of what is out there. We should, therefore, admit that 'culture is not an ethically neutral entity, and cultural change cannot be a matter of ethical indifference.'[43] In this matter, too, we would be wrong to insist on a rigid dichotomy between so-called cultural facts and cultural values, between cultural patterns and configurations on the one hand, and, on the other, moral sentiments and standards. Our very apprehension of the natural world is never so detached that it is not imbued with moral impressions, and this is more so in the cultural domain which the religious shadow overhangs, so that, contrary to Hume's scepticism, we may remedy an agnostic empiricism with what Troeltsch calls the a priori of reason, or what Newbigin calls teleology. Something of this teleology may act as a prescriptive rule to mitigate and illuminate entropic contractions within cultures.[44] Thus systemic breakdown would be pre-empted or mitigated by a moral safety valve that allows the two opposite streams, the one being prescribed, or even normative behaviour, and the other forbidden conduct, to meet without permanent harm. Some examples: incest might be a major offence for which horrendous sanctions apply, but the rules of consanguinity might be flexible enough to make second-cousin incest less serious than incest between first cousins or siblings. Similarly, fertility laws might be extremely stringent, so stringent

43. Lesslie Newbigin, 1978, *The Open Secret*, Grand Rapids: Wm. B. Eerdmans, repr. 1981, 161.

44. Freud asserts that cultural ideals, and the achievements that fostered them, are of a narcissistsic nature, giving pride and satisfaction to members, though narcissism also foments discord and enmity. If this is so, then we are left with cultural confusion and contradiction as endemic and ultimately destructive forces. *Future of an Illusion*, 1975, 13.

that barrenness, especially if it should become common, might threaten an unacceptably large number of people with a form of social death, in which case the definition of fertility would be expanded to incorporate a more flexible rule of adoption of nieces and nephews and other collateral relatives.[45] In those ways a culture would take steps to devise conceptual and qualitative equivalents for social and biological relationship.

Thus would a culture act to resolve what Bernard Williams calls 'the Archimedean point', namely, a species of scepticism that turns out to be unreasonable, or at any rate untenable.[46] That is why we cannot take literally what George Orwell said in a different connection, namely, that ethical scepticism has 'exploded a hundred tons of dynamite beneath the moralist position, and we are still living in the echo of that tremendous crash',[47] since all such scepticism would, at least in meaningful community life, be mitigated by social realism and common sense. A similar moral realism still suffuses our consciousness though the sappers pursue us even at the moon. Consider the extreme case of the community of ancient Israelites who, in a pinch, would rather go to the Philistines to have their swords sharpened than give in to relativistic compromise.

There may, therefore, be an important clue (and it is only as clue that I pursue the subject here) in the fact that as human beings we continue to believe in the progress of humanity through qualities of humaneness, compassion, philanthropy, generosity, peace and tolerance, making those among the chief attributes of the cultural project, all of which suggests a moral ethos for the cultural enterprise as such. The Promethean cultural rebirth we thus seek hints sufficiently at a loss we suffered at an earlier time to make retrieval a moral issue rather than a matter only of natural mutation. It is thus reasonable to conclude that our projects of retrieval are connected to the moral rehabilitation of the human enterprise, a retrieval in which we remain the subject matter of the rehabilitation and the agents for effecting it. This double role should result in a corresponding double awareness,

45. My own brother was adopted thus by a childless maternal relative.

46. Bernard Williams, *Ethics and the Limits of Philosophy*, Cambridge, Mass.: Harvard University Press, 1985, 22–29.

47. George Orwell, *A Collection of Essays*, New York: Harcourt Brace Jovanovich, 1953, 65.

and thus in an important break from the chain of natural causation. The flaw we perceive in the cultural scheme is not simply a missing piece in our biological equipment, but a sense that by and in ourselves something is missing, that our wish for cultural deliverance is a symptom of a redeemable insecurity in our primordial unconscious, something so profoundly embedded in the roots of being and so wide-ranging in its consequences that we propagate it in the stem and branches of everything we construct, and must thus confront it at source. That source is our unique and precious affinity with the sovereign moral law. Therefore the challenge we face in culture is not so much that of empirical completeness, of the accumulation of physical data and the extension of technological mastery, as of an acute sense that our empirical rationalism seems to have its tendrils hedged with a moral screen, rough-hew them how we will. How can our empirical tree flourish when its roots are so entangled? If cultural purpose amounts to anything more than quantitative measures and the human enterprise more than the sum of its biological functions, then we are right to include spiritual and intellectual activity in our descriptive inventory, to rate gravity concealed below and behind the roots as of equal moment as the elements above. Our cultural jungle is penetrated by trails that would bring us finally to our moral sense, though at present we feel extended, and expended, in cultured tasks of personal orienteering that bring us back to where they found us.

Indeed the phenomenon that has accompanied the rise of culture consciousness is henotheist faith, of belief in culture as the source of ultimate values, so that while belief in the supernatural has declined, or, which is perhaps more common, has come under attack, faith of a less self-interested kind has moved in to take its place. Consequently, the total number of believers and nonbelievers may not have changed much; what has changed significantly has been the relative position of the two categories, with modern cultural believers and religious sceptics reversing roles with their premodern predecessors. Just as believers of a different era took for granted the plausibility of their worldview, so cultural protagonists today assume a corresponding plausibility for their presuppositions. Neither side can afford to doubt what it believes in. Such certainty is the hard crust under which the moral life finds refuge, with the nonreligious person drawing from such moral reserves without accountability. When our intellectual guides prescribe for us the confidence of humanism, the fatalism of realism, or the despair of naturalism, in fact they are leaving in place this sense that their description is morally evocative, even provocative, that cultural diagnosis includes a yearning for moral truth, that erosion and sedimentation in culture are symbols of fatigue and renewal that evoke death and resurrection and the glorious consummation. It is not adequate with regard to our destiny that we grin and bear it, curse and resist, or else grasp and transcend the flux, but that we understand our response to be a reading of the 'facts' guided by intelligence not originated in 'facts'. At the point where our thoughts and actions are dissected by the forces of life we have to respond in ways that preserve and promote our authentic selfhood and humanity. We cannot afford at such moments the luxury of detached scepticism and objective disengagement. The point has been well made that ethical scepticism is very different from scepticism about the material world, for the 'ethical involves more, a whole network of considerations, and the ethical sceptic could have a life that ignored such considerations altogether.'[48]

This is one of the reasons the methods of rational demonstration cannot, I believe, take the full measure of culture, since, as Arnold has shown, culture is at heart a spiritual phenomenon, a matter of inner intention. I do not think, furthermore, that the issue lies in psychological moods, with mental orientation able to resolve the difficulty. The psychoanalytic approach to the issue of human happiness might, for instance, explore human character in terms of moods, such as optimism, depression, alienation, fear, gloom, contentment, gratification, etc., without that in any way being related to ethical questions. A sadistic person, we recall, might enjoy inflicting suffering on others, his mood at the time being one characteristically of accomplished satisfaction. If we made mood the only criterion of character, it would not help us to differentiate between good and bad or right and wrong: a person may be successful at stealing and derive great comfort

48. Bernard Williams, *Ethics and the Limits of Philosophy*, 25.

and profit from it though it be at someone else's expense.[49]

One kind of religious response to the phenomenological and epistemological challenge of culture is an abandonment of initiative, for it sets out to imitate empiricism and set up 'laws and axioms' that are beyond dispute, using, or appearing to use, the rules of demonstration to sweep aside any basis for doubt.[50] That such a religious path is beset with difficulties is acknowledged when the proponents shift in the next stage to dealing with sin, for they propose as its remedy redemption through the emetic use of self-reproach. Religious subjectivism may be just as bereft of any ethical foundation as the secular force that feeds it, which is why instrumental mysticism, with its tendency towards self-moralization and psychic proofs, remains a problem for prophetic religion. It therefore follows that any sensible religious response must gather and nurture the numerous hints and clues in the language of progress and of the perfectibility of human institutions that Enlightenment thinkers and their successors employed and bring them into convergence with the vision of a transcendent moral order. And, as John Oman has observed:

> . . . a higher morality is closely interwoven with a higher religion; and there is no form of religion in which there is not some beginning of a higher value for man and his society and some measure of better rule than impulse and better motive than fear or favour or any form of self-interest. [Even if we attend to his animal ancestry,] in man at any stage, the sense of the holy, however sunk in mere awe, the judgment of the sacred, however fettered in the

49. Freud observes in this regard: 'There are countless civilized people who would shrink from murder or incest but who do not deny themselves the satisfaction of their avarice, their aggressive urges or their sexual lusts, and who do not hesitate to injure other people by lies, fraud and calumny, so long as they remain unpunished for it.' *Future of an Illusion*, 1975, 12. Fear in those circumstances would be based on an apprehension of a prescriptive code.

50. It is relevant to consider how Lord Russell, for one, took up the issue of mathematical certainty, thinking it might offer knowledge that was 'indubitable', only to abandon it 'after some twenty years of very arduous toil' because 'if certainty were indeed discoverable in mathematics, it would be in a new kind of mathematics . . .' *Autobiography*, 725. The attempt at a comparable kind of risk-free knowledge in religion is destined to fare no better. Newman sees the issue differently, saying 'there is no ultimate test of truth besides the testimony born to truth by the mind itself.' Ian Ker, *John Henry Newman*, Oxford: Oxford University Press, 1990, 618–50, 646.

> material, and the sanction of the Supernatural, however beclouded by magic, make man's conduct in some sense moral, a standing above the mere flux of impulse and circumstance, and an estimate of himself, his fellows and his ultimate environment which is not measured by material advantage.[51]

The Culture Crisis: The Problem of Truth and Value

I said in the opening paragraph of this chapter that my generation of undergraduates adopted the cultural project as the enlightened, rational alternative to religion, believing that we could advance the cause by the principles of cultural relativism, and rejecting any reciprocity between cultures, since cultural reciprocity would open the door to cultural meddlesomeness, as with Christian missions. I want now to return to that theme and show how scientific positivism and the anthropology developing from it performed for us the functions of a religion, that is to say, an idealized construction of value-free cultural practices that we defended like sacred dogma against the obscurantist moralizations of religion.

In his penetrating inquiry into the history of anthropological science, David Bidney plotted the rise within the discipline of what he calls its natural science claims.[52] Modern anthropologists made what to them was an important distinction by committing themselves to facts and laws and leaving philosophers and humanists to deal with values, a distinction that gained currency only in the nineteenth century. By contrast, Renaissance thinkers believed in human perfectibility in time, assuming that human beings could, under divine providence, perfect themselves and their institutions. There was general confidence of an inevitable progress from primitiveness to civilization as from darkness to light, with few limits set as to what people could achieve in culture in contrast to nature with its morally deficient, blind alleys. At that stage the optimist and the pessimist both shared the confidence in human instrumentality,

51. Oman, 1931, 388.

52. David Bidney, 'The Concept of Value in Modern Anthropology,' in *Anthropology Today: An Encyclopedic Inventory*, Chicago: University of Chicago Press, 1953, 682–699.

the only difference being that the optimist discounted any possibility of regression while the pessimist felt eternal vigilance was needed to prevent a slide into the barbaric past. The optimism that was characteristic of the Renaissance was overthrown by an Enlightenment cynicism that hardened into an antireligious stance, placing religion, particularly the clerical maraboutic forms of it, in the domain of the irrational and obscurantist. The work of Edward Gibbon (1737–94), as we shall see in a subsequent chapter, fits into this combative mould, and its historical roots reach back to the Republican morality of the French Revolution in which the ideas of Socrates, Marcus Aurelius and Cicero were declared the new religion of deism known as Theophilanthropy. Its advocates intended it to replace the refurbished Christianity of Rousseau. Its doctrines were God, humanity, fraternity and immortality. Napoleon in 1801 ended the brief reign of this religion when the state adopted a contrived amalgam of Rousseau and Christian idealism. However, its ideas maintained a hold on the intellectual elites, so that even as late as 1905 when the church-state Concordat came to an end, the antireligious rationalism eventually reasserted itself. The most substantial division of knowledge and reality in the Enlightenment formulations is the division between the progressive, rational principles which conform to natural reason, and, on the other hand, unnatural, barbaric customs and conventions that conflict with natural reason. This was a major departure from the views of Renaissance thinkers who were not afraid to stake the entire enterprise on the issue of human perfectibility, with human beings performing a custodial responsibility under divine providence.

A further important shift occurred when, under the impact of scientific positivism, particularly that of Auguste Comte (1798–1857), modern anthropologists believed they could 'arrive at a knowledge of man's nature through a comparative study of culture history. Psychological laws were to be discovered as the final product of the study of comparative culture history, and they were not to be regarded as the presuppositions of historical study. Man was to be known through a study of culture history, not culture history through a study of man.'[53] They conceived a

53. Bidney, 1953, 684.

progression from theology to metaphysics and finally to science which for Frazer was itself a phase still to be overtaken by an undefined stage. The next operational shift was to deduce the idea of God from effects in natural phenomena, that is to say, to make religion the illicit product of faulty reasoning, a logical false step that depends on nature though it erroneously imagines there is a necessary supernatural reality lurking in the shades. In this view the moral code is a function of geography, of cultural context. In the famous words of Pascal: 'Three degrees of polar elevation overturn the whole system of jurisprudence. A meridian determines what is truth', so that, as someone else said, 'somewhere east of Suez there ain't no ten commandments.' The new Comtian advocates felt the real truth is that the laws of nature, being rational and progressive in the humanist sense, are more than adequate to take the place of divine providence. Thus, while appearing to keep an open mind about what might succeed science, scientific positivism was still dogmatic about excluding religion from any enlightened human dispensation.

Arthur Schlesinger Jr, whose historical works we read in college, for example, could take it for granted that relativists have the truth on their side and that the advocates of the religious law have been the purveyors of darkness and death.[54] However, as a correspondent rightly noted, relativists are not as impeccable as they claim: the commandment, 'Thou shalt not kill', as an absolute rule is a fundamental safeguard of life. 'It's only when you add exceptions making it a relative prohibition that the slaughter begins.'[55] In all its confident swagger this, then, was the reductionist relativism we inherited in our undergraduate educa-

54. Arthur Schlesinger Jr, 'The Opening of the American Mind', *The New York Times Book Review*, July 23 1989. Schlesinger used strong terms to put down religion, accusing it of intolerance, bigotry and self-centredness. But it is well to remember that he cites with approval Reinhold Niebuhr's neo-Calvinist morality as essential for de-absolutizing secular and mundane structures, and the human instrument as finite and provisional vis-à-vis God's absolute and universal purpose. Niebuhr's central conviction about human power and institutions being always precarious and fragmentary is, says Schlesinger, indispensable to democratic values and historical realism. In fact Niebuhr's position can be traced back to the Reformers and, before them, to Pauline theology, pioneers of the 'absolutism' Schlesinger otherwise pillories.

55. F. Paul Wilson in letter to the editor, *New York Times Book Review*, 13 August, 1989.

tion, kept alive by a cultural rage against moral universals or uniqueness, with cultural pluralism and relativity replacing earlier assertions about universal stages and types. The position of Ruth Benedict, a student of Franz Boas, expresses very well the new attitude. She and her colleagues saw things differently. For them, 'historic cultures, whether literate or preliterate, were regarded as aesthetic patterns or configurations, each of which is a legitimate expression of the potentialities of human nature. There is, it was held, no absolute normality or abnormality of social behavior; the abnormal is only that which is divergent from the cultural pattern of the community.'[56] However, such a construction of the cultural project was grounded in a specific liberal democratic cultural ethos and did not, therefore, abandon either the unilateralism of Enlightenment rationalists or the inductive principles of the positivists, a problem that dogged many cultural relativists. The problem came to a head during World War II when the US War Department convened a special meeting of cultural anthropologists to get help in psychological campaigns against German National Socialism. One of these anthropologists objected to the purpose of the meeting on the grounds that scientific anthropology, being an objective discipline, carried no ethical biases as such, and therefore could make no value judgments. 'He went on to say that if the Germans preferred Nazism, they were entitled to that preference, just as democratic Americans are entitled to their own different preference,' because 'preference is simply an expression of [the] cultural milieu' in which we find it.[57]

A similar issue was involved when Melville Herskovits, a leading scholar of cultural anthropology, was confronted with the practical task of producing a charter of universal human

56. Bidney, 1953, 688.

57. Reported by James Luther Adams in his Introduction to Troeltsch, *The Absoluteness of Christianity*, 1971, 7. Robert Redfield, a cultural anthropologist and a participant at the meeting, tried, however, to split the issue, on the one hand, between scientific objectivity and its determinist ethical, or nonethical, consequences, and, on the other, the actions of free and moral human agents. Redfield's solution aggravates, rather than resolving, the problem, because if cultural relativism disqualifies moral judgment by its superior objective scientific method, then moral judgment is spurious and as such inferior, and vulnerable, to demonstrable objective facts.

rights for the United Nations. Herskovits adopts a concrete form of philosophical idealism, and identifies himself with the statement of Cassirer that 'experience is culturally defined',[58] not just 'conditioned'. Herskovits continues: 'Even the facts of the physical world are discerned through the enculturative screen so that the perception of time, distance, weight, size and other 'realities' is mediated by the conventions of any given group.'[59] For Herskovits there simply is no other reality than the social reality, and this absolute rule was the nemesis courting his theory of cultural relativism. Herskovits anticipates this criticism and says that our slowness or failure to concede the truth of cultural relativism is because we are bogged down in 'the ethnocentric morass' of a puritanical religious culture. Yet such an outburst does not rescue his scheme, merely repeats his denunciation of religion and relies on us to propagate the prejudice.

At the behest of the executive board of the American Anthropological Association, Herskovits drafted a document on human rights for the United Nations in 1947. In the statement Herskovits made three salient points: (a) that individuals realize their potential only through culture, (b) that cultures are unique and different with no valid scientific standard of objective evaluation, and (c) that standards of judgment are relative to the culture from which they derive. Consequently there can be no universal absolute moral codes, and therefore the attempt to impose a Universal Declaration of Human Rights on all mankind is scientifically invalid and morally indefensible.[60] It must have been awkward for Herskovits to feel that his natural impulse to want to uphold certain liberal democratic codes for life and conduct and for maintaining standards of human decency against possible abuse by nondemocratic regimes must give way to 'scientific' scruples of cultural noninterference.

The crux of the problem for cultural relativists is that in their concern to reject the unhealthy consequences of Western cultural and religious imperialism they reverted to a form of ethnocentrism in which other cultures are given licence to be a

58. Melville Herskovits, *Man and His Works*, New York: Alfred A. Knopf, 1948, 27. Cited also in Bidney, 1953, 689.
59. ibid., 1948, 63.
60. Bidney, 1953, 693.

law unto themselves and thus to be ethnocentric, with the stage set for proliferating plural cultural ethnocentrisms. The relativists have thus replaced the progressive ethnocentrism of the Enlightenment with their own serial ethnocentrism, with both sides retaining unilateral advantage and never really shaking free of historical particularity except, that is, by an illegitimate idealist route. It is hard to see how you could have cultural relativism without ethnocentrism. When Boas and Benedict, for instance, argue that the only scientific basis for intercultural harmony is mutual recognition of cultural equality and tolerance for difference,[61] it is not entirely clear whether such a basis, laudable in itself, is 'culturally determined'. In which case its converse, of prejudice and intolerance, could conceivably also be 'culturally determined', with no yardstick with which to adjudicate the matter. Nor is it clear how you could have unmitigated cultural relativism alongside any notion of absolute progress. Such would be the outcome of rigid adherence to 'facts and laws'.[62]

The Theological Issue

All of this leaves us with an acute problem in defining values. Full-blown cultural ethnocentrism is unacceptable because, relativists insist rightly, it encourages us to demean and devalue the cultures of others. Yet if our values are themselves culturally determined, then prejudice and domination and ideas of 'subjectivity' and 'objectivity' cannot be judged except as 'enculturative screens', and that simply will not do. Cultural relativists have forced themselves into their own Procrustean bed by insisting that our choice is between a doctrine of fixed absolutes and one of historical cultural relativity, since in cultural determinism there is no logical connection between specific cultural facts and a general moral code, so that any meaningful choosing on our part is at best

61. ibid., 1953, 688, 690.

62. Troeltsch observes in this connection: 'The doctrine of endless progress, or rather the theory of endless change, is a groundless prejudgment that seems plausible only to people who have consigned all metaphysical ideas regarding a transcendent background of history to the status of illusion – and with such ideas the religious belief in the unity and meaningfulness of reality.' Troeltsch, *The Absoluteness of Christianity*, 94.

arbitrary, or else self-interested, but in either case a choosing that is a conditioned rather than an independent moral act. It still remains an issue that human beings across cultures practise moral judgment and appeal to ethical rules, however diverse and different the contexts, and if that were not the case we would have bilnd conformity, aimless historical wandering, and worse. It would complicate matters, with the relativist, for instance, robbed of any virtue that might acrue to a worthy cause. Unless a fresh term is introduced into the equation we cannot escape the empirical dilemma of cultural relativism, namely, how in pursuit of progressive values we can move from what *is* to what *ought* to be. That 'middle' term is not a 'fact' we can scoop up nor a 'law' that belongs with ordering the relationship of inanimate objects, but an intellectual lever that takes us somewhere different from where it found us. That is how I would propose to proceed, to recognize that the cultural project, in being spiritual and intellectual, is at heart a theological matter, that reason is only secondarily human and primarily divine, not the wear and tear of nature's exterior drapery but its sap and fibre. Culture, 'whether personal or communal, is not reducible to genetics or ethnicity because man is always capable of transcending his origins, that is, of ending his journey in a different and better place than he began it.'[63]

Steiner's observation on the connection between theology and modern cultural projects is appropriate here, especially because it also deals with the issue of Enlightenment rationalism and nineteenth-century logical positivism. Steiner argues that the special way in which we read a text today, comment, critique and interpret it, derives directly from the study of Holy Scripture. He continues:

> Our grammars, our explications, our criticisms of texts, our endeavours to pass from letter to spirit, are the immediate heirs to the textualities of Western Judeo-Christian theology and biblical-patristic exegetics. What we have done since the masked scepticism of Spinoza, since the critiques of the rationalist Enlightenment and since the positivism of the nineteenth century, is to borrow

63. Levenson, 'The God of Abraham . . .', 19.

> vital currency, vital investments and contracts of trust from the bank or treasure-house of theology. It is from there that we have borrowed our theories of the symbol, our use of the iconic, our idiom of poetic creation and aura. It is loans of terminology and reference from the reserves of theology which provide the master readers in our time (such as Walter Benjamin and Martin Heidegger) with their licence to practice. We have borrowed, traded upon, made small change of the reserves of transcendent authority.'[64]

Steiner calls the misuse of religion by our secular, agnostic civilization an 'embarrassed act of larceny', involving as it does the act of drawing from a source while loudly trumpeting its bankruptcy, or, on the subject I now wish to treat, robbing the religious metaphysic to service a political metaphysic, for that is how the modern national state has emerged in Western consciousness. Thus in his penetrating analysis of the state as the symbol of 'the life-energy of the European race', Troeltsch shows the serious moral deficiences of cultural ethnocentrism expressed in political institutions, including the state. The ethnocentric state elevates military science and bureaucratic rules to a transcendent ethic, giving directions and goals in human affairs an absolute normative status. Troeltsch says that we must be able to live as human beings, which might become the legitimate subject of the state, but that we live not for the sake of mere physical existence but for the sake of ideas and ideals from which the state derives its ultimate meaning and value. He insists that the state as the possessor and user of power ought to come under the authority of what he termed 'the indestructible moral idea'.[65] Troeltsch goes on to argue that the separation of state and culture has allowed the state to push aside higher culture or otherwise harness it to its own interest, while higher culture for its part, sundered from a political ethic, is inclined to become escapist, the society of Orphic initiates.

Nationalism often acts to fuse the otherwise separate impulses

64. Steiner, *Real Presences*, 20.

65. Ernst Troeltsch, *Religion in History*, Minneapolis: Fortress Press, 1991, 176. Troeltsch was born in 1865 and died in 1923.

of culture and politics, and to produce a sentiment indistinguishable from the religious. Nationalism offers people a creed every bit as potent as religion, with love and devotion to one's people and country a competitor in the altruistic sense with faith in God and the hereafter. Honour and duty thus arise from citizenship nearly as faithfulness and submission arise from religious faith, for both prove their claims from the personal sacrifices individuals are constrained to make. Nationalism in this understanding effectively combines persuasion with sanction, self-denial with personal vindication, natural ties with acquired skills, the struggle for existence with giving one's life, and so on. 'By thus identifying oneself with the state, one no longer needs to fear any superior power, except possibly God; in this sense of inviolability, one experiences a value that transcends egoism because it [i.e., the value] relates not to the individual but to the whole, and is made possible by an intense self-discipline and personal subjection.'[66] The state in these circumstances would come to regard 'itself as a source of ethical value and moral obligation. It can (and often does) invest this claim with all the pathos of moral sentiment.'[67] Yet, as Troeltsch admits, nationalism that is thus sacralized and absolutized becomes a source of the demonic and the depraved, in Europe and elsewhere,[68] including programmes of 'ethnic cleansing'.

Taking up a similar theme, the American philosopher, William Ernest Hocking, identifies the grounds for a limited theory of state sovereignty, saying that the state furnishes the conditions under which people can make themselves. The state, he argues, is necessary to enable rational planning to take place, including planning for the future. However, this future-planning function of the state, Hocking says, is perceived as representing 'man's longer will' and is consequently given an objective status, leading to the wrong conclusion that the state is capable of civilizing human beings, of leading us out of ignorance and stagnation into knowledge of the future and progress. Hocking spoke confidently of the state as the political community having its counterpart in the religious community which embraces the 'totality of the

66. Troeltsch, *Religion in History*, 179.
67. ibid. 68. ibid.

ultimate state of man, representing a dimension which the state cannot reach.'[69] The state, in Hocking's view, does not speak for the cosmos but for a community of people limited in scope and wisdom. In spite of that, he says, the expectation has grown of the state's superior right to conceive and speak for the attainable good life, leading to the view that it is the Church, not the state, that will in time wither away. This, Hocking insists, is the secular hypothesis: the state will satisfy human nature and succeed in its work. Yet, Hocking cautions, the state is inadequate in itself: it 'depends for its vitality upon a [spiritual] motivation which it cannot by itself command.'[70] The religious case against the doctrinaire state is a solid one, because 'religion is the affirmation of the anchorage in reality of ideal ends'.[71] The very nature of the secular, pragmatic state is that it is a human, finite contrivance, 'and the gap between the finite and the infinite remains – infinite. If . . . it is with the infinite that we have always to do, the state must be infinitely short of complete competence.'[72] In which case, the state's finite capacity would turn oppressive once it assumes the prerogatives of the infinite. 'A strong State without a strong Church, as recent events have vividly shown, will inevitably assume some, and perhaps most, of the attributes of unchecked absolutism.'[73] On the face of it, then, it seems scarcely possible to repudiate the moral law in favour of absolute sovereignty in nature or in politics without disastrous consequences for persons and societies.

Thus when Aristotle reflected critically on what might be involved in transcending our natural limitations and thus securing our felicity as human beings, he did the best he could in the circumstances and left the door open to a theological inquiry. He suggested that we aspire to the fount itself and not be content with the mere trickle of the natural order.[74]

69. William Ernest Hocking, *The Coming World Civilization*, London: George Allen & Unwin, 1956, 2.

70. ibid., 6. 71. ibid., 30. 72. ibid., 44.

73. Kenneth Grubb, review article, 'The Relations of Church and State', *International Review of Missions*, vol. 36, no. 142, April, 1947.

74. Aristotle held that intellectual inquiry and the ordinary life of civic virtue would indeed harmonize by a natural teleological development, but he misses the cultural factors that might warp such a process.

> If happiness is activity in accordance with virtue, it is reasonable that it should be in accordance with the highest virtue; and this will be the best thing in us. Whether it be reason or something else that is this element which is thought to be our natural ruler and guide and to take thought of things noble and divine, whether it be itself also divine or only the most divine element in us, the activity of this in accordance with its proper virtue will be perfect happiness.[75]

The comment of C. S. Lewis, that 'when we are forced to admit that reason cannot be merely human, there is no longer any compulsive inducement to say that virtue is purely human' articulates an insight that returns the arc to its point of maximum tension, marking a fitting consummation of Aristotle's design.[76]

Similarly, when Bacon writes of God's book and God's works as two necessary sources of knowledge, he allows the view that the pen as reason is mightier than the spade, and higher than 'centaurs and chimeras', the gods of whim and fancy. We should see that 'human reason in the act of knowing is illuminated by the Divine reason.'[77] This is so because reason in that sense has to break free sufficiently from the chain of causation to be at the behest of what it knows. It is the characteristic of the knower as subject that, as al-Ghazálí (1058–1111) would express it with reference to religion, the believer's 'heart has reasons his reason does not know'.[78] Thus the chain of causation in which we lock up all of nature turns out to have a key in the insight of reason: it is that insight that gave us by inference the chain in the first place. As Chesterton remarked concerning the pervasive anti-Aristotelian material determinism of our day, it is absurd to claim that people are rational and objective because they come to no

75. *Nicomachean Ethics*, bk, X, chp. 7.

76. Lewis's statement may be read not as seeking to rescue Aristotle's teleology but as concerning itself with the nature of thought as such.

77. C. S. Lewis, *Miracles: A Preliminary Study*, London & Glasgow: Fontana Books, 1963, 26–7.

78. Cited in Averroës, *The Incoherence of the Incoherence* (*Taháfut al-Taháfut*), vol. i, ed. & tr. Simon van den Bergh, London: Luzac & Co., 1954, xxxvi. Al-Ghazálí, an effective apologist for Islamic orthodoxy, made use for that purpose of the methods of the scholastic philosophers.

conclusion, and that religion is subjective and untrustworthy for bringing us to conclusions. Such a claim, Chesterton points out, is based on 'the quite unproved proposition of the independence of matter and quite improbable proposition of its power to originate mind.'[79] There is a certain tautology such unexamined assumptions produce, such as that no intelligent person would believe in religion, and therefore intelligent persons who do (such as Pasteur, Newton, Faraday, Einstein or Newman) cease to count as such, or, as Chesterton puts it, 'first you challenge me to produce a black swan, and when I produce a score you rule them all out because they were black. Yet the conclusion to which religion would bring us presses hard even on our resistance, namely, the awesome grandeur of Cosmic Reason as our Creator and Maker.' Lewis puts it as follows:

> In so far as thought is merely human, merely a characteristic of one particular biological species, it does not explain our knowledge. Where thought is strictly rational it must be, in some odd sense, not ours, but cosmic or super-cosmic. It must be something not shut up inside our heads but already 'out there' – in the universe or behind the universe: either as objective as material Nature, or more objective still. Unless all that we take to be knowledge is an illusion, we must hold that in thinking we are not reading rationality into an irrational universe but responding to a rationality with which the universe has always been saturated.[80]

79. G. K. Chesterton, *All Things Considered*, 1908, repr. Philadelphia: Dufour Editions, 1969, 137. Emerson writes confidently of nature as mental life, so that 'in the mass and in particle, Nature hastens to render account of herself to the mind'. 'The American Scholar' in Stephen E. Whicher, ed. *Selections from Ralph Waldo Emerson*, Boston: Houghton Mifflin Co., 1960, 65. Compare that view to that of John Stuart Mill who wrote: 'the appearances in nature forcibly suggest the idea of a maker (or makers), and therefore all mankind have believed in gods', although Mill goes on to say that these appearances also contradict the idea of a perfectly good maker. John Stuart Mill, *Journals and Debating Speeches*, Collected Works of John Stuart Mill, 1988, vol. xxvii, London: Routledge: Toronto: University of Toronto Press, 659.

80. C. S. Lewis, 'De Futilitate', chap. in his *Christian Reflections*, 65. We may observe that it is part of the rational structure of reality that the physical universe

In the final analysis the religious view that creation has a purpose and that we as human beings hold it in moral stewardship may be decisive for any enlightened cultural project, in the same way that the inflexibility of both the right-wing romantic 'return to nature' and the left-wing ideological reductionism could be its ruin. This would explain why even the imaginative synthesizing of an exalted reason and an idealized beauty to create an aesthetic harmony appears to have failed because both reason and beauty were torn from their common moral framework, so that Voltaire's 'cultivated garden' (*il faut cultiver notre jardin*) seemed as much like the valley of dead bones as Montaigne's dry cynicism (*il nous faut abestir pour nous assagir*). Retreat in the one instance is answered by defiance in the other, and in both cases we have merely *homo mensura* ('man as the measure of all things') as first and last resort. Lessing tried to make a virtue of this sense of forlorn heroism in the following words:

---

was born in time, created as such, and participates in the temporal conditionality of existence, assuming life, growing, aging, dying and coming to life in the relentless thrust towards its completion. This view of the universe stands right at the heart of Christian theology, in contrast to the timeless notions of philosophical idealism. This timeless view of nature is analogous to the view of nature as necessary, rather than only as contingent. It is as such that Emerson, for example, would wish to promote Nature in the upper case. 'The astronomer discovers that geometry, a pure abstraction of the human mind, is the measure of planetary motion. The chemist finds proportion and intelligible method throughout matter; and science is nothing but the finding of analogy, identity, in the most remote parts. The ambitious soul will sit down before each refractory fact; one after another reduces all strange constitutions, all new powers, to their class and their law, and goes on forever to animate the last fiber of organization, the outskirts of nature, by insight. Thus to him, to this schoolboy under the bending dome of day, is suggested that he and it proceed from one root; one is leaf and one is flower, relation, sympathy, stirring in every vein.' Emerson, 'The American Scholar', 66. To that extent Emerson has jettisoned any notion of the historical character of the world, finding truth in the 'inner life, a life stripped of the past because it was conceived by a regenerate soul in nature', says his biographer. Evelyn Barish, *Emerson: The Roots of Prophecy*, Princeton: Princeton University Press, 1989, 174. Bertrand Russell (1872–1970) rejects this Hegelian monism, saying it collapses everything into the subject-predicate form. *Autobiography*, London: Unwin Paperbacks, 1975, repr. 1989, 674. It is, however, difficult to reconcile Russell's high ethical idealism with his hedonism, his complaint against all that makes 'a mockery of what human life should be' with his call for indulging the passions in ecstasy.

> If God were to hold in His right hand all truth, and in His left the single, ever-living impulse to seek for truth, though coupled with the condition of eternal error, and should say to me, 'Choose!' I would humbly fall before His left hand, and say, 'Father, give! Pure truth is, after all, for Thee alone . . .'[81]

This kind of herosim belongs not with the nature of the facts as we know them but with the moral sense that transcends nature. We may recall the words of John Stuart Mill that all the things for which human beings are hanged or imprisoned for doing are routinely committed by nature, including 'hundreds of hideous deaths' that surpass the cruelty of a Domitian. 'All this,' Mill pleads, 'Nature does with the most supercilious disregard both of mercy and of justice.' (*Essay on Nature*). Such a plea appeals to the tribunal of our heart and brings us up against the moral grain. A line in the liturgy of the East Syrian Church expresses the sentiment well when it affirms: 'Thou hast clothed us with a moral nature which our trespasses ever painfully oppress.' The quest for the cultural ideal, then, contains this melancholy strain, defying us to set a course that would not eventually rejoin the main tributary in which all streams renew themselves by discharging their moral tribute. Some of that impulse still stirs in the depths even of apparent indifference and other forms of moral sluggishness, the thin blue line that separates us from the nature of Mill's description. And it is precisely what makes religion, even religion in its deterrent form, in what it repudiates, qualitatively different from rational defiance or self-indulgence in which the enterprise can be no greater or higher than what would be at stake in a heroic self-vindication, as in Wagner's Wotan. There is a real qualitative, moral change involved in the religious life, because '[the] moment that some things are sacred, man has begun to live in the world which provides for him the substance and the sanction of his ideals: and the change appears as much in the quality of his disloyalty to them as of his faithfulness . . .'[82]

If, for example, the whole Western enterprise consists in nothing other than heroic exploits of self-assertion, then, of

81. Rolleston, *Life of Lessing*, 1889, chp. xvii.
82. Oman, *The Natural and the Supernatural*, 1931, 388–89.

course, the historical facts of the Western encounter with other cultures and societies could with justice be read as unequivocal facts of violence and domination. If, on the other hand, Western Christianity, though sharing in all the cultural forms of the larger society, was nevertheless not ultimately synonymous with those forms, then Christianity in its locally appropriated forms would introduce some ambiguity into cultural encounter, such that there would be ambivalence, paradox and other unintended consequences resulting from the encounter. This would not deny the real destruction and harm that accompanied Western expansion abroad, including missionary denigration of non-Western cultures, but it would not give all the initiative to the West. While we cannot deny Christianity as a cultural captive of the West, with missionaries, for example, more often than not being agitated by cultural differences and seldom excited by genuine religious similarities, we may discover in that coalescence of religion and culture how a similar process would be repeated to the advantage of non-Western populations whose particular appropriation of Christianity would mobilize and enshrine the local idiom.

Thus the question we must deal with in subsequent chapters is whether the Western cultural project is so flawed that contact with other cultures imperils those cultures to the same extent. Modern historical examples of the West's violent intrusion into other societies do not, on the face of it, encourage a different conclusion, and it would be disingenuous in the extreme to pretend otherwise. Yet, unless we were to adopt a rather extreme view of comprehensive indigenous defeat, it seems reasonable to think that some pockets of resistance remained within which local initiatives could prosper and bear fruit, with or without Western encouragement. If that were the case, it would make Western cultural contact one factor, albeit a fundamental factor, in the total historical picture whose focus might now be local interlocutors and the agency role they assumed as translators, interpreters, vademecums, colporteurs, teachers, writers, preachers, catechists, secretaries, and so on, not an insignificant shift of emphasis in the light of alleged Western control and monopoly of the subject.

Furthermore, if we were to shift our attention in that way, it would move us beyond the easy stereotypes of oppressor and oppressed, or of victimizer and victim, stereotypes that have made so much of the scholarly literature in the field so repetitive and predictable. Missionaries have been handy scapegoats for Western political imperialism, with historians only too ready to enter the breach on the side of angels. The indigenous refocusing, however, might assist us to vary the diet, as it were, to cut back on foreign bulk and increase local intake. We must afford to concentrate on the indigenous meat between the formal sandwich of colonialism and mission if we hope to say anything new or different on the subject, as I personally hope.

Thus when we assess whether Western contact has had a harmful or beneficial effect on non-Western populations, whether, to take even more specific forms of the question, modern Western Christian missions in Africa have damaged or advanced local cultural practices and aspirations, we emerge with a rather complex understanding, one that throws new light on the question of whether culture contact can be completely innocent and neutral, in which case so-called 'contact' is a misnomer, or whether, as I would argue, contact can be mutually beneficial as well as harmful. The proponents of innocent culture contact deny its possibility and thus invoke the harmful alternative. That view is what has carried the main charge of expounding and explaining the work of Christian missions, including the process of religious conversion, in Africa and elsewhere. Yet, unless we were to assume the victim view of non-Western populations, it would seem remarkable that missionary contact should always and everywhere lead to the same unvarying result of leaving the Western initiative triumphant and unchallenged while Africans grovelled in unmitigated defeat. Historical realism should discount such a wholesale displacement of human originality and the creative impulse it spawns, a realism borne out, indeed, by the records themselves. We should now move forward to explore the specific and concrete dimensions of what has until now tended to be promoted in the guise of hostile sweeping generalizations.

2

'They Stooped to Conquer':* Cultural Vitality and the Narrative Impulse in Missionary Translations

Introduction

I would like in this chapter to pursue two main themes: the idea of mother tongues being at the root of cultural narrative, and vernacular Scriptural translations of Western missionaries as the machinery of mother tongue literacy in Africa and elsewhere. Two further related issues are the nature of Christianity as an essentially 'translated' religion linguistically and theologically, and the continuity of that 'translated' theme in vernacular religious translation in the Christian West and how that influenced narrative development in the West. The essentially 'translatable' nature of Christianity, to be more fully discussed in the following chapter, and the Western comparison are the two folds between which I attempt to place the African material, both to show thematic continuity and contextual specificity. I now wish to push beyond many of the considerations of the previous chapter, beyond culture as a problem for philosophical idealism, and go on to the material and historical content of the cultural narrative. In particular, I would like to demonstrate with some concrete examples the connection between the Christian process and narrative impulse. We should proceed to examine the bond between 'the noble character of common speech' that was such a distinctive trait of Bunyan's art and the common stirrings of soil, blood and breeding that have been the narrative force behind the vernacular translation of the Christian Scriptures.

Expressing a sentiment that might stand as a flagship for Renaissance humanism, Erasmus (d. 1536) spoke of the social and cultural effects of making Christian Scriptures available to

*An adapted version of this chapter was published in *Research in African Literatures*, Summer, 1992.

ordinary as well as exotic people in their own tongues. He had the vision not that farmers, fishermen and weavers should abandon plough, shore and shuttle and flock to the academy, but that translating the Scriptures would help achieve for the common and humble people the humanist ideal. Aware of the revolutionary social implications of his view, Erasmus defended himself by arguing that the religion of Christ is imbued with a populist, republican principle, for whereas, in his words, 'the mysteries of kings, perhaps, are better concealed', those of Christ are meant to be 'published as openly as possible'.[1]

It is not necessary to pursue this sociopolitical theme in order to appreciate the profound cultural and linguistic consequences of extending to vernacular languages the authority of Scriptural status, not to say anything of the detailed, copious labour necessary to reduce these languages to writing and to furnish them with a scientific apparatus. It is that cultural/linguistic subject I want to pursue in a thematic way here, using African, Western and other examples to marshal and develop the subject.

I should, however, say my methodology of focusing on the vernacular involves a shift from those who *brought* the message to those who *received* it. In the examples we shall be considering of translating the Christian Scriptures into the vernacular, we find, among other things, that indigenous conceptions and idioms modified considerably the terms of Western encounter with non-Western cultures.

The African Crucible

The awakening of communities and individuals towards a sense of opposition to colonial overlordship in fact has been one of the momentous consequences of vernacular translation in Africa. Two powerful currents arising from a common source in Europe swept through Africa by divergent channels. Colonial rule carried the current of foreign legitimacy, with the corollary that local leaders and institutions are inadequate, while Christian missions,

1. Desiderius Erasmus, *Christian Humanism and the Reformation*, Selected Writings, with the life of Erasmus by Beatus Rhenanus, ed. John C. Olin, New York: Harper Torchbooks, 1965, 96–7.

or at least those so involved, adopted the vernacular, making it the basis for religious work as well as for the wider cultural expression in relation to which specific religious responses could be elicited. Thus the missionary goal of establishing the spiritual kingdom produced materials that Africans used in order to pursue cultural goals here and now. Henceforth, as Africans faced the unforeseen situation of forcible foreign rule, they found that the accompanying foreign Christianity possessed the unsuspected antidote to the loss represented by colonialism, and since Christianity could ostensibly be adopted as evidence of capitulating to foreigners, it was an effective disguise for the cultural resistance it made possible. There is little doubt about the role of missionary institutions in creating and guiding the sentiment for the national cause, and a Christianity that commended itself through mother tongue projects afforded Africans a unique opportunity for bicultural competency. Ultimately mother tongue sentiments fused with the revolutionary message of the Bible concerning the *impartiality* of God towards all peoples and races and then inveighed against residual obstacles created by continued colonial rule and the doctrine of white racial supremacy.

It should be said that in some significant instances missionary translators themselves stumbled on the significance of mother tongue primacy even before Africans came to a similar realization. As one missionary argued, the experience gained from translating the Scriptures into African languages was decisive for the conviction that no insuperable barrier existed against adopting these languages as mediums of instruction in schools, languages that were 'rich, flexible, expressive, musical, capable of infinite development'.[2] Therefore, 'to insist upon an African abandoning his own tongue and to speak and read and think in a language so different as English, is like demanding that the various Italian peoples should learn Chinese in order to overcome their linguistic problem.'[3] In time, missionary confidence elicited a corresponding African attitude and the two sides coalesced into

2. Edwin W. Smith, *The Golden Stool: Some aspects of the Conflict of Cultures in modern Africa*, London: Holborn Publishing House, 1926, 302.
3. Smith, *Golden Stool*, 303.

a common conviction to break surface in organized activity. There was, consequently, a remarkable historical coincidence between vernacular development and mother tongue aspirations that were the early forms of nationalist ferment. Here, too, the political and social implications of Erasmus's observations find parallels.

Two general ideas growing out of the vernacular translation ferment and having considerable impact on Africans may be identified here. One was how the Christian religion, or at any rate its Protestant forms, separated itself from the need to employ a special professional language, especially any arcane, elitist form reserved for religion and excluded from the mundane, workaday world. Secondly, ordinary Africans, including women, came to perceive that in principle they suffered no stigma of a ritual or cultural nature to prevent them from participating in the religious life. From the perspective of those receiving the message, the indigenous enterprise became necessary for religious and moral fulfilment, so that communities and individuals that henceforth stood affirmed as without stigma before God saw fit to demand equality of treatment before colonial rulers. Their religious insight, bound up with mother tongue awareness, found political expression.

That Africans conceived a narrative continuity in religion, more pervasive, more all-embracing and more comprehensive still than the Western view of it as a separate department of life, is undoubted, and it allowed them to relate Christianity to the whole system of life. Thus one schoolteacher in Africa responded to missionary inquiries about where religion and other forms of indoctrination occurred in the syllabus in this way:

> We teach it all day long. We teach it in arithmetic, by accuracy. We teach it in language, by learning to say what we mean – 'Yea, yea, and nay, nay.' We teach it in history, by humanity. We teach it in geography, by breadth of mind. We teach it in handicraft, by thoroughness. We teach it in astronomy, by reverence. We teach it in the playground, by fair play. We teach it by kindness to animals, by courtesy to servants, by good manners to one another, and by truthfulness in all

> things. We teach it by showing the children that we, their elders, are their friends and not their enemies.[4]

If some missionaries saw and welcomed the liberating and renovating effects of vernacular literacy, there were others who saw and feared it. In much of French and Portuguese-speaking Africa, for example, vernacular Scriptural translation was discouraged, in large part because the authorities suspected it of fomenting the nationalism they abhorred. The slow painful emergence of vernacular projects in culture, language and literature, or the highly ambivalent attitudes that have long prevailed in these and other countries, shows the importance of mother tongue consciousness to the modern culture of Africa. The point was underscored by one assessment which states that 'hardly any writing is done in the vernaculars' in former French, Belgian and Portuguese territories, in contrast to English-speaking Africa where 'indirect rule and the concern of Protestant missionaries to make the Bible available to native populations have encouraged the new writers' attachment to their mother tongues.'[5] Thus, in this matter, the negative proves the argument as well as does the positive, for disallowing the vernacular because it incites mother tongue aspirations concedes its power.

These considerations make explicit the issues involved in the methodology employed in our analysis and it calls us to recognize indigenous criteria for cultural and artistic creativity rather than looking to imported models only. If Africans were merely to protest at foreign influence without a sense of their own unique vernacular voice, they might succeed in proving they have been dominated but scarcely that they are creative agents of their own destiny. Yet anyone familiar with Africa can testify to the great reserves of talent and enterprise that even current economic gloom has failed to dissipate entirely.

4. Cited in Smith, *Golden Stool*, 311.

5. Albert S. Gérard, *Four African Literatures: Xhosa, Sotho, Zulu, Amharic*, Berkeley & Los Angeles: University of California Press, 1971, 382. Edwin Smith also observed that the French, the Belgians and the Portuguese adopt policies that suppress African languages 'not on educational, but on political grounds'. Smith calls it 'an injustice'. Smith, *Golden Stool*, 301–2.

Historical Precedents and Comparative Perspective

Whether or not they intended it, therefore, missionary translators gave consecrated value to the vernacular by investing it with a Scriptural tradition. It would be useful with a few early historical examples to show how such linguistic work leads to wider cultural interest, examples that would help to position the subject adequately. Coptic Christianity is a good illustration. From about the middle of the third century, Coptic villages along the Nile began converting to Christianity. At first Greek was the predominant language of religion and scholarship, having been in wide currency in neighbouring Alexandria, the home of the famous Catechetical School. But the language was viewed as foreign. As the new religion gained ground it spawned the need to move beyond Greek, or the little of it that was employed, and in the late fourth century and early in the following, steps were taken to produce material in the vernacular allowing Egypt to make its unique contribution to Christianity. As the Yale scholar and first occupant of the position the present writer is privileged to fill, Kenneth Scott Latourette, put it: 'In Egypt it was the successful effort to provide the masses of the population with a literature in the speech of everyday life which halted the exclusive use of the alien Greek for the written page and which stimulated the development of an alphabet which could be quickly and easily learned by the multitude in place of the ancient hieroglyphics which could be the property only of the few. Through this medium Coptic Christian literature came into being, largely the work of monks.'[6]

A similar phenomenon occurred in Ethiopia, where by the middle of the seventh century, the great vernacular work in Amharic and Ge'ez within the Ethiopian Orthodox Church had been accomplished. It gave Ethiopia a powerful national and cultural sense of her heritage[7] and was an effective barrier against wholesale Islamization.

6. Kenneth Scott Latourette, *A History of Christianity*, 2 vols., revised edition, New York: Harper & Row, vol, i, 250–51.

7. Taddesse Tamrat, *Church and State in Ethiopia: 1270–1527*, Oxford: Clarendon Press, 1972; also E. Ullendorf, *Ethiopia and the Bible*, London: Oxford University Press, 1988; Asa J. Davis, 'The Orthodoxy of the Ethiopian Church', *Tarikh*, 1967, vol. 2, no. 1; Getatchew Haile, 'A Christ for the Gentiles: the Case of the za-Krestos of Ethiopia', *Journal of Religion in Africa*, 1985, vol. 15, no. 2.

Parallel developments were taking place in Europe itself. In the Carolingian empire, for instance, significant attention was being devoted to the vernacular cause, with mission again providing the impetus. A modern scholarly evaluation of the Frankish Church identified the vernacular work as a force in the rise of German national sensibility.

> The impetus to write the vernacular still came from the mission-field and to it the emperor [i.e., Charlemagne] had something to say. There can be no doubt that to him, as to all his contemporaries, the language of Christianity in the liturgical sense remained Latin, one of the three sacred languages . . . But the Anglo-Saxons and the Goths had shown that the language of religious exposition could be vernacular; and this was to be encouraged . . . Most significant . . . are the very large number of vernacular glosses, sermons, hymns and confessions that survive . . . This wide-ranging reach of the written vernacular for religious purposes through the Carolingian world is of first significance . . . That people should understand underlies a large part of all surviving vernacular translation of the period.[8]

One individual who strengthened this vernacular effort was Otfrid von Weissenburg, active between 863 and 871. He appealed to the people to remain faithful to the vernacular cause and to adopt measures to ensure its faithful transmission. The criticial account of his work says he called on his learned contemporaries 'who knew how to think and who can be encouraged through the vernacular to read more for themselves. Moreover, he combines learning with piety with great technical skill; something which no one had hitherto attempted in German on such a scale. Like the *Heliand* [sic.] poet, Otfrid moved within the Germanic thought-world of warrior ethos, loyalty and obedience, the lord-man relationship.'[9]

Such pioneer religious translation work was the force that sparked the great cultural impulse of northern European tribes,

8. John Michael Wallace-Hadrill, *The Frankish Church*, Oxford: Clarendon Press, 1983, 378ff.
9. ibid., 386.

articulating afresh older cultural themes and examples in the midst of religious change. Matthew Arnold is correct to credit what he calls the northern Barbarians with a leavening influence on Western cultural refinement, but Barbarians only *after* their fateful encounter with Christianity.[10] The translated manuscripts themselves are a unique historical source as well as being literary specimens that helped set the pace for wide-ranging cultural innovations.

One of the most explicit and ambitious attempts during this early period to adopt the vernacular was the effort in Moravia, where, in the ninth century, two Byzantine missionaries went to work. These were Constantine-Cyril, who died young at forty-two (Feb. 869), and his brother saint, Methodius (d. April 885). They were both committed champions of the vernacular. They invented the Slavonic alphabet, known after its creator as the Cyrillic alphabet, the standard usage in the Eastern Orthodox Church, including Russia. Of the wide-ranging effects on Slavonic society and culture of the vernacular translation inaugurated by Constantine-Cyril and developed by Methodius, a modern authority summed it up as follows:

> His translation is in many ways an adaptation of the peculiar genius of the Slavic idiom elevated to a literary language and to the needs of the young Moravian church . . . Constantine was well acquainted with the translations of the Gospels into other eastern languages . . . He stressed his intention of translating the Gospels as accurately as possible, respecting, however, the difference in expression and in the meaning of certain words of both languages. In such cases he thought himself entitled to a more independent rendering of some of the passages in order to be able to explain the true meaning of the original.
>
> In his translation Constantine followed the principles expounded in his treatise. Slavic philologists recognize the excellent qualities of his translation, which reveals a very deep knowledge of the Greek and Slavic languages and of

10. Matthew Arnold, 'Culture and Anarchy', chap. 3, *Selected Prose*, Penguin Classics, 1987.

> their character. The translation is sometimes not verbal, as Constantine tried to make Greek expressions more understandable to the Slavic Christians . . . Constantine introduced his translations of the four Gospels in a special poetic composition . . . *We read there a passionate appeal to the Slavs to cherish their books written in their own language* . . . this was the first translation of the Gospels into a vernacular language to appear in the West.[11]

Modern commentators trace the idea of the unique character of Czech-Slavic culture and national identity to the vernacular translation work of the ninth century. The modern scholar, Weingart, for example, affirms that 'This Czech-Slavic type of culture was of paramount importance for the preservation, or at least, for the strengthening of the national character. If the Czechs did not succumb to Germanization as quickly and to such an extent as the Wends [i.e., the Slavs of eastern Germany], this is indeed due to the growth of the Czech Old Church Slavonic letters.'

On the occasion of the 1100th anniversary of the Moravian Mission, His Beatitude Dorotheos, Metropolitan of Prague and All Czechoslovakia, held the vernacular work of Constantine and Methodius as responsible for preserving the Slavic national idea. He commented: 'The testament of Orthodox Moravia, left to us by St Methodius, has been the keynote throughout the history of our nation; it has become the guide of the Slavic idea . . . Methodius and Cyril helped to develop the culture of Great Moravia, especially the language . . . thus uniting [the] separate Slavic tribes into well-organized states. In so doing, they [awakened] in the nation a sense of national self-awareness.'[12]

In the subsequent history of the Eastern Orthodox Church, this vernacular emphasis distinguished its own mission into other cultures. For example, St Stephen of Perm (1340–96) led a

11. Francis Dvornik, *Byzantine Missions among the Slavs: SS Constantine-Cyril and Methodius*, New Brunswick, N.J.: Rutgers University Press, 1970, 117ff. Emphasis added.

12. Metropolitan Dorotheos, 1985, 225, 219. I have reorganized the passages in the interests of logical coherence, with resulting awkward pagination.

mission to the Zyrian tribes of the northern forest, creating a Zyrian alphabet and translating some religious works into the language. He encouraged vernacular literacy.[13] A long period of regression followed with imperial Russia intervening, but in the nineteenth century Orthodoxy's vernacular policy was revived with the production of a modern Russian translation of the Old Testament by the versatile Macarius Gloukharev (1792–1847), coupling that with a translation of Western works.[14] And then Nicholas Ilminski (1821–91), a brilliant linguist who also studied Arabic in Cairo, carried the vernacular cause among the Russian Tartars whose language he treated not as a subspecimen of Arabic, as had been the wont, but as a language in its own right. The story is told of an elderly Tartar who was so struck by the genius of Ilminski's translation that he felt it affirmed the best in his culture. Thus, when he heard devotions in Ilminski's translation, he 'fell on his knees . . ., and with tears in his eyes thanked God for having vouchsafed to him at least once in his life to pray as he should.'[15] The devout Tartar had been stirred in the depths of blood, soul and tongue. Ilminski illuminated what he called 'the living tongue of the Tartars'[16] by investing it with Scriptural esteem, so that the popular, everyday language of the people was connected directly to 'their deepest thought and religious consciousness'.[17]

'It is in us, in our blood'

It is the same vernacular note that sounds like a drumroll in the rise and spread of the sense of social and cultural self-awareness, not in some refined if ephemeral Pan-African cultural project that is inclined to overlook linguistic and social particularity, but in the detailed, single-minded missionary cultivation of vernacular specificity, including the preservation of dialectical distinctions.

One missionary linguist who left a permanent mark on the African vernacular scene was Johannes Christaller, a Basel missionary of German origin who arrived in Ghana in the 1840s

13. James J. Stamoolis, *Eastern Orthodox Mission Theology Today*, Maryknoll, New York: Orbis Books, 1986, 26f.
14. ibid., 30f. 15. ibid., 32. 16. ibid., 33. 17. ibid., 33.

and soon after embarked on an enormous translation project that took him deep into the intricacies of Akan life and culture. His work has been received by modern Ghanaians as a manifesto of cultural nationalism. After Christaller left Ghana in the mid-1870s to return to Basel, he continued with his vernacular work. One of the fruits of his labour was an impressive compilation in 1879 of some 3600 Twi proverbs and idioms that provides an invaluable and unique insight into the Akan worldview. The British anthropologist, R. S. Rattray, produced an abridged and translated version of the proverbs for the Oxford series on African literature. In the preface to the collection Christaller acknowledged the great wealth of wisdom whose source, he felt, was no other than the Creator of the universe, a view which left the Akan and other Africans unbeholden to Western cultural scruples. He wrote: 'May this collection give a new stimulus to the diligent gathering of folk-lore and to the increasing cultivation of native literature. May those Africans, who are enjoying the benefit of a Christian education, make the best of the privilege; but let them not despise the sparks of truth entrusted to and preserved by their own people, and let them not forget that by entering into their way of thinking and by acknowledging what is good and expounding [sic.] what is wrong they will gain the more access to the hearts and minds of their less favoured countrymen.'[18]

In 1881 Christaller published his much acclaimed Twi dictionary, *Dictionary of the Asante and Fante Language: Called Twi*, a monument of indigenous scholarship and an impetus to cultural revitalization. The Twi dictionary systematized and articulated a wealth of linguistic and cultural materials, and established bonds of relationship and mutual influence among neighbouring languages and societies. Combined with the grammar of the Twi language that Christaller also wrote, the Twi dictionary gave the Akan an important instrument for cultural self-awareness in the context of the advancing machinery of colonial subjugation.

Christaller also helped found a paper, *The Christian Messenger*, in Basel in 1883, devoted to the promotion of Akan

18. Cited in Dr J. B. Danquah, *The Akan Doctrine of God*, London: Lutterworth Press, 1944, 186.

culture and social life. From 1905 to 1917, when it was transferred to Ghana, it published articles in Twi, Ga and English, and covered local as well as international events, such as the news of the Russo-Japanese War of 1905 – an event in which there was considerable local interest – Halley's Comet of 1910 and the sinking of the *Titanic* in 1911. As I had occasion to write elsewhere, 'The use of the vernacular to report on world news and instruct its readers in local affairs was a major contribution of the paper, for it suggests that its audience could keep abreast of happenings without literacy in the European languages.'[19]

David Asante, a native of Akropong, Ghana, and trained between 1857 and 1862 at Basel, inherited Christaller's devotion to the vernacular cause. Commenting on Christaller's translation of the Psalms into Twi, Asante, evoking the sentiments of the elderly Tartar, testified: 'The Psalms are translated perfectly and brilliantly. Nobody can read this translation without deep feelings of awe. They resemble in many ways the songs of mourning [*Kwadwom*] in our Twi language; the Twi people will be glad to read them. May the Lord give His blessing to your labours. I want to congratulate you personally and in the name of Africa. May the Lord give you strength for more such work.'[20]

Such pioneer linguistic work was important for reinforcing the indigenous narrative predilection, as Asante's work makes clear. He translated many works from the German and English into Akan, including John Bunyan's *Pilgrim's Progress*, that perennial of the genre. His significance for Ghanaian letters and literature is considerable. 'But such is the preoccupation of Ghanaian biographers with 'merchant princes' and nationalist firebrands that, outside a small circle of the Presbyterian Church and an entry in the *Encyclopaedia Africana*, not much is known of such pioneers as Asante. Yet in the translation of the Bible and in his other books he helped to introduce new concepts, new words and phrases into Ghanaian literature.'[21]

19. Lamin Sanneh, *Translating the Message: The Missionary Impact on Culture*, Maryknoll, New York: Orbis Books, 1989, 2nd printing, 1990, 180.
20. Cited in Hans W. Debrunner, *A History of Christianity in Ghana*, Accra, Ghana: Waterville Publishing House, 1967, 144.
21. Andrew W. Amegatcher, 'Akropong: 150 Years Old', *West Africa*, July 14, 1986, p. 1472.

Another local pioneer was Carl Christian Reindorf who wrote in 1889 a history of his people, *The History of the Gold Coast and Asante*, a work that embodied two major innovations. It was first written in Ga, the vernacular of the Ghanaian coast, and, second, it made extensive use of oral traditions as a source comparable to documentary evidence, thus representing the kind of historical methodology that scholars thought they were pioneering in the 1960s. All of this immense vernacular work had a predictable effect on national sentiment.

Indeed, almost as a response to that vernacular theme in Christaller and David Asante, a local quasi-political organization was founded, called the Reference Group, comprising educated Akan who pressed for the retention of the vernacular in church and social life. For it, too, religious insight sought a political channel. Its members were, therefore, considered the early pioneers of African nationalism.[22]

In the case of South Africa a similar vernacular process can be discerned, and, given the historic controversy there, we should expect the Erasmian criticism of elite monopoly of truth to assume a particularly explosive form wherever vernacular sentiments are aroused. The turning point came when missionaries adopted the African name for God, so that the Zulu word *UnKulunkulu*, for instance, was adopted for the God of the Christian Scriptures. Nothing in their previous training or religious preparation had prepared the missionaries for such a momentous move or its consequences. God is the great archetypal theme in African narrative life, since the first stories about the race and its lapsarian afflictions come out of that source, the paradigmatic story in the light of which other stories can be told and retold. In the vernacular field setting, it turns out, the missionaries were overtaken by Africans who had heard of God and the special forms by which knowledge of this God assumes the dimensions of narrative understanding. No wonder many missionaries felt themselves pre-empted; the story of their arrival among the people, though a major historical event, was, on the level of narrative, a pale reflection of the myths and legends that spoke of spirit and matter and of good and evil.

22. Lamin Sanneh, *West African Christianity: The Religious Impact*, Maryknoll, New York: Orbis Books, 1983, 2nd printing, 1990, 150.

The religious and theological aspects of vernacular translation, strictly considered, belong to a later stage of our discussion. What is clear now is that missionary transmitters, having stooped to conquer the native idiom, mobilized African sentiments and commenced a transformation process in society and culture by paying close and sustained attention to mother tongues, including furnishing a documentary apparatus for their understanding. There was change involved in this, for while it might be possible in the pre-Christian period for Africans to think of God in highly refracted social and ethnic terms, now a new scale of identity was introduced that included critical self-reflection in the transcribed medium of language, a language, in the bargain, that retained the marks of the people's tongue. Unless we were to allow ourselves to be deterred by the scruples of anthropological innocence or cultural superiority, we must concede that through the vernacular channel Africans entered an immensely important stage of human consciousness in which the printed word and native diction combined in elucidating the encounter not just with the brave new world of the West but with ancient forms that always told of God's far from certain mindfulness for the race and tribe. Anyone who has learnt first to think and write in the mother tongue has an advantage that subsequent exposure to a foreign medium can only reinforce rather than displace, and if the mother tongue were to be saturated with popular sensibilities of Scripture, then we would have a social reality of remarkable endurance. Religious thought and reflection, and whatever else is involved in conversion, would in that context normally carry the seeds of social and cultural innovation.

What is illuminating in the indigenous cultural process then, is how the Christian Scriptures, cast as a vernacular oracle, gave the native idiom and the aspirations it enshrined a historic cause, allowing Africans to fashion fresh terms for their own advancement and possibility. As a result, language was organized and integrated with the simplest and most eloquent rules, with the terms of everyday speech stripped of foreign or gnostic conceit and made available to men, women and children without regard to economic or social status – and in some significant cases challenging such status. It was the kind of intellectual revolution that in the West produced the idea of the primacy of conscience, and thus of the free individual as the linchpin of redemption and social emancipation. In Africa, by contrast, it produced a fresh narrative cultural sensibility set in the context of family, tribe and nation.

In any case, having come that far and adopted, for example, the Zulu word for God, missionaries were committed to documenting relevant instances of observance, ritual, ceremony and practice, in the process furnishing invaluable ethnographic details and evidence. In the beginning some of them put up a dogged resistance to radical indigenization, including imposing on African converts humiliating sanctions for using mother tongues and practising other native customs on missionary premises. That was how missionary insensitivity collided with the pride Africans came to develop as the natural outcome of mother tongue literacy. By that stage the beast of the tribe was beyond taming, one consequence being that even the seclusion of mission enclaves failed to secure final immunity against indigenous claims.[23] Whether in the short or long run, the vernacular crucible forged the very image and substance of what did survive and endure from the missionary enterprise. The meticulous and painstaking business of learning African languages, of producing very careful scientific linguistic materials as an aid to translation, including the creation of alphabets – all this constituted landmarks that belonged with the native patrimony. They redefined Africa's material and intellectual values by placing them solidly within the general language of human consciousness, and it is a matter of incalculable significance that on the historic front line of cross-cultural encounter, Europeans should meet Africans not just as vanquished populations but as inalienable possessors of their own languages. It may not have averted eventual European mastery of the continent, but at least it introduced greater ambiguity into the encounter than would otherwise have been the case.

Thus before the first complete Zulu Bible was produced in 1883 by the American Board of Commissioners for Foreign Mission, there had been a generation or so of preparatory work.

23. I have examined this question of missionary enclavement in 'The Yogi and the Commissar: Christian Missions and the African Response', *International Bulletin of Missionary Research*, January, 1991.

In 1850, Hans Schreuder published a grammar of Zulu, followed in 1855 by the Anglican Bishop John Colenso's grammar. In 1859, Lewis Grout of the American Board produced in Natal his own grammar of Zulu.

Similar concentrated attention was paid to Zulu dictionaries. In 1855 Perrin's dictionary was published, and in 1861 Colenso's *Zulu-English Dictionary* came out, and in 1880 Charles Roberts produced a similar work. Colenso was prominent in a landmark event in the history of the Zulu language when in 1859 he visited the Zulu King Mpande. He took with him two Zulu schoolboys, Magema and Ndiyane, and a schoolteacher, William. Following their visit they published a book containing accounts in Zulu of the meeting with the king. The three texts written by Magema, Ndiyane and William were the earliest published contribution by a Zulu to the language.[24] Professor Nyembezi's general observation is worth reiterating here, namely, that missionary translation was connected with indigenous cultural revitalization. He says it was not simply that 'missionaries concerned themselves primarily with grammars, dictionaries and the translation of the Scriptures, [as that] some of them recorded folk-lore, proverbs and valuable historical material.'[25] C. M. Doke, whose pioneering and definitive studies of Zulu[26] take in the missionary factor, in his review of the development of Bantu languages has also drawn attention to the indispensable role of Bible translation in establishing these languages. Beginning with early Portuguese missionary translations in the seventeenth century, through Moffat, Krapf and Livingstone in the nineteenth century, and to Pilkington, W. H. Murray and Alexander Hetherick in the twentieth, an unprecedented linguistic enterprise was carried through that transformed the face of modern Africa. Doke admits, 'The story of this achievement of translation work, if written, would constitute a stirring romance. It will never be realized what privation, intensity of purpose, continued study, painstaking labour and pious devotion all this has meant, often in unhealthy

24. C. L. Sibusiso Nyembezi, *A Review of Zulu Literature*, Pietermaritzburg: University of Natal Press, 1961, 3f.

25. ibid., 3.

26. One of his first linguistic works is still considered a classic: Clement M. Doke, 1926, *The Phonetics of the Zulu Language*, a special publication of

climate, amid active opposition, with weak equipment or lack of support.'[27]

John Colenso was representative of those Western missionaries who saw that vernacular translation of the Scriptures opened the door into creative regions of the culture. For example, when he visited the Zulu king in 1859, Colenso had each of his three Zulu companions subsequently write an account of the event in Zulu, because, Colenso reasoned, it would encourage them to 'make a first attempt at keeping journals in their own language, which might be useful in showing how some of our proceedings looked from a native point of view',[28] a native point of view that naturally would leave its stamp. One of the results was that Colenso found a deep natural piety in some of the Zulu material of these journals, with a strong rhythmic structure that lent itself to measured metre. Colenso commented: 'The words run almost of themselves into rhythm and he [William Ngidi, one of his Zulu companions] has since thrown them into a metrical form, which is here added, in translation, as a specimen of a Zulu Hymn, written by a native.'[29] Here is the hymn itself:

> My brethren, let our weapons,
>   Our warlike weapons all,
> Be beaten into ploughshares
>   Wherewith to till the soil;
> Our shields, our shields of battle,
>   For garments be they sewed,
> And peace both North and Southward
>   Be shouted loud abroad.
>
> Northward, I say, and Southward,
>   And far on every side,

Bantu Studies, Journal devoted to the Scientific Study of Bantu, Hottentot, and Bushmen, vol. II, July, Johannesburg: University of Witwatersrand Press.

27. C. M. Doke, 'Scripture Translation in Bantu Languages', in C. M. Doke and D. T. Cole, *Contributions to the History of Bantu Linguistics*, Johannesburg: Witwatersrand University Press, 1961, 110.

28. John W. Colenso, *Bringing Forth Light: Five Tracts on Bishop Colenso's Zulu Mission*, Pietermaritzburg: University of Natal, and Durban: Killie Campbell Africana Library, 1982, 51.

29. ibid., 194.

Through Him who ever liveth,
  The Father of our Lord,
Who is our very Father;
  And, as for evil all,
Through Him let all be peaceful,
  I say, let all be good.

Our soldiers be they gathered,
  For those who others harm;
For those, who seek to injure
  The men who live in peace, –
Gathered to make the highways
  That go from land to land,
Till every tribe shall utter,
  'He is, indeed, our Lord!

'He is the Lord, our Master!
  He is the Lord our God!
He is the Lord Almighty,
  Who liveth evermore!
Yes! dead is now all evil!
  Goodness alone abides!
For Jesus Christ has conquered,
  Who's risen from the dead.

'Through Him we too, my brethren,
  The world have overcome;
Have vanquished it entirely,
  With all its evil things.
Yes! dead is now all evil!
  Goodness alone abides!
For He, of Good the Father,
  He liveth evermore.

'The father died of evil,
  And evil too, is dead;
Now ever lives all Goodness,
  Now ever lives all Love;
And Northward and Southward,

And far on every side,
Peace lives, and lives forever,
The Peace of Christ our Lord!'[30]

At face value this hymn shows great religious spirit, using all the well-known rules of reversal in Scripture of the weak made strong, the bellicose meek, the last first and the lowly exalted, and taking in one hand all the great themes of faith and goodness and turning them over to the power of story-telling and praise-singing to bring Africans into their own favour. But we should also anticipate the critics of mission who argue that the hymn exhibits all the classic marks of African acquiescence to white supremacy, although I think that is off the mark. In any case, such critics insist that here is proof, if proof be needed, of Christianity taming Africans, of missionaries placing natives under supervised guidance, with the Zulu hymnwright giving vent to sentiments that would please his new masters. It is the kind of invasive subversion of African culture that missionary translators had set out to achieve, we are told.[31] The difference between such gestures and the native reflex, such critics say, is tantamount to the difference between the private and amusing gambols of a lion cub and the wild thunder of the tribal hunt that has tasted blood.

Yet this taming, if taming it be, this apparent socializing of the savage nerve, is, I would urge, the captivity of the beast in its native habitat, of Africans infusing from a stream to which the primordial paths of hunting and gathering had led them. The sound and tones of native speech, of which the English translation can convey an impression only as vivid vibrations, may now carry a new theme and burden, but they bear still the stamp and pace of ancient energy. The difference now is that the bush is inhabited by more exotic, more tempting game by virtue of which old tools and skills are redesigned, not discarded. And Christian Africans, even the successfully Westernized ones, whose tones so

30. ibid., 194–5.
31. Jean and John Comaroff, *Of Revelation and Revolution: Christianity, Colonialism and Consciousness in South Africa*, Chicago: University of Chicago Press, 213–30. This book is a sophisticated presentation of the classical theory of Christianity as a tool of colonial subjugation, and of Africans as victims. As such, the book represents the European metropolitan viewpoint, the viewpoint of the transmitters over against the recipients of the message.

reassured as well as threatened the cultivated halls of Europe, made their presence felt, like uncaged beasts following the scent. There is a much greater difference between traditional Africa and the secular West, say, than between Africa and the Bible, a difference that could gravely distort our image of African Christianity were we solely to view Africa, as we have tended to, from our Western vantage point. Traditional Africa, we might say, and say so without defending it here and now, has her hand given in religion, waiting for the written oracle like the Israelites the promised land. Few things, we recall, are as natural to Africans as religious commitment the written form of which, when it emerged, transcribed the intentions of the inbred variety. As someone wrote approvingly in a different connection, the African seems 'to be so made as to worship a book. It comes as a new thing to him, but it is not strange to his mind that a material object can convey a message from the unseen world.'[32]

In effect, Western scruples about religion, including the overzealous missionary advocacy that assumes unbelief as the point of departure, imposes on Africans a scepticism that does not belong with their understanding of the subject, or does not belong in the same way or to the same degree. To answer such scepticism Africans have had to switch to the terms of an imposed idiom, sometimes successfully, in any case self-consciously, and almost inevitably in ways adapted to social and ethnic experience. Whatever the response and however it was mediated, the Christian religious encounter tended to be accompanied, and induced, by indigenous self-reflection and expression, a self-reflection that thrives on the remembered past rather than its forgotten past. As psychology has taught us, it is the forgotten past, the dim, undeciphered images buried we forget where that enslave us, not the images and symbols summoned by effort and choice. This is a truth that thoughtful missionaries appreciated.[33]

32. Edwin W. Smith, *The Golden Stool: Some Aspects of the Conflict of Cultures in Modern Africa*, London: Holborn Publishing House, 1926, 226. Georg Simmel made much of the idea of literacy as a form of secrecy. *The Sociology of Georg Simmel*, ed. & tr. Kurt H. Wolff, New York: The Free Press, and London: Collier-Macmillan, 1950, repr. paperback, 1964, pp. 352–55.

33. For example, Edwin Smith, a veteran missionary of Southern Africa, wrote about this, saying, 'The personality of the African is rooted in the past – the past of the African's own race. He cannot be treated as if he were a European who

What we can observe, however, is the definite process by which some Western missionaries have slipped out of their own primitive scepticism to embrace the African confidence, a process that marked people like John Colenso. He was led to observe that Africans are also caught up in the same narrative sweep of God's dealings with humanity as the West. He spoke thus:

> I believe that, by thus meeting the heathen, half way, as it were, upon the ground of our common humanity, and with the recollection that humanity is now blessed and redeemed in Christ . . . we may look for far greater success in Missionary labours, and far more of stability in the converts that may be made, than by seeking to make all things new to them – to uproot altogether their old religion, scoffing at the things which they hold most sacred, deriding the fears, which alone have stood to them, for so many years long, as the representatives of the spiritual world.[34]

It was that John Colenso in his African transformation, the missionary domesticated in Africa, who came to exert a mutually transforming influence upon Africans of his time and place, especially through long-standing contacts he had with native agents, one of whom was Magema Fuze, a convert in the late nineteenth century who went on to write a valuable account in the mother tongue of his Zulu people, *Abantu Abamnyama* (*The Black People*). The book was finally published in 1922, and a critical modern translation in English came out in 1979. Fuze's observations have been recognized for their unique ethnographic, linguistic and historical importance, while he himself 'stood at the frontier of the clash of cultures, values and interests. In fact the teacher's [i.e., Colenso's] tolerance and sympathy towards

---

happened to be born black. He ought not to be regarded as if he were a building so badly constructed that it must be pulled down, its foundations torn up and a new structure erected on the site, on a totally new plan and with entirely new materials. Any such attitude is psychologically absurd.' Smith, *Golden Stool*, 295.

34. Jeff Guy, *The Heretic: A Study of the Life of John William Colenso: 1814–1883*, 1983, 45. This biography is considered by critics far superior to anything that has hitherto appeared on Colenso.

local customs and attitudes laid an even greater responsibility and difficulty upon the convert. That he did not violently resist, that he did not completely capitulate, that he thought about the problems and came to his own conclusions, as these early chapters most clearly reflect, is a tribute to the man and to the many Zulu people like him.'

The account continues: 'A major interest of the book is the way in which Fuze lives in several worlds at once. He came to Bishop Colenso's mission station, Ekukhanyeni (the place of enlightenment), from a country background, the influence of which remained with him throughout his life. The care and accuracy with which he describes the details of Zulu rural life suggest not only that he was still in sympathy with it, but that he was still in constant touch with it, even at the mission . . . It is clear that it was the wider world of the mission that fostered a wider sense of identity and nationality . . . on his travels through Natal and Zululand on mission business, [Fuze] gained a wider view than he could have gained from his original circumscribed background. It is also clear that the mission gave him a stronger sense of Zulu nationalism, for it was through the mission that he became acquainted with the Zulu royal family and with the issues borne by emissaries backwards and forwards across the Tugela River . . .'[35] Thus did Fuze weave together in his own life and work the several distinctive strands of the traditional and the Christian, the local and the national, the Zulu ethnic impulse and its wider African ramifications, the force of cultural particularity and of historical unity. The editor of his book feels constrained to conclude: 'The historical and sociological value of Fuze's book lies largely in the way it "straddles the several worlds he inhabits" and shows "the linkages he forges between them".'[36]

The matter of Fuze taking up residence at a mission station is relevant to the argument as to whether or not missions created indigenous alienation in their effort to impose the religion they knew and trusted. In Fuze's case his attention was turned not inward, to the routines and affairs of the mission station, but

35. Magema M. Fuze, *The Black People: And Whence They Came*, 1922, repr. Pietermaritzburg: University of Natal Press, and Durban: Killie Campbell Africana Library, 1979, p. xi.
36. ibid., p. xii.

outward, to events and matters in the wider society. His book is copious evidence of his roots in his own society, with mission residence serving as a hidden platform for the enactment of a drama and story in which local interlocutors held centre stage. No doubt if Fuze had spoken even half as eloquently about what went on at Ekukhanyeni, for example, it could, conceivably, have illuminated the fascinating world of the internal dialogue between missionaries and Africans, and perhaps thereby have revealed how indigenous influences had worked upon missionary presuppositions and attitudes. The attention would have shifted to missionaries and perhaps revealed the familiar paradox that Africa suffered less from the weaknesses of missionaries than from their strengths, for powerful people may learn by experience and incentive to get the better of their weaknesses, whereas they fail by their strengths, which in the mission field included too close a supervision of affairs without leaving much initiative to Africans. Robust Christianity would under such circumstances become a function of distance: the farther away from the mission station the better the prospects.

On the other hand, it may say something of real value that his exposure to Christianity at the mission produced in Fuze such careful and thoughtful interest in the constructive and imaginative resources of culture, a primary sensibility refined with cumulative narrative wit. Thus we seem to have, on the level of power relations, not the forcible uprooting of Africans and their barracooning in mission stations, but the vernacular transformation where local impulses are stirred and deepened and carried forward as articulate themes. We have, therefore, at Colenso's Ekukhanyeni an example of how Africa began the process of domesticating Christianity, expressing through it indigenous themes and convictions even while Christianity itself was causing alterations in old habits and notions. If missions had adopted a deliberate policy of advancing Africa's native aspirations, then they could not have chosen a more effective instrument than the mother tongue, mainly because mother tongues represent the African advantage, and were for that reason least compatible with the rhetoric of inferiority missionaries directed at African culture. For those missions that chose to employ mother tongues for what they imagined would be business as usual, had in fact, knowingly or unknowingly, adopted the indigenous cause as the operative factor in mission, and the business of mission under those circumstances became the business of people like Fuze. No one can read his book without recognizing someone in deep touch with his own roots, as confident about where he and his people came from as about where they were going. His infectious humour, his uncontrived candour, his sense of realism about human possibilities, his natural flair for idioms matured in the cultural crucible, his alertness to what animates and constrains his people, their ideals and fears, their strengths and weaknesses, all these things and more leap from the page. In Fuze's hands the light of genuine affirmation falls naturally on the Africa he knew so well, including the one that was being born with his aid.

The effects of mother tongue adoption and development have been far more beneficial to the cultures affected than those that attach to suppression and neglect. Even in the most ambiguous cases, such as when a linguistic federation is willed into existence against local criticism and opposition, or when an excise levy is imposed on local customs to bring them into line with imported strictures, the controversy generated often produces important intellectual materials about historical forms, the issue of origin and affinity, the nature of language as an attribute of the human mind, and comparative links with the West. In any case, let not a subtle, avuncular protectiveness push us to the point of claiming that Africans are inherently incapable of coping with Western contact and criticism and should, therefore, be made the exception to the rule of maturity through historical struggle. We would be in danger of promoting such a view were we to disallow any possibility for complexity in indigenous categories and values and Africans' ability to draw comparisons and contrasts from their own resources.

Thus when the Yoruba clergyman, the Rev. Samuel Johnson, wrote his magnificent *The History of the Yorubas* in 1897,[37] he devoted considerable space in his introductory remarks to a discussion of linguistic matters pertaining to Yoruba. He expounded his theme with the use of scientific, literary, historical,

37. The book was finally published in 1921, reprinted in 1969, London: Routledge & Kegan Paul.

religious, social, political, geographical and economic examples. He also described the contributions of European scholars, missionaries, clergymen and other interested writers by virtue of which the African heritage had been improved and strengthened. Samuel Johnson in his own person, too, proves that even a Western 'denomination' of his individual appellation could not deny or suppress his Africanness so long as his mother tongue continued to enjoy the detailed, sustained attention of missionaries and Africans like himself.

We have to conclude from such evidence that the arrival of Christian missions contributed often in unexpected ways to fresh cultural combinations and permutations, with people like Johnson and Fuze, for example, finding a vocation within that. However, if it is not facile, it would be plain dishonest to claim that such initiatives in the culture came only with the missionaries, for they most assuredly did not. Indeed, in many important cases missionaries encouraged and rewarded in their converts an uncritical imitation of the West, with some hapless missionaries paying a personal price of flagrant cultural insensitivity. It is a theme Noel Coward has caricatured with merciless humour in the musical *Pacific*, some of the lines of his doggerel running thus:

> Poor Uncle Harry having become a missionary,
> found the natives' words rather crude.
> He and Aunt Mary swiftly imposed an arbitrary ban
> upon them shopping in the nude.
> They all considered this silly and decided to rebel,
> They burnt his boots and several suits,
> which made a horrible smell.
> The subtle implication was that Uncle could go to hell.[38]

Any concentration on the full record of the missionary movement would have to include such examples of missionary high-handedness, and also, as Vilakazi eloquently puts it, the numerous instances of distortion by missions of African social relations by altering relationships and networks of affiliation. In many

38. Cited in Julian Pettifer and Richard Bradley, *Missionaries*, London: BBC Books, 1990, p. 20.

places the Church became 'a new form of organization, usurping the functions previously performed by traditional institutions'.[39] Church organization introduced new rules and patterns of administration, bureaucracy, formal procedures, communication, correspondence and record-keeping. It might be right to press the view from such a situation that Christianity allowed missionaries to mount a systematic assault on Africa's ancient dispensation and put in its place a replacement civilization: schools, hospitals, clinics, chapels and scientific methods of agriculture, health, communication and commerce. Undoubtedly such power would arouse in even the most saintly of missionaries feelings of superiority over Africans.

Images abound of children in Africa or Papua, New Guinea, or anywhere else, playing cricket, working diligently at their table manners or comporting themselves to the measured jig of Scottish country dance, all their consecrated hours witnessed by a bucolic missionary chapel on the hill and a long way from the village. How many African choirs have not laboured gallantly at the strains of Gounod or Handel while the harmonic rhythms of a different music throb in their veins? These or even worse travesties can be recounted ad nauseam.

However, what can be stated equally unambiguously is that imported accomplishments would be a lukewarm contender with vernacular originality of native wit and wisdom. As a commission into the use of African languages in schools reported, 'the mother tongue is the true vehicle of mother wit.'[40] And in any case, it is a fact that under missions, creative impulses in the vernacular could be documented with precision and consistency and their intellectual connections with projects of national and historical importance demonstrated.

It goes without saying that there is an inconclusiveness as well as an element of ambiguity in the task of transcribing the mother tongue, especially when you are doing so for the first time. It is difficult enough to attempt to cover all the ground of current usage, let alone try to delve into deep and obscure pockets of memory to identify and retrieve half-forgotten treasures.

39. Absalom Vilakazi, *Zulu Transformations: A Study of the Dynamics of Social Change*, Pietermaritzburg: University of Natal Press, 1962, 94; also 97ff.
40. Cited in Smith, *Golden Stool*, 303.

Furthermore, the translator would wish to compile a catalogue and inventory not just of the vocabulary and grammar of the language but the infinite number of occasions on which people use and produce language. The principles for organizing, explaining, interpreting and utilizing hitherto unwritten languages are, to complicate matters, similarly innumerable. Yet something really unexpected and incalculable happens when a mother tongue is furnished with a new transcription and launched under its own steam. It moves not just to the formulas of imitation, subjugation and conformity contrived for it, but to the free rhythms and resonances of its hidden life and logic. One impulse in it is charged with more significance than all the nonbiodegradable erudition that buoyed up imported classics in colonial Africa.

One other matter should not escape attention. In the field of Bible translation as such, there is a built-in principle of progressive improvement in the versions that are produced. If the job is done well enough, a newly translated version will establish itself and discourage further translations from occurring too soon, or occurring in any way that might challenge existing forms, as happened with the King James' version. On one level this might not be bad in itself, since any new translation would have to compete with a tough, worthy predecessor. On the other hand, it can be predicted that forms and idioms that had been successfully pioneered in scriptural translation would, even without further Bible translation, take on a life of their own in fields outside the religious, fields as varied as literature, music, art, psychology and customary law. With mother tongue literacy, the die is cast. Literacy is an incomparable catalyst for cultural change, ushering in transformations far beyond any obvious agenda of the formal curriculum. Under the circumstances we would have no choice except to leave the door open to new possibilities and developments, precisely the space any dynamic cultural project requires in order to flourish and succeed. I do not see how we can exclude this possibility for African culture once we concede the historical fact of the mother tongue projects of missions. In any case, I argue this to be true.

To turn to another example, Robert Moffat (1795–1883) was fairly representative of his age too, and so something of his personal story may reveal clues into the cultural dynamics of missionary translation. No sooner had he arrived in South Africa early in 1817, than Moffat was confronted with the language barrier. Very little systematic work had been done in the indigenous languages, apart from Cardoso's catechism of 1624 and that of Pacconio and de Couto of 1643. To remedy the situation, Moffat decided to go and settle among the Africans, which he did in 1827. He acquired fluency in Setswana and was able to preach in that language. From this time on, Moffat became the sponsor of translation and publication in the language. When he had done a translation of the Gospel of Luke, for example, he rode four hundred miles to Cape Town with the manuscript in his pocket to try to find a printer, and when he found a printing press its rather archaic state was aggravated by the unavailability of printers with adequate skill. It left Moffat little choice but to learn the skill himself, which he proceeded to do. The printing press gave Moffat an effective tool for advancing the cause of Setswana vernacular literacy and confirmed him in the front ranks of world vernacular pioneers.

Moffat found that he could not successfully or unthinkingly assume Western theological terms for the vernacular, and decided instead to follow the internal logic of Setswana in the rendering of religious concepts and ideas. 'The Sechuana language,' he confessed, 'though exceedingly copious, is of course deficient in theological terms . . . This at first occasioned considerable difficulty; but research has convinced me, that the language itself possesses an ample source of suitable words to convey with wonderful clearness, the language and meaning of the Scriptures.'[41]

Apart from the theological issue, Moffat saw a similar problem in persisting with the Western ecclesiastical tradition for Africa. In particular, the denominational sectarianism such as had marked modern European Christianity was, he felt, out of place in the faithful transmission of the message in the vernacular idiom, an idiom as yet untainted with credal uncharitableness. 'I have studiously avoided,' he testified, 'giving the slightest tinge to any rendering in favour of any creed.'[42] It is very difficult if, for

41. Cited in Doke, 1961, 111.
42. Doke, *loc. cit.*

example, in an African language the word for 'church' means the same as community, as it most assuredly does in many, to use it also to mean 'stranger' or 'excluded outsider'. Whatever the case, Moffat's biographer wrote: 'In the famous library at the Bible House in London there is a memorial window figuring great translators: William Tyndale, Jerome, Cyril and Methodius, Martin Luther, John Eliot, William Carey, Robert Morrison, Henry Martyn, and – Robert Moffat, who takes his place naturally in the far-shining company, most of whom were greater scholars than he, but none of whom surpassed him in single-hearted devotion.'[43] Moffat claimed much less for himself, content merely to say, 'I felt it to be an awful thing to translate the Book of God.'[44]

The work of translating the Scriptures also involved being out of step with Western cultural suppositions and proceeding on the terms of indigenous societies and at their pace. Dr Henry Callaway, a pioneer missionary translator in Zulu, spoke of his experience of having to defer to 'native experts' even though he was impatient to press on with the job. In a letter he admitted: 'I have a "committee" of natives sitting on the translation! Each of the three natives has a translation by someone else in his hand, and I read ours, verse by verse. We do not get on very fast, but I am quite satisfied with what we have done. It corroborates me in the belief that hitherto nothing has been printed which at all approaches to what ours will be when completed.'[45]

It is in the very nature of Scriptural translation that sooner or later revisions should follow, and older forms and conceits, having exhausted their staying power, yield place to new. Such a process developed in African language translations, though often it was a slow process, either because the earlier versions, such as had happened with the Authorized (King James) Version in English, had succeeded too well to be easily dislodged, or because new experts were slow to arrive on the scene, or both. In any case, revision work helped to carry forward the impulse for cultural renovation by inscribing new words and concepts into the

43. Edwin W. Smith, *Robert Moffat, One of God's Gardeners*, London: Student Christian Movement, 1925, 245.
44. Doke, loc. cit.
45. Cited in Doke, 1961, 115.

cultural memory and bringing them into fruitful convergence with past usage and custom. Although we can criticize what may sometimes appear to be the stifling effects of Scriptural translation on new initiatives and the spirit of independence, especially where we find a slavish adherence to older versions, we must be balanced even here. We need to remember the contrasting case of neoclassical literature in the European Renaissance when writers before Shakespeare, Corneille and Lope de Vega copied ancient forms mechanically without a true appreciation of the function of such works. Aristotle and Seneca were pillars of conformity then, not stimulators of free imagination. What we can say, therefore, is that when it came to be done, revised translations necessitated augmenting existing resources, raising and refining standards and widening areas of contact and affinity – precisely the sort of intellectual activity by which a culture propagates itself and overcomes the potential hazard of foreign assimilation. Eventually, when Western contact became the single most important fact for modern Africans, and assimilation unavoidable, it was vernacular self-understanding that acted as reassurance and blunted considerably the sharp prongs of Western intrusion.

The question whose deafening echo has settled on the field like a thunderclap is the view that Christian missions opened the way for the suppression of African and other cultures, a view which, if correct, leaves us with the notion of Africa as a victim, together with a corresponding derivative understanding of her cultures. In fact, the missionary and the colonizer in Africa might be likened to Virgil's Juno and Jupiter on Olympus deciding the fate of Rome before a victorious Troy. The missionary, like Juno, acquiesced in the conquest of Africa, but the ground he, or, through him, the African convert yielded to the colonial Jupiter is actually reserved for native speech and dress. In Virgil's hands, the Trojan invasion is absorbed and naturalized into the subjugated Latin culture, so that the cultural weapon, what Virgil calls simply 'the tongue of their fathers and their ancient ways', more than compensates for the march and thunder of Jupiter's foreign cohorts. Virgil's perspective of representing the cause of the vanquished carries this vernacular sentiment, and in the harsh, bitter conditions of foreign defeat the Latin tongue is invoked to allay ultimate disenchantment. In that sense his words ring with future assurance:

Never command the land's own Latin folk
To change their old name, to become new Trojans,
Known as Teucrians; never make them alter
Dialect or dress. Let Latium be.
Let there be Alban kings for generations
And let Italian valour be the strength
Of Rome in after times. Once and for all
Troy fell, and with her name, let her lie fallen.[46]

Such a device Virgil employs to transcend the phantom of imperial subjugation. Similarly, the fact of Western colonial suppression of Africans would undoubtedly have been far harsher, more comprehensive and longer enduring without the mitigating effects of missionary projects of mother tongue literacy, and the narrative flash they kindled in people's hearts, whatever motives missionaries shared or did not share with colonialists.[47]

One indication that commitment to mother tongue literacy alerted missionaries to the political aspirations of the subject races was contained in a specific policy directive by Dr Robert Mann, the colonial superintendent of education in South Africa. In 1864, he proposed making an appropriation from the colonial Reserve Fund in the form of an annual grant for schools with the prerequisite that all instruction be in English. Rufus Anderson, the secretary of the American Board of Commissioners for Foreign Mission at the time, opposed the plan partly on the grounds that government sponsorship of mission schools would bring them under government control and end their independence,

46. Virgil, *The Aeneid*, Robert Fitzgerald's translation, New York: Penguin Classics, 1990, Bk. XII, lines 830ff, p. 398.
47. The prototype colonialist is Cecil Rhodes who, in his 'Confession of Faith' in 1877, spoke of 'English' colonialism as the messianic destiny of his race. He lamented the loss of America, saying there might be time to avert a similar thing elsewhere, if necessary even with secret designs to reclaim America! Rhodes was convinced of the English being 'the finest race in the world and that the more of the world we inhabit the better it is for the human race.' He continued: 'Africa is still lying ready for us[.] [It] is our duty to take it. It is our duty to seize every opportunity of acquiring more territory[,] and we should keep this one idea steadily before our eyes[:] that more territory simply means more of the Anglo-Saxon race[,] more of the best[,] the most human, most honourable race the world possesses.' Cited in John Flint, *Cecil Rhodes*, Boston: Little, Brown, 1974, 248, 250.

suggesting government and mission were not necessarily natural allies on the ground, and partly that English would then supplant Zulu. Daniel Lindley, an American missionary, took up these objections and expanded on them, in particular the language issue. He said while he understood that it was natural in an English colony for government to want to promote English and for the need for whites and blacks to have a common language, and that, equally importantly, for Africans to acquire fluency in English as the language of government and administration, he was opposed to dropping Zulu altogether. 'The time is probably much nearer to us than it is to our friends in some New England States when black men with certain qualifications will be allowed the right of suffrage,' he speculated innocently, but Christianity could not dispense with Zulu. He would settle for a compromise: the gospel would be preached in Zulu; translating the Bible into Zulu would continue; other Zulu literature would continue to be produced; English would be taught only to those who could already read and write Zulu. So he settled on the slogan: 'Some English for some Zulus.'[48] For even the English instruction they would give, Lindley insisted, the mission agencies would refuse to accept payment from government because, he said, such instruction would be done not for money or pandering to government 'but for the good of the Zulus'.[49] Missionary practice in such regard retained the advantage for the African.

So the question of Christian collaboration with colonialism looks very different from the angle of the vernacular paradigm, especially when we remind ourselves that in societies unbroken by technological impact, language and culture are inextricably intertwined, so that the missionary effort in reducing these languages to writing and pioneering their development in other ways produced indigenous repercussions in numerous creative fields. It thus followed that 'the same missionaries who promoted "modernization" of African languages through codification in writing, standardization, and diffusion of printed texts also used language to defend traditional culture.'[50]

48. Edwin W. Smith, *The Life and Times of Daniel Lindley (1801–80)*, London: The Epworth Press, 1949, 388.

49. Smith, *Lindley*, 389.

50. Johannes Fabian, *Language and Colonial Power: The Appropriation of Swahili in the Former Belgian Congo 1880–1938*, Cambridge: Cambridge

David Livingstone, the famous Scottish missionary who dominated the world of missions in his day and beyond, reflected on the value of language as a bearer of Christianity, a reflection that alerted him to the distorting effects of Western contact. Scriptural translation, he thought, would activate the wider Christian process and help preserve the culture before (and after) it had come into contact with domineering Europeans, and it ought, therefore, to be encouraged. He contended:

> It is fortunate that the translation of the Bible has been effected before the language became adulterated with half-uttered foreign words, and while those who have heard the eloquence of the native assemblies are still living; for the young, who are brought up in our schools, know less of the language than the missionaries; and Europeans born in the country, while possessed of the idiom perfectly, if not otherwise educated, cannot be referred to for explanation of any uncommon word.[51]

Livingstone paid close attention to what might be implied by the adoption of the vernacular for Scriptural translation. He called attention to Robert Moffat's translation of the Setswana Bible, saying Moffat had demonstrated the superiority of Setswana, so that 'the Pentateuch is fully expressed . . . in fewer words than in the Greek Septuagint, and in a very considerably smaller number than in our own English version.'[52]

All this led Livingstone to appeal to the norm that had also constrained the framers of the American Constitution, namely, that 'all men', Africans included, are endowed by their Creator

---

University Press, 1986, 78. One guarded study of the subject is nevertheless prepared to present the view that missionary expertise in African languages grew naturally out of a commitment to African particularity, and in the process it led to the creation of 'oral literature texts [that] often come closer to the ideals of contemporary scholars than do those of [European colonial] administrators.' Ralph Austen, 'Africans Speak: Colonialism Writes: The Transcription and Translation of Oral Literature Before World War II,' Boston University Discussion Paper AH Number 8, 1990, p. 3.

51. David Livingstone, *Missionary Researches and Travels in South Africa*, London: John Murray, 1957, 114.

52. Livingstone, 1857, 114.

with basic inalienable possessions, above all the gift of humanity which is not a matter of selective attainment. Livingstone insisted:

> The existence, therefore, of the various instruments in use among the Africans . . . indicates the communication of instruction at some period from some Being superior to man himself . . . The argument for an original revelation to man, . . . though quite independent of the Bible history, tends to confirm that history. It is of the same nature with this, that man could not have *made* himself, and therefore must have had a Divine Creator. Mankind could not, in the first instance, have *civilized* themselves, and therefore must have had a superhuman Instructor.[53]

It is the more reasonable conclusion to claim for the African genius the same divine status that we do for Europeans than to give credence to the theory that Africans subsisted in a state which would otherwise prove fatal to all the descendants of the race. Africans are not an exception to the human race, a thought that would be an unacceptable affront to the Creator. Thus it was that Livingstone felt that even though they stood outside the Graeco-Roman civilization, Africans, too, participated in the general human process.

> Language seems to be an attribute of the human mind and thought, and the inflections, various as they are in the most barbarous tongues [thinking here, perhaps, of the clicks], as that of the Bushmen, are probably only proofs of the race being human, and endowed with the power of thinking; the fuller development of language taking place as the improvement of our other faculties goes on.[54]

The veteran missionary, Edwin Smith, a translator of the Ila New Testament in Zambia, stated the reasons, as he saw them, why Scriptural translation seeks in authentic mother tongues the sources and forms of cultural originality, of why the translation

53. David and Charles Livingstone, *Narrative of an Expedition to the Zambesi and its Tributaries and of the Discovery of the Lakes Shirwa and Nyassa: 1858–1864*, New York: Harper & Brothers, Publishers, 1866, 533–34.
54. Livingstone, 1857, 114.

avoids artificial or foreign materials that restrict the range to current or contemporary fashion. He observed that:

> Men need two kinds of language, in fact; a language of the home, of emotion, of unexpressed associations; and a language of knowledge, exact argument, scientific truth, one in which words are world-current and steadfast in their meanings. Where the mother tongue does not answer both needs, the people must inevitably become bilingual; but however fluent they may succeed in being in the foreign speech, its words can never feel to them as their native words. To express the dear and intimate things which are the very breath and substance of life a man will fall back on the tongue he learnt not at school, but in the house – how, he remembers not. He may bargain in the other, or pass examinations in it, but he will pray in his home speech. If you wish to reach his heart you will address him in that language.[55]

Introducing a subject of pivotal interest and relevance to creative literary activity the world over, the reference to 'home speech' as the pulse of the imaginative life identifies the heart of the cultural process. It was alluded to by Christaller in speaking about 'the sparks of truth entrusted to our people', those flashes of matured brilliance and insight conveyed to us in the innumerable tiny vessels of custom, usage, sign and symbol, and the myriad other artful means that are our bequest. It was also pointed out by Professor Diedrich Westermann of Berlin and a former missionary to Africa, who wrote:

> Language and the mental life are so closely connected that any educational work which does not take into consideration the inseparable unity between African language and African thinking is based on false principles and must lead to an alienation of the individual from his own self, his

55. Edwin Smith, *In the Mother Tongue*, London: British and Foreign Bible Society, 1930, 8. Oliver Wendell Holmes pithily expressed a similar sentiment thus: 'Language is a solemn thing; it grows out of life, out of its agonies, its wants and its weariness. Every language is a temple in which the soul of those who speak it is enshrined.' *The Autocrat of the Breakfast Table*.

> past, his traditions and his people. If the African is to keep and develop his own soul and is to become a separate personality, his education must not begin by inoculating him with a foreign civilization, but it must implant respect for the indigenous racial life, it must teach him to love his country and tribe as gifts given by God which are to be purified and brought to full growth by the new divine life. One of these gifts is the vernacular, it is the vessel in which the whole national life is contained and through which it finds expression.[56]

The great and costly work of William Tyndale (c. 1494–1536) and Miles Coverdale (1488–1568) in giving us the English of the Scriptures, and thus helping to open a worldwide channel for the language, is a relevant reminder to us of the intellectual roots of a medium we have learnt now to take for granted. In a work on the Igbo language, the achievement of Tyndale and Coverdale in creating the vernacular English Bible is quoted in support of pioneer language development.[57] The English Bible, in being simple and succinct, became the repository of those sparks and impulses that have animated the soul of a people. There are only about 6,000 words in the English Bible, compared with Shakespeare's considerably greater output, (some sources putting it as high as 32,000) so economical and direct was the language of the Bible. This point of economy was remarked on by John Ruskin in his comments on Sir Philip Sidney (1554–1586). 'Sir Philip Sidney,' Ruskin wrote, 'will only use any cowboy's or tinker's words, if only they help him to say precisely in English what David said in Hebrew; impressed the while himself so vividly by

56. Diedrich Westermann, 'The Place and Function of the Vernacular in African Education,' *International Review of Mission,* January 1925.

57. Rev. G. E. Igwe and M. M. Green, *Igbo Language Course: Book III: Dialogue, Sayings, Translation*, Ibadan, Nigeria: Oxford University Press, 1970, 69. The authors cite the words of I. Williams as follows: 'No book has had an equal influence on the English people. Apart from its religious considerations, it gave to all classes alike an idiom in which the deeper emotions of life could be recalled. It gives grace to the speech of the unlettered and it entered into the style of the most ambitious writers. Its phrasing coloured the work of poets, and its language has so embedded itself in our national tradition that if the Bible is forgotten, a precious possession will be lost.' This quote is given in Igbo in a parallel translation (68–70).

the majesty of the thought itself, that no tinker's language can lower it or vulgarize it in his mind.'[58]

William Wordsworth (1770–1850) recalls the words of Erasmus with the following poetic lines:

> But to outweigh all harm, the sacred Book,
> In dusty sequestration wrapt too long,
> Assumes the accents of our tongue;
> And he who guides the plow or wields the crook,
> With understanding spirit now may look
> Upon her records, listen to her song.

Walt Whitman (1819–1892), himself an architect of language, speaks in his *November Boughs* of the translated Bible as the bearer and symbol of the creative impulse. He affirms: 'I've said nothing yet of the Bible as a poetic entity, and of every portion of it . . . How many ages and generations have brooded and wept and agonized over this book! . . . Translated in all languages, how it has united the diverse world! Not only does it bring us what is clasped within its covers. Of its thousands there is not a verse, not a word, but is thick-studded with human emotion.'

Joseph Addison (1672–1719), the editor of the short-lived but influential periodical, *The Spectator*, reflected thus on the legacy of the Bible in Western literature and letters:

> Homer has innumerable flights that Virgil was not able to reach, and in the Old Testament we find several passages more elevated and sublime than any in Homer. After perusing the Book of Psalms, let a judge of the beauties of poetry read a literal translation of Homer or Pindar, and he will find in these last two such an absurdity and confusion of style, with such a comparative poverty of imagination, as will make him sensible of the vast superiority of the Scripture style.

Speaking of 'beauty', the literary critic, Henry Bradley, pointed out that the word 'beautiful' did not exist in English literature

58. Cited in *The Influence of the English Bible upon the English Language and upon English and American Literatures*, New York: American Bible Society, 1947 edition, 7.

until Tyndale used it.[59] Hilaire Belloc, the English writer and a stern judge of Tyndale, admitted, nevertheless, that Tyndale 'had created the glories of English prose', and that Tyndale's 'rhythms had begun to vibrate in the minds of a younger generation', as his 'spirit still moved through' the majestic cadences of the language.[60] In his *Grammar of New Testament Greek*, Professor A. T. Robertson remarks on the creative force of the language of the Bible. He says, 'The Christian spirit put a new flavour into this vernacular and lifted it to a new elevation and dignity of style that unify and glorify the language.'

It is not necessary to recount here the tragic fate of Tyndale in stooping to the English vernacular for Scripture since the consequences of his achievement are undeniable. Sir Arthur Quiller-Couch in his Cambridge lectures pointed to what he considered the self-evident matter of our Bible being a translated book. Isaiah, he said, did not write the cadences of his prophecies as we know them; Christ did not speak the cadences of the Parables or of the Sermon on the Mount as we know them. 'These have been supplied by the translators. By all means let us study them and learn to delight in them; but Christ did not suffer for . . . the cadences invented by Englishmen almost 1600 years later.'[61] Quiller-Couch then took a panoramic view of the development of the language and assessed in that the role of the translated Bible, in particular, the *Authorized Version*. He says the English Bible

> . . . has cadences homely and sublime, yet so harmonizes them that the voice is always one. Simple men – holy and humble men of heart like Izaak Walton and Bunyan – have their lips touched and speak to the homelier tongue. Proud men, scholars – Milton, Sir Thomas Browne – practise the rolling Latin sentence; but upon the rhythm of our Bible they, too, fall

59. Henry Bradley, *The Making of English*, New York & London: Macmillan, 1904, 220.
60. Hilaire Belloc, *Cranmer, Archbishop of Canterbury, 1533–1556*, Philadelphia: J. P. Lippincott & Co. 1931, 193f. Though his literary reputation is acknowledged, Belloc is less worthily regarded by historians.
61. Quiller-Couch, *On The Art of Reading*, 1920, 137.

> back . . . The precise man Addison cannot excel one parable in brevity or in heavenly clarity; the two parts of Johnson's antithesis come to no more than this: 'Our Lord has gone up to the sound of a trump; with the sound of a trump our Lord has gone up.' The Bible controls its enemy Gibbon as surely as it haunts the music of a light sentence of Thackeray's. It is everything we see, hear, feel, because it is in us, in our blood.[62]

It is in us, in our blood It is a sentiment passionately expressed by Thomas Carlyle when he wrote: 'Of this one thing, however, be certain: wouldst thou plant for Eternity, then plant into the deep infinite faculties of man, his Fantasy and Heart! wouldst thou plant for Year and Day, then plant into his shallow superficial faculties, his self-love and arithmetical understanding, what will grow there.'[63] That sentiment might stand as the motto of the vernacular cause. Speaking with reference to the early modern Catholic missions to India, the biographer of the Jesuit, Robert de Nobili, a seventeenth-century Italian missionary, underlined his vernacular commitment, saying de Nobili 'was aware that no amount of learning [which in de Nobili's case was considerable] could replace the deepest springs within the soul, fed by blood, tradition and climate, and crystallized in a mother tongue.'[64] Adolf Deissmann, in his Haskell Lectures at Oberlin College, spoke of the New Testament idiom as being 'the underground stream of the people's language', not a shrine for 'the mysteries of kings' and the upper classes.[65]

We might add to all these examples the testimony, cited in the Introduction, of Robert Louis Stevenson. He spoke of the cultural importance of missionary translations of the Bible and other literary materials for the Samoan people among whom he settled in the nineteenth century. He testified:

62. Sir Arthur Quiller-Couch, *On The Art of Reading: Lectures Delivered in the University of Cambridge*, Cambridge: Cambridge University Press, 1920, 155–56.
63. Cited in Smith, *Lindley*, 387.
64. Vincent Cronin, *A Pearl to India: The Life of Robert de Nobili*, London: Rupert Hart Davis, 1959, 173.
65. Adolf Deissmann, *The New Testament in the Light of Modern Research: The Haskell Lectures, 1929*, New York: Doubleday, Doran & Co. Inc., 80.

> Well, after this excursion into tongues that have never been alive – though I assure you we have one capital book in the language, a book of fables by an old missionary of the unpromising name of Pratt, which is simply the best and the most literary version of the fables known to me. I suppose I should except La Fontaine, but L.F. takes a long time; these are brief as the books of our childhood, and full of wit and literary colour; and O, Colvin, what a tongue it would be to write, if one only knew it . . . Its curse in common use is an incredible left-handed wordiness; but in the hands of a man like Pratt it is succinct as Latin, compact of long rolling polysyllables and little and often pithy particles, and for beauty of sound a dream.[66]

We might recapitulate and reconsider here the theme of the social and ideological implications of Bible translation, something that could play into the hands of sectarians and the arbiters of political correctness. Lewis makes an observation that is relevant, to the effect that 'all translations of scripture are tendentious: translation, by its very nature, is a continuous implicit commentary. It can become less tendentious only by becoming less of a translation.'[67]

Conclusions

In conclusion, we should draw an important distinction between missionary translations of the modern era and Enlightenment views. Enlightenment scholars defended translation on the grounds that all languages obeyed the same laws of reason, so that the diversity and variety of idioms merely concealed an inner uniformity of structure, which translation, in their view, supported. For that reason, Enlightenment writers felt a duty to write a universal grammar in order to break free of contingent restrictions in pursuit of the universal efficacy of abstract general categories. The Enlightenment view was that cultural differences conceal

66. Robert Louis Stevenson, *The Works of Robert Louis Stevenson: The Vailima Letters*, Edinburgh: Longmans, Green & Co., 1897, p. 46. For Stevenson's comments on Bible translation see H. J. Moors, *With Stevenson in Samoa*, London, N.D., 69.
67. Lewis, 'Drab Age Prose – Religious Controversy and Translation', *English Literature in the Sixteenth Century*, Oxford, 1954, 157–221, 206.

and thus distort the truth of one humanity – a view that is akin to the prevailing monism, and would, if followed to the letter, make imitation and arid conformity the rule and ideal for narrative construction.

It is a departure from this point of view that Scriptural translations saw cultural and linguistic distinctions as arguments for recognizing the vernacular paradigm, so that no one language or culture might promote itself as the universal exclusive norm. Thus it was that in missionary translations even minute dialectical differences were noted, bringing variety and diversity into creative convergence with pluralism.[68] This had momentous consequences for African culture and literature, for that was how Africa's languages for the first time came to possess a literature of their own, namely, the vernacular Scriptures, even though we deem them unworthy of Shakespeare or Milton.[69] There was, of course, a worldwide general ambition motivating missionary translations, namely, to secure converts for the Church, often with Western cultural criteria for the Church so understood. However, it is interesting to reflect that critics of missions thought the idea of cultural relativism would effectively demolish the case for missions, yet cultural relativism as empirical practice was what distinguished missionary linguistic research and development. The variety and diversity of the plethora of languages employed in Scriptural translation promoted, as nothing else has, cultural specificity and particularity, the notion the Enlightenment found such a stumbling block to its intellectual claims. The mother tongue projects of missions turned the soil for a harvest of enormous indigenous proportions, generating projects more distinguished by their 'common tellurian' bias than by uprooted assertions of missionary rhetoric. Thus cultural relativism was scarcely consistent with itself when it opposed interference in

68. Holger Pedersen argues in this connection that modern linguistic science is a child of Christian missionary activity. Holger Pedersen, 1962, *The Discovery of Language: Linguistic Science in the Nineteenth Century*, tr. John Webster Spargo, 1959, Bloomington, Ind.: Indiana University Press.

69. Saul Bellow, the Nobel laureate, attacked African culture precisely for not having produced a Western literary prototype, evidence, he thinks of intrinsic inferiority. 'Who is the Tolstoy of the Zulus? The Proust of the Papuans? I'll gladly read them,' he sneered.

African societies on the principle of the absolute autonomy of these societies, an idea that, because it assumes these societies to be a cul de sac and to share in an original innocence, actually breeds ethnocentrism. However ambiguous the record, it can be said that a Scripturally based mother tongue assurance became a salient part of the missionary record, and a pluralist Africa was thereby reinvigorated. Thus neo-Enlightenment scruples concerning original innocence would, if allowed, promote the kind of ethnocentric extremism that conflicts with the logic of pluralist particularity, of the 'one' and the 'many'. Cultural relativism, in fact, became the holding position of the left-wing rump of Enlightenment progressivism, for it promoted non-Western cultures as exotic representations of forms that had reached their most developed stage in the West, thus returning by a downward spiral to the ethnocentric exclusiveness it fought so single-mindedly.[70]

By contrast, mother tongue particularity was a direct consequence of missions' careful development and promotion of vernacular languages in Africa, and from that we come upon the springs of cultural particularity and renewal, the very basis on which significant literary and artistic creation in Africa have gone forward and entered the wide stream of world history. The modern Christian missionary impulse staked the enterprise as much on the viability of local cultural forms as on the outcome; and by attending first to the essential linguistic and cultural undercarriage of the message and leaving the ultimate outcome to an indefinite future, as Livingstone urged on his missionary colleagues, the conveyers of the message put in place a formidable mother tongue Juggernaut which time and opportunity favoured. An enduring cultural awakening resulted from this, and allowed local populations to devise for themselves projects of cultural renewal and intellectual awakening often going far beyond the narrow walls of membership in the Church. It does not discredit the missionary enterprise to say that one of its fruits was the preservation of mother tongue aspiration, so that were we to shift attention to

70. For a recent discussion of how language origins might be located in a single universal tongue see Robert Wright, 'Quest for the Mother Tongue: Is the Search for an Ancestor of all Modern Languages Sober Science or Simple Romanticism?' *The Atlantic*, April, 1991, 39–68.

other aspects of the Western missionary encounter in order to discredit it, we would overlook perhaps the most critical frontier of the encounter, namely, the missionary pioneering of languages.

Consequently, we may make the following observation, that the real life and vitality of numerous African languages are no different in kind or degree from what is true for long-established literate societies: all languages are particular vehicles by which human beings construct meaning, transmit the heritage and in other ways communicate, some vehicles more widely used and articulated and more ably serviced with texts and resources than others, but all of them serving an identical need and purpose. The great importance that Christian missionaries attached to mother tongues, therefore, was no small contribution to the advancement of the cause of the general human enterprise.

It is not enough to look upon such linguistic and cultural materials as the triumph of field anthropology, as proof that the 'one' God of religious doctrine became demystified in the 'many' names of language and practice. Rather, we should see how religious doctrine acted to remove from hitherto unwritten languages the constrictions of the episodic and anecdotal without suppressing their inner power and vitality. The coping stone of the narrative structure was the personal testimony in which biographic and autobiographic vignettes are set down with intimate familiarity, sometimes with conventional dullness and didactic sterility, at other times girding at moral seriousness, yet often bringing to bear all the worth of what the Apostle called 'the inner man', a subject of limitless possibility, as St Augustine has taught us. We owe these linguistic pioneers, missionary as well as African, an incalculable debt for being the architects of the new consciousness which a maturing humanity ranks among its most prized possessions. Thus even if we were to confront these languages with what we regard as universal cultural and religious symbols, these would be expressed, at least in the setting of the vernacular Scriptures, hymns and prayers, with the force and immediacy of solemn but homebred familiarity, the actual domestication of those narrative impulses that are the plausibility structure of all creative human experience. We might amend the words of Charles Lamb (1775–1834) to the effect that if

Shakespeare were to come into the room, we should, by choice, perhaps all rise, but if a work by its vernacular force were able to stir us in the depths of blood, soul and tongue, we should, like the venerable Tartar, greet it devotedly on our knees. It is time now to examine the religious and theological aspects of the Western missionary encounter as an expression of the wider global cultural process.

3

Gospel and Culture: Theological and Religious Reflections*

Introduction

A popular but erroneous view has been promoted in several quarters regarding the naturalness of separating gospel and culture, with the assumption that by that procedure Christians can get at the *gospel* pure and simple. However, this is no more possible than getting at the kernel of the onion without the peel. The *pure* gospel, stripped of all cultural entanglements, would evaporate in a vague abstraction, although if the gospel were without its own intrinsic power it would be nothing more than cultural ideology congealing into something like 'good manners, comely living, and a sense that all was well,' as James Truslow Adams declared of New England Unitarianism.[1] If Christianity could be turned into a *pure Platonic form*, as is evident in some forms of theological liberalism, then it would be religion fit only for the elite, whereas if it were just a cultural disguise it would breed only commissars of cultural codes. The real challenge is to identify this intrinsic power without neglecting the necessary cultural factor.[2]

It is important to call attention to the fundamental character of Christianity as a force for cultural integration. Several paradoxes

* A version of this paper appeared in Philip C. Stine, ed., *Bible Translation and the Spread of the Church: The Last 200 Years*, Leiden, New York, Copenhagen, Cologne, 1990. E. J. Brill.

1. James Truslow Adams, *History of the United States*, vol. ii, p. 227. The Unitarian-Universalist movement has also been described, tongue in cheek, as 'the fatherhood of God and the brotherhood of man in the neighborhood of Boston.'
2. This is relevant to arguments of Christianity as a subject of Western cultural captivity. While the Western 'translation' of the religion domesticated the gospel, in its subsequent transmission and expansion abroad Christianity breached its Western walls.

point to this fact. The first is that Christianity is almost alone among world religions in being peripheral in the place of its origin. Ever since Pentecost and the Antiochean breakthrough, Christianity has turned its back on Jerusalem and Bethlehem, regarding them as secondary signposts, with the consequence of the religion becoming preponderant in regions once considered outside God's promises. The Christian religious psyche was purged of the 'Promised Land' fixation, so that believers have almost to err to revert to any one centre to the exclusion of others.

The second paradox is that Christians are unique in abandoning the original language of Jesus and instead adopting Greek in its 'Koine', and Latin in its 'Vulgar' forms as the central media of the Church.[3] Except in extremist sectarian groups, Christians never made the language of Jesus a prerequisite for faith or membership in the fellowship. It is this linguistic revolution which accounts for the entire New Testament canon being written in a language other than the one in which Jesus preached.[4] Thus it is that translation, and its attendant cross-cultural implications, came to be built into the historical make-up of Christianity. Another striking paradox is the contention by Christians that God's eternal counsels are compatible with ordinary, everyday speech.[5] This view cuts across the tendency in some parts of early Christianity to cast the religion into an elitist gnostic discourse. Christianity in the mouth of Jesus was the divulging of the secret design of God,[6] and Christian faith the public attestation to that fact. Of course, Jesus did not just turn

3. For a scrupulous account of the language issue in the Bible, see Matthew Black, 'The Biblical Languages', *The Cambridge History of the Bible: vol. i, From the Beginnings to Jerome*, eds., P. R. Ackroyd and C. F. Evans, Cambridge: Cambridge University Press, 1970, repr. 1988, 1–29.

4. Edward Gibbon writes, 'The authentic histories of the actions of Christ were composed in the Greek language, at a considerable distance from Jerusalem, and after the Gentile converts were grown extremely numerous.' Gibbon, *Decline and Fall of the Roman Empire*, vol. i, 432.

5. Martin Luther is quoted as dismissing theologians as irrelevant to Bible translation. Instead the translator must 'ask the mother in the home, the children on the street, the common man in the marketplace about this, and look them in the mouth to see how they speak, and afterward to do our translating.' Cited in Jean Bethke Elshtain, review article, 'The American Battlefield', *First Things*, no. 23, May, 1992, 69–72, 70.

6. Mark iv: 22; Luke viii: 17; John vii: 4; xviii: 20; W. Pannenberg, ed., *Revelation as History*, New York: Macmillan, 1969, 141ff.

plain speaking into expressive individualism, but rather made it the vehicle of his teachings.

This view of religious language as belonging to the ordinary, commonplace world of men and women, and even of children,[7] is not necessarily shared by the other religious traditions which in fact are inclined to make a virtue of elitist secrecy, of a professional cultic language understandable only to the elite initiated few. The Christian attitude to religious language places right at the heart of things the idea that people, especially ordinary people, should understand,[8] a view with momentous consequences for social and cultural awakening, with people feeling that the social enterprise as such is not discontinuous with God's universal plan.[9] It is one of the great historical truths of our day that otherwise obscure tribes, without a claim to cosmopolitan attainment, should find in indigenous particularity the sole grounds for appeal to international recognition. It is the Christian promotion of this indigenous particularity with the vernacular translations of missions which laid the basis for the modern nationalist phenomenon.

A final paradox, with practical implications for ecumenical relations, is the universal phenomenon of Christians adopting names for themselves without the explicit warrant of the founder of the religion or of the New Testament itself. The proliferation of

7. Erasmus wrote defending public and popular access to the Scriptures. Erasmus, *Christian Humanism and the Reformation*, 96–97.

8. Adolf Deissmann, a scholar of the New Testament, argued that the old literary style of classical Attic differed markedly from the New Testament style in its elaborate and cultivated refinement, whereas in the New Testament 'the underground stream of the people's language springs up powerfully into the daylight . . . Jesus spoke of the light and the candlestick, of the city on the hill, of father and child, bread and fish, egg and scorpion, of asking and giving, of seed and crop, of hunger and thirst. No long sentences, no speculative questions, transparent, pithy, plastic . . . The linguistic estimation of the New Testament shows us that our Holy Book in its classical, creative period is in close contact with the middle and lower classes and in sharp contrast to the old artificial Atticistic culture which struggled for a new lease of life in the surrounding world.' Deissmann, *The New Testament in the Light of Modern Research: The Haskell Lectures*, Garden City, New York: Doubleday, Doran & Co. Inc., 1929, 80, 94.

9. Commenting on the revolutionary implications of the vernacular Bible, the English historian, G. R. Elton, noted the role it regrettably afforded the common folk. Elton, *Reformation Europe: 1517–1559*, Cleveland, Ohio: Meridian Histories of Modern Europe, 1964, 52.

denominational names and religous orders is the staple of all Christianity, whether from the left and low, or the right and high. This again is in sharp contrast to the other major world religions, and especially with those that have a missionary tradition such as Islam. The name, 'Muslim', for example, is shared by all the followers of Islam, whatever the real differences in culture, custom, history, language and nationality, with explicit Qur'ānic sanction for the rule.[10] Christians, on the other hand, identify themselves by a variety of religious labels, from Anglican to Zionist, with Methodists, Orthodox, Presbyterians and others making up the middle ranks. Instead of decrying this phenomenon, or applauding it in Islam, it is our duty to understand it within the general context of the *translatability* of Christianity.

In these factors of paradox lies the central issue concerning the relationship between gospel and culture. In many quarters people assume that gospel and culture would make a right combination in the Third World, that is to say, the 'inculturation' or otherwise integration of Christian teachings with the culture would be a healthy thing, while a similar combination of gospel and culture in the West is wrong or harmful. Consequently, Western Christian missions have come in for severe criticism because they bring this combination of gospel and culture into the Third World where they suppress indigenous expression. A logical position, however, should see that the successful Western cultural transformation of Christianity indicates a similar possibility for the Third World, and, conversely, that the harmful consequences of the cultural adaptation of Christianity in the West will in time extend to the Third World as well.

This symmetrical argument brings us to what it is that makes culture both a natural ally and a natural foe for the gospel. It does not really matter whether we are speaking of culture in the West or in the Third World in this regard. In all situations the gospel seems to find its natural congruence within the cultural stream while at the same time encountering there its most serious obstacles. I should like to expound this theme in two complementary stages, first dealing with the positive aspect before turning to the negative. In the concluding stages of the chapter I shall synthesize the positive and negative aspects and examine their

10. Qur'án xxii: 77–78.

religious and theological significance. My aim is to pioneer a methodology, not produce a comprehensive statement.

The Positive Force of Gospel and Culture

One of the most forceful presentations of the cultural basis of Christianity is the work of the German scholar, Ernst Troeltsch, whose book, *The Absoluteness of Christianity* has had an enduring impact on subsequent generations of scholars.[11] Troeltsch's central argument is that the gospel and Western culture are indistinguishable to the extent that people cannot speak of the one without implying the other. Two pessimistic conclusions are drawn from this: first, that Christianity has become so culture-specific that it is incommunicable cross- culturally; and second, that non-Western converts face the doubly impossible burden of 'Westernization' and 'Christianization' simultaneously.

Troeltsch's position has been implicitly but nevertheless seriously questioned by several contemporary Western scholars. The historian Arnold J. Toynbee, for example, has argued that the 'Westernization' of Christianity represents only a historical phase in the expansion of the religion. Taking the Hellenic transformation of the Church as the Western paradigmatic shift, Toynbee pressed for a fresh view in which the Greek scientific metaphysic of the first four centuries of the Church no longer holds sway for people today whose worldview may be different. For one thing, the cumulative scientific construction of the universe today demands a shift of interpretation. For another, the West itself is in process of being relativized by new forms of culture and civilization.[12] Toynbee's own views on disentangling Christianity from Western culture have not gone unchallenged,[13] but few people can

11. Ernst Troeltsch, *The Absoluteness of Christianity and the History of Religions*, trans. David Reid, Richmond: John Knox Press, 1971.

12. Arnold J. Toynbee, *An Historian's Approach to Religion*, London and New York: Oxford University Press, 1956, pp. 129ff. See also his *Civilization on Trial*, New York: Oxford University Press, 1948 and *Christianity among the Religions of the World*, New York: Charles Scribner's Sons, 1957. Toynbee wrote in that last title about the need 'to purge our Christianity of its Western accessories', pointing to the admirable example set by Christians in seeking to divest Christianity of its Western cultural accretions (pp. 92–3).

13. See, for example, Albert Hourani, *Europe and the Middle East*, Berkeley & Los Angeles: University of California Press, 1980, chapter 7: 'Toynbee's Vision of History,' 135–60.

doubt the essential soundness of his reasoning that the West no longer holds monopoly on God's design for the world.

This same idea is forcefully expressed in the words of another Western scholar, R. G. Collingwood. He said that under the levelling impact of Christianity, the West in its Graeco-Roman manifestation ceased to be the centre of the world, ushering in a Copernican revolution in which the universal historical process becomes everywhere and always of the same kind, which is 'the general development of God's purpose for human life. The infusion of Christian ideas,' he continues, 'overcomes not only the characteristic humanism and substantialism of Graeco-Roman history, but also its particularism.'[14]

The third writer who also tried to place the West within a comparative worldwide Christian perspective is William Ernest Hocking who gained notoriety as chairman of a revisionist mission report which caused tremors in mainstream Christian quarters.[15] Hocking approached the matter of the West's relative status in terms of the diversity and particularity of human experience and in terms of the evolving nature of Western ideas and institutions themselves. He focused in this sense on the intrinsically limited, rather than absolute, nature of the state as safeguard for human freedom. Rare among Western philosophers in taking history seriously, Hocking confronted without, however, resolving the question about the challenge of historical pluralism for what may be regarded as the theological core and essence of Christianity.[16] Similar rumblings concerning

14. R. G. Collingwood, *The Idea of History*, London & New York: Oxford University Press, 1946, repr. 1966, p. 49.

15. William Ernest Hocking, *The Coming World Civilization*, London: George Allen & Unwin, 1958. The layman's report was published as *Rethinking Missions*, New York: Harper & Brothers, 1932. This report provoked, among other things, the leading Dutch theologian of the time, Hendrick Kraemer, to write his influential work, *The Christian Message in a Non-Christian World*, 1938.

16. Hocking, *Coming World Civilization*, 134ff. Hocking senses that particularity is indispensable to authentic Christian expression, but seems undecided about whether local grounding of the faith is unavoidably in conflict with universality. Taking Quakerism as an example, he said that few people will doubt Quakerism has 'best caught the genius of a particularity that is also universal' (p. 135). He then relates Quakerism to Catholicism, saying that they 'together bear their partials of a truth, which includes the truth of a continuing historical community of aggressive caritas at once material and spiritual'

the relative position of the West in world history can be discerned in the writings of Marshall Hodgson[17] and E. H. Carr,[18] to cite only two further examples.

The cultural formulation of religion, and of Christianity in particular, represents a formidable intellectual legacy in our world. Much of the confidence by which this legacy is promoted stems from the peculiar role of the Church in promoting, or in being perceived as promoting, culture. The spectacular success of Latin, for example, shows the Church as the preserver and guardian of the Western tradition.[19] In the Carolingian empire, to take a different example, Christianity fostered the use of the vernacular. A leading champion as we saw earlier was Otfrid von Weissenburg, who devoted himself to promoting the vernacular cause for both religious and secular purposes. He found it necessary to direct his attention to his contemporaries 'who knew how to think and who can be encouraged through the vernacular to read more for themselves.'[20] Furthermore, as Christopher Dawson has shown, in spite of the Latin hegemony in the Church, Christianity in northern Europe in the medieval period was linked to the vernacular stimulus.[21]

The early Christians were themselves in no doubt about the essential pluralism of the religion they adopted and drew comfort from the thought. Justin Martyr (c. A.D. 100–165), for example, a Palestinian born of settlers in Neapolis (Nablus), remarked:

(p. 135). It is clear that Hocking is trying to juggle the interests of Christianity as a dynamic historical phenomenon alongside those of Christianity as a fixed dogmatic system, and then inferring from that tension a progressive element largely constituted as 'internal advance in self-understanding'. This way of dealing with the issue dissolves historical diversity into an idealist construction and is, therefore, in the final analysis unsatisfactory.

17. Marshall G. S. Hodgson, 'The Interrelations of Societies in History', *Comparative Studies in Society and History*, v, 1962–63, 227–250.

18. E. H. Carr, *What is History?*, New York: Alfred A. Knopf, 1962, repr. 1964, in particular chapter vi, 'The Widening Horizons'.

19. See W. H. Frend, *The Rise of Christianity*, Philadelphia: Fortress Press, 1984, p. 560.

20. John Michael Wallace-Hadrill, *The Frankish Church*, Oxford: Clarendon Press, 1983, p. 386.

21. Christopher Dawson, *Religion and the Rise of Western Culture*, London: Sheed and Ward, 1950, p. 115.

'For there is not a single race of human beings, barbarians, Greeks, or whatever name you please to call them, nomads or vagrants or herdsmen living in tents, where prayers through the name of Jesus the Crucified are not offered up to the Father and Maker of the universe.'[22] In his famous letter to the Emperor Trajan, Pliny the Younger alluded to the enormous social diversity existing within the Christian movement, making the religion extremely difficult to check in its spread and appeal. He also implies that Christian activity has acted to rejuvenate the older traditions, an important point to which I shall return presently. He wrote alarmingly:

> People of every age and rank and of both sexes will continue to be gravely imperilled. The contagion of that superstition has infected not only cities (*civitates*) but villages (*agros*) and hamlets; but it seems possible to check and correct it. It is clear, at least, that the temples which had been deserted are again frequented, and the sacred festivals long intermitted are revived. Sacrificial victims for which purchases have been rare are again in demand.[23]

Another early source, the anonymous *Epistle to Diognetus*, a third-century source in spite of claims that it was written in A.D. 124, takes an upbeat, positive view of Christian cultural interface. It says:

> The difference between Christians and the rest of mankind is not a matter of nationality, or of language, or customs. Christians do not live apart in separate cities of their own, speak any special dialect, nor practise any eccentric way of life . . . They pass their lives in whatever township – Greek or foreign – each man's lot has determined; and conform to ordinary local usage in their clothing, diet, and other habits . . . they are residents at home in their own

22. Cited in J. Spencer Trimingham, *Christianity among the Arabs in Pre-Islamic Times*, London: Longman; Beirut: Librairie du Liban, 1979, p. 94. Edward Gibbon cites the same material in *The Decline and Fall of the Roman Empire*, N.D., New York: Modern Library, 3 vols., vol. i, p. 438.

23. Moses Hadas, ed. & tr. *A History of Rome: From Its Origins to A.D. 529 as Told by the Roman Historians*, New York: Doubleday Anchor Books, 1956, p. 131. Also *The Letters of Pliny the Younger*, ed. & tr. Betty Radice, New York: Penguin Books, 1969, repr. 1985, pp. 293–95.

> countries . . . they take their full part as citizens . . . For them, any foreign country is a motherland, and any motherland is a foreign country.[24]

Ancient statecraft, in some contrast to modern forms of exclusive nationalism, saw cultural pluralism as necessary for a strong and vigorous society, with Christianity as the engine for this. For example, when Hungary was transformed from 'the Magyar robber state' 'into the Apostolic Kingdom that was to be the eastern bulwark of Christendom', its founder, St Stephen, seeking to emulate Rome whose greatness he attributed to its encouragement of pluralism, declared: *nam unius linguae, uniusque moris regnum imbecile et fragilum* (for weak and fragile is a kingdom that has only one language and custom).[25] There may, of course, be the usual Constantinian peril of coopting Christianity as an accoutrement of state policy, in Hungary or anywhere else, but the issue here is Christianity as a positive force on the front line of cultural interface. As such, it is the opposite of the popular notion of Christianity as ruthless cultural iconoclasm. This introduces the second, negative stage of the interface of gospel and culture.

The Negative Force of Gospel and Culture

In his great work on the Roman Empire, the eighteenth-century historian and rationalist, Edward Gibbon, formulated the thesis, now conveniently lodged in the Western liberal temper, that Christianity dealt a mortal blow to the Empire by introducing endemic provincialism and fostering subversive congregational

24. *Early Christian Writings: The Apostolic Fathers*, tr. & ed. Maxwell Staniforth, New York: Penguin Books, 1968, repr. 1982, 176–77.
25. Christopher Dawson, 1950, 137. Dawson's own views on Christianity and culture have come under attack. Commenting on similar ideas that Dawson presented in his book *Beyond Politics*, T. S. Eliot took him to task for saying that the extent of Christians creating culture should be limited to participation in the voluntary organization of culture, which in a liberal democratic society is the political party. T. S. Eliot, *Christianity and Culture: The Idea of a Christian Society and Notes Towards the Definition of Culture*, New York & London: Harcourt Brace Jovanovich, 1968, 59–61. Eliot's own independent proposals smack too much of the status quo in some enlightened rehash to be but a derivative moralization.

particularism at the local level.[26] Gibbon goes on to elaborate on the subversive motives of Christians towards the Empire, saying that Christians considered 'every disaster that happened to the empire as an infallible symptom of an expiring world,'[27] as if the mere fact of Christians *thinking* ill of the Empire *caused* disaster to follow even if we assume Christians *thought* in that particular way. At any rate, Gibbon made colourful assertions about Christianity as the enemy of enlightened progress, saying that culture in its noble rebirth would discard the religion as the butterfly the chrysalis. Sir James Frazer, who in anthropological science belonged to the Intellectualist School, picked up these views and embellished them with a wealth of ethnographic detail, using evidence of Christianity's open frontiers with Paganism as signs of a shared irrational defect.[28] In Frazer's evolutionary model, magic, religion and science followed each other in an ascending, superseding order,[29] with the religious gadfly destined to be extinct in the evolutionary process as such. Frazer's great erudition concealed the otherwise all too obvious fact that his materials were largely wrenched from any organic context and reconstituted into a massive logical structure which, by its sheer energy and brilliance, carried forward the rationalist polemic against Christianity. And there are, even today, innumerable variations on this polemical theme, with Edmund Leach, another British anthropologist of Cambridge, Frazer's own university, calling for the overthrow of religion and the full emancipation of human beings from the fetters of dogma.[30]

In a curious way this negative view of Christianity was gratuitously promoted by Christian scholars themselves, even though for them the focus is on the power of Christianity to succeed where others failed, or were thought to be failing. An eloquent proponent of this view is the German scholar, Ulhorn.

26. Edward Gibbon, *The Decline & Fall of the Roman Empire*, New York: Modern Library, N.D., 3 vols., vol. i, 671–726.
27. ibid., 405–6.
28. James Frazer, *The Golden Bough: Part IV: Adonis, Attis, Osiris: Studies in the History of Oriental Religion*, 3rd ed., London: Macmillan & Co., 1914, 300–301.
29. See Evans-Pritchard, 1965, referred to above.
30. See Edmund Leach, *A Runaway World?*, BBC Reith Lectures of 1967, London: BBC Publications, 1968.

Writing in 1882, he postulated: 'Had the stream of new life issuing from Christ encountered ancient life when the latter was still unbroken, it would have recoiled impotent from the shock. But ancient life had by this time begun to break up; its solid foundations had begun to weaken . . .'[31] This became the thundering theme in Eric Dodds's influential book[32] which elicited a counterrejoinder in an edited work.[33] Dodds's main argument is that 'For the people of the Empire it was a time of increasing insecurity and misery; for the Church it was a time of relative freedom from persecution, of steady numerical growth, and above all of swift intellectual advance.'[34] The basic outline of Christianity under this negative thesis is that cultural opportunism enabled the new religion to profit from the crisis and misfortune whose causes lay outside the religion. Dodds put it in sensational terms as follows: 'From a world so impoverished intellectually, so insecure materially, so filled with fear and hatred as the world of the third century, any path that promised escape must have attracted serious minds. Many besides Plotinus must have given new meaning to the words of Agamemnon in Homer, "Let us flee to our own country." That advice might stand as a motto for the whole period.'[35]

In his scholarly study, Kenneth Scott Latourette of Yale advances an identical argument. 'Had Christianity been born in a vigorous young culture whose adherents were confident of its virtues,' he hypothesized, 'it might have met a different fate.'[36] However, in their different ways, these writers base their reasoning on evidence that is by no means unequivocal. For example, Latourette, scrupulous to the hilt, admits that Christianity had encountered a vigorous Neoplatonism which 'had the

31. Ulhorn, *Die christliche Liebsthätigkeit in der alten Kirche*, p. 37, cited in Adolf von Harnack, *The Mission and Expansion of Christianity*, New York: 1908, 2 vols., vol. i, 22n.
32. Eric R. Dodds, *Pagan and Christian in an Age of Anxiety*, New York, 1970: W. W. Norton.
33. Robert C. Smith and John Lounibos, eds., *Pagan and Christian Anxiety: A Response to E. R. Dodds*, Lanham, Md.: University Press of America, 1984.
34. Dodds, *Pagan and Christian*, 106.
35. ibid., 100–101.
36. Kenneth Scott Latourette, *A History of the Expansion of Christianity*, 7 vols., vol. i, New York: Harper & Brothers, 1937, 163–64.

endorsement of a much larger proportion of the upper classes than did the eventual victor.'[37] For his part, Gibbon signalled the conversion of people from what he called 'the advantages of natural endowment or fortune.'[38] As demonstrated also in the works of Augustine, Christianity gave evidence of having encountered a massive cultural and intellectual tradition in the Graeco-Roman world, an encounter bearing the hallmark of challenge rather than opportunism.[39]

We can evaluate the arguments of the negative impact of Christianity on culture by saying that the religion in its spread seems to encourage local revitalization. This does not contradict the views of someone like Gibbon; it merely calls into question his operative assumption about culture and civilization being synonymous, with Christians showing a contempt for both by their misguided faith in immortality.[40] However, local revitalization, especially in the form of organized community life and responsibility, may sometimes come into conflict with the structures of centralized control. If that is what Christianity has meant in the Graeco-Roman world, then the Christian conflict with the Empire should be assessed differently rather than in terms of the alleged anarchy of Pietism.

As I have tried to show, Gibbon shares his negative evaluation with many Christian writers who wish to paint a more positive picture of Christianity but who nevertheless assume that Christian universality is compromised by local particularity, an assumption with a venerable pedigree in German philosophical idealism. William Ernest Hocking, the American philosopher, for example, was disinclined to see anything of much value in the 'localization' of Christianity, so that when he considered Western Christianity he baulked at the notion on the grounds that the Western component was evidence of unacceptable 'local' adaptation. His words bear citing in full.

> Western religion has, for over three centuries, had the unique advantage of constant intercourse with a science

37. ibid., i, 164.
38. Gibbon, *Decline*, vol. i, 440–441.
39. St Augustine, *Confessions*, Penguin Books, New York, viii, 2, 4, 5. Also *City of God*, New York: Penguin Books, 1972, Book X, pp. 371–426.
40. Gibbon, *Decline*, vol. i, 402.

> and philosophical activity independent of itself, and yet relevant to its being. Largely through this free intercourse it has moved toward solving insights which, made part of its own vital impulse, promise to give it curative impact on any modern society. Yet this whole historic process, and its involvement in western culture, may tend to localize it. And if Christianity as a whole is distinctively western, its significance for world civilization is – I will not say nullified from the start, but discontinued.[41]

The fact of the matter is that the localization of Christianity is an inevitable and indispensable aspect of the religion qua religion, and that without that concrete, historical grounding Christianity becomes nothing but a fragile, elusive abstraction, salt without its saltness. That is the problem that dogs all attempts at defining the core of the gospel as a propositional truth without regard to the concrete lives of men and women who call themselves Christian. And it is precisely the historical concreteness of Christianity that makes cross-cultural mutuality possible and necessary. A sort of 'United Nations' of the essence of Christianity is actually an oxymoron, with essence contrasted with the existence of 'individual nations' presupposed in a 'United Nations'. World solidarity and national particularity are not incompatible opposites, although they become problematic when we make them into ideological causes. I believe it is this ideological difficulty that Christian realism about the proper relationship of the general and particular, of fact and significance and culture and gospel can help resolve, an issue to which I shall return.

Theology and the Cultural Front Line

In the heated and sophisticated discussion about religion and culture, there is a recurrent idea that religious truth is inseparable from culture, not just in the fortuitous way culture entangles religion but in the drastic sense that the cultural configuration of religion is also its final and essential form. In this view, cultural markers in the religious life signify not just religious reality but in fact constitute the reality itself, forms whose content is no more

41. William Ernest Hocking, *World Civilization*, 80.

or less than how that content is symbolized. There is, however, something of a jump, or at any rate an awkward transition at this point, for if it is contended that on the one hand religious traditions are themselves cultural refractions of God and on the other that such refractions are symbols that do not hold anything independent of themselves, then we would have a reinforced circularity in which God is only a formal point of reference, useful for poetry and linguistic convention perhaps, but otherwise superfluous as an independent reality. Thus, to speak of God in terms exclusively as a form of human cultural encounter would be only an unnecessarily complicated, roundabout way of describing the human enterprise as cultural forms in different modes of apprehension. What is not clear in this procedure is whether 'God' is a metaphor for the general principle of unity that cultural symbols *signify*, or whether the concrete forms of *representation* themselves undergo a sort of intrinsic mystical transformation at the same time as they refract and in other ways project the idea of God. Either way, material objects would acquire rather inconsistent powers: they would form and shape reality; they would emanate or otherwise reveal reality, and they would generate ideas and theories with which we apprehend, explain and in other important ways sort them out. This would be fetishism and would be clearly absurd: tobacco does not also contain grains that tell us about lighting, smoking or worshipping it, nor do mountains and streams from their mass and dynamism give us logical charts or catechisms about contours and scales. It is only in relation to specific religious ideas and ritual action that material objects acquire symbolic meaning. Yet a good deal of the discussion of religion and culture is marked by a contradiction pretty close to this logical repetitiveness, and intelligent people have found themselves swept along by the sheer force of repetition. When we in turn strip and materialize cultural forms to construct our categories of the real and ideal, we exploit a procedure incapable of enlightening us about either, for the argument forces us to take as real ideal notions and their cultural configuration, with the result that cultural perceptions become philosophical conceptions, qualitative analogies, literal facts and representation identity. We do not stop to ask ourselves how cultural forms can be both *modifiers* and *subjects*, the path and the destination at the same time, how abstract or freely exchangeable forms of representation can also congeal as the incarnate substance and subject of what they represent. This is at the heart of the issue of cultural relativism, including the unwarranted step of inferring moral relativism from descriptive ethnography. I shall deal with this matter in my concluding observations on history and cultural innocence.

The great nineteenth-century Sanskritist and historian of religion, Max Müller, referring to this phenomenon of reducing religion to its cultural forms, once spoke of religion as 'a disease of language', a phrase that haunted him in later years. Müller meant by that the tendency of metaphorical language employed in a religious context to harden and obscure the original and concrete experience and its attributes which gave the initial impetus to language. For example, the striking idea that a memorable event once occurred at dawn may come down in metaphorical language as 'Apollo loved Daphne; Daphne fled before him and was changed into a laurel tree.' In this account Apollo is a solar deity, and Daphne, the Greek for a laurel tree, was dawn. The story would then be transformed into the sun chasing away dawn. It is called the Solar Myth. The process at work here, according to Müller, is the personification of experience and its attributes as deities. Thus *nomina* become *numina*.[42] Or, to take another example, the king dying in a Western battle may become mythologized as the symbol of the sun setting in the west, while Apollo killing the python would be an allegory of summer driving out winter. Müller believed, therefore, that philology (he was professor of comparative philology at Oxford) would be a necessary instrument to remedy the defect, or at any rate the natural tricks, of langauge. But his theory sounds unconvincingly as if the disease and its cure are the same.[43]

42. St Augustine ridicules a version of this idea (*City of God*, Bk. vi, chaps. 8 & 9). Oman similarly rejects the conjecture on the grounds of *numina* not 'being individual and personal, like the polytheistic deities, but rather manifestations of one mysterious, awe-inspiring diffused potency.' He continues: 'How this vague unity of awareness, which was felt as a whole at every point of interest, as space at every point of perception, came to be broken up into powers corresponding to a wide range of organized interests and graded values, is a question as difficult as it is important.' Oman, *The Natural and the Supernatural*, 391.

43. On the general matter of religion as a cultural system, see the chapter of that title in Clifford Geertz, *The Interpretation of Cultures*, New York: Basic Books, 1973. On Max Müller, see Evans-Pritchard, 1965, and his posthumous *A History of Anthropological Thought*, ed. André Singer, New York: Basic Books, 1981.

It seems reasonable to say that cultural formulations of God are possible because God is available in the first place as the prior category, rather than that culture feeds on itself to produce a sacral category, like water and vapour.[44] However we look at it, the mountain can scarcely worship the mouse of its own labour.

G. K. Chesterton, with his penchant for playful, if revealing paradox, says the issue is not how nature, or culture for that matter, gave us our idea of God, but how God gave us our idea of nature and culture. He contends that much of our reductionist hostility to religion in general is fuelled by our prior commitment to deny Christianity in particular, so that with the same unilateral stubborness we bring other religions and cultures to an equal fate.

> The god was never a symbol or hieroglyph representing the sun. The sun was a hieroglyph representing the god . . . No human being was ever so unnatural as to worship Nature. No man however indulgent (as I am) to corpulency, ever worshipped a man as round as the sun or a woman as round as the moon. No man, however attracted to an artistic attenuation, ever really believed that the Dryad was as lean and stiff as the tree. We human beings have never worshipped Nature; and indeed, the reason is very simple. It is that all human beings are superhuman beings. We have printed our image upon Nature, as God has printed His image upon us. We have told the enormous sun to stand still; we have fixed him on our shields, caring no more for a star than for a starfish. And when there were powers of Nature we could not for the time control, we have conceived great beings in human shape controlling them. Jupiter does not mean thunder. Thunder means the march and victory of Jupiter. Neptune does not mean the sea; the sea is his, and he made it . . . Heathen gods mean nothing, and must always mean nothing, to those of us that deny the Christian God.[45]

44. This is no more convincing than that John Smith in general has become Lieutenant Smith in particular. 'Or, as the name first came from the function, it is as when the ancestral anvil is forgotten in the name of Smith and the owner is on his way to a peerage.' Oman, *The Natural*, 390.

45. G. K. Chesterton 'The Priest of Spring', in *Stories, Essays and Poems*, London: Everyman's Library 1935, no. 913, repr. 1965, 163. With character-

Religious people may therefore respond that while they employ culture to represent God as transcendent being, the God who is so represented may not be identified with some cultural manifestations to the exclusion of others, so that partial cultural representation does not become the comprehensive criterion of God. Such a Christian position would allow cultural access and utilization without making end and means identical.

Consequently in the detailed and specific responses religious people make, it can be said that God is connected to culture, but, in the general scheme of salvation history, God is connected to culture not in the descriptive sense as a figure of identity but in the normative one where the plan is to bring everything under subjection to Christ.

This may sound at once threatening and inconclusive, threatening because it rejects cultural systems as in any sense definitive of truth, and inconclusive because it perceives culture as inseparable from the truth.

However, we can reply that the truth of God is finally destroyed if it becomes absolutely synonymous with corresponding cultural forms. The fundamental question, then, is whether the truth of God has also to be capable of being conceived beyond – and through – all cultural systems if it is to amount to anything more than ethnocentrism, though if it bypassed culture altogether the truth would be nothing more (or less) than subjective idealism.

This philosophical dilemma is in fact the paradox that made the cross-cultural front line the source of much creative innovation and religious practice, for in that context cultural forms are upheld in their plural diversity without their being absolutized in their unique particularity. The great historical forms of culture are thus refined and consummated through the milieu of mother tongue translation and set against the background of common ethical accountability. It was in this way that historical forms of culture became more than a multiplicity of disconnected episodes; they

---

istic brilliance Chesterton develops the same theme in his book, *The Everlasting Man*, London: Hodder & Stoughton, 1925, especially chapter V, 'Man and Mythologies', and chapter VI, 'The Demons and the Philosophers.'

became coherent links in the chain all human beings depend on for communication, self-understanding and moral education.

This is the 'instrumental' view Christianity in its worldwide expansion has promoted with regard to languages and culture. It grows out of the Christian view of who and what God is, and its effect has been to endow the religion with a pluralist ethos at the heart of the gospel.

It is important to spell out what is the particular, peculiar Christian understanding of culture, and to do this from the perspective of the New Testament. The primitive Christians inherited from Judaism the Law and the synagogue as the exclusive standards of religious truth. However, from their subsequent understanding of the life and work of Christ, they came to a fresh view concerning God's impartial activity in all cultures. The watershed for this new understanding was Pentecost which set a seal on mother tongues as sufficient and necessary channels of access to God,[46] a piece of cultural innovation that enabled the religion to adopt the multiplicity of geographical centres as legitimate destinations for the gospel. Christians continued to cherish their Judaic roots in the context of growing pluralism within the Church, a pluralism at the core of which is the principle that no culture is the exclusive norm of truth and that, similarly, no culture is inherently unclean in the eyes of God. So Jews, Gentiles, Barbarians, Scythians, Cypriots, Arabs, Goths, Ethiopians, Copts among others, were all to be found rubbing shoulders at prayer, worship and in acts of mutual succour. In time, too, numerous intellectual streams discharged their share into the Church, so that Aquinas could speak of the great advantage that accrued to the Church from the fact that the Fathers and early apologists had been Pagans. The Christian movement confidently, if not always consistently, adopted many diverse kinds of materials, including *Gnostic* sources, placing early Christian thought within a pluralist context, and this kind of eclecticism was the natural outgrowth of the gospel having been 'translated' out of Galilean Aramaic and Hebrew into country (*Koine*) Greek, so that, as I observed earlier, most of the early converts had no living knowledge of the primary language

46. Acts 2: 6, 8, 11.

of the preaching of Jesus. Clearly the early Christians understood that the language issue may be detached from the question of faithfulness to the message of Jesus Christ, and that gives us an important clue into culture as 'instrumental'.

Two major consequences for the religious status of culture may be characterized as, first, the 'relativization' of all cultural arrangements, and, second, the 'destigmatization' of all Gentile or taboo cultures. Thus would transcendent truth subsume cultures and mobilize them at the same time. Taboo cultures, regarded through time and eternity as outside the pale of salvation, came thus to qualify as among the first fruits of God's impartial dealings with humanity. These two consequences became the heritage that opened the way for teeming pluralism and diversity of view in the community, with Christians drawing on a complex assortment of cultural materials to define and undefine themselves, something which has relevance for issues of denominational identity.

In a recently discovered letter written from Nicopolis on the Dalmatian coast to his friend Darius at Rome, for example, Severus draws attention to the character of the fledgling religion. The letter was written sometime in the early third century. Severus and his friend had been in the habit of comparing notes on the Christian movement, a hobby that blossomed into a genial rivalry between them, in which connection the enigmas from Nicopolis would be variations on a theme. 'I have a tale to tell you,' Severus arouses his friend's curiosity, 'that will surpass even your most fantastic account of Christians in Rome. Since our common fascination with this new and outlandish religion drew us together and we dedicated ourselves to chronicling the spectacle of these Christians, our competition for news of this curious fellowship has been played largely on a level field. But you must admit, my friend, that my posting to Nicopolis has put me at a decided disadvantage. Yet, despite the odds, I've topped you this time.' And then he went on promptly to recount the details of a debate attended by Christians about estabishing a new seminary syllabus. He called the Christians 'diverse and fractious', and the proceedings 'such a circus'. He continued, 'Open dissent had shattered the illusion of conformity, and the steady tone of authority was overwhelmed by buzzing more fierce than a thousand angry hornets. How these people could agree that the sky is blue, my friend, let alone what to teach their leaders, is beyond my powers of understanding . . . What fun!'[47]

All these materials suggest that in the early centuries the new religion moved forward like an oriental caravanserai, with its complex baggage of exotic teachings, baffling mysteries, colourful sounds and an eclectic ethical code, leaving the authorities to whistle in the dark about the unshakable foundations that have ordered the community, fixed the beliefs and set the common practices. In the jumble and tumble of social encounter, Christians spoke a bewildering variety of languages, with the new experience again and again exciting bursts of separatist fervour. In this respect, at least, Christianity was a major cultural as well as religious revolution whose force has endured into our own time. Its basic outline is extremely simple: from the point of view of God's 'plan of salvation', all cultures are equally valid, if equally inadequate.

It is pertinent to ask what sustained this important change and what its lessons are for Christians today. If Pentecost was the monument to the salvific potential of mother tongues, then St Paul was the pre-eminent person who carved his name on that monument. Paul understood completely the specific and general implications of Pentecost, and was equally prepared to stake his reputation on what Pentecost stood for. The effect of the gospel, Paul affirms, was to 'de-stigmatize' the culture and the people associated with it: Jews, Gentiles, Barbarians and provincials all now stand on an equal footing under God's salvific purpose. Judgment had come upon the world, upon the Jew first, but also upon the Gentile, to wit, that the terms of one people's self-understanding, though invaluable for knowing God's intentions, are not, however, the absolute or exclusive norm for others. And so those matters, such as dietary regulations, circumcision and holy days, which are central to Jewish particularity, should nevertheless not be constituted into a principle of exclusion from, or participation in the fellowship.[48] Similarly, Gentiles are under notice not to make an exclusive norm of their own cultural

47. 'Ancient Letter Discovered: The Seminary Crisis at Nicopolis', *Christian Century*, Febr. 5–12, 1992, 116–7, 116.
48. Romans 14, 5–23.

particularity, that is to say, not to reduce religion to cultural ideology and thus indulge in self-absolutization.[49] Essentially, Paul says, nothing is unclean in itself,[50] or, to put it in contemporary language, sacrality is not intrinsic to culture or nature but is something with which the religious person invests cultural or natural objects when they become religious subjects. Thus has Wilfred Smith rightly observed that religious symbols in themselves have no intrinsic merit. 'The religiousness of religious symbols,' he says, 'and of the tradition that they constitute does not lie in those symbols or that tradition. These, it turns out, may be of stunningly diverse sorts, of no constant shape or style. It lies rather in the involvement with or through those symbols of those persons or groups whose lives are ordered in relation to them. That involvement leads far beyond the symbols themselves, demanding or making possible the totality of the person's or group's response, and affecting their relation not only to those symbols but to themselves, to their fellows,'[51] and to God. It follows, then, that Paul would want to urge the believers to respect cultural practices *for the sake of each other* because of the God who gives them all things. God in Jesus Christ, the Apostle teaches, affirms our particularity in all its forms. But there is a major, fundamental qualification, namely, that form of cultural particularity which absolutizes and thus excludes is itself 'excluded'. Ethnic individuality, yes, but ethnic divinization, no.

It is from this position that Paul builds the majestic structure of Christian pluralism in Romans 12 and I Corinthians 12. 'Christianity thus came to adopt a plurality of cultures as

49. ibid., 3: 9; 11: 22; *Gal.* 3: 28–29.

50. Romans 14: 14. Also *I Cor.* 7: 18–20 where the Apostle attempts specifically to 'relativize' circumcision, that is, to strip the custom of its normative overload, seeking neither to ban it nor to enjoin it. His procedure introduces a fundamental qualification into his earlier exhortation, in his words, to keep the commandments of God (second half of verse 19), especially if those commandments included the observance of circumcision.

51. Wilfred Cantwell Smith, 'Philosophia, as One of the Religious Traditions of Humankind: The Greek Legacy in Western Civilization viewed by a comparativist', in *Différences valeurs hiérarchie: textes offerts à Louis Dumont*, Jean-Claude Galey, ed.: Paris: École des Hautes Études en Sciences Sociales, 1984, 253–279, 265.

natural extensions of the religious proclamation without surrendering the 'instrumental' view of culture. This is both a simple and delicate matter. Culture, however lofty or privileged, remains in the Pauline account an instrument and channel under God's undivided sovereignty. Yet that sovereignty, being 'one', is itself mediated to us through the 'many' bottlenecks of culture.[52] Thus Christians hallow culture by the paradox of denying its intrinsic sacrality, and elevate it by opposing its idolization. It is part of the Pauline achievement that it enables us thus to reconcile the 'one' and the 'many'.

The Christian encounter with culture has provided us with the first rigorous, not to say modern, critique of culture, and that legacy, whatever its chequered history, has endured through the centuries. The religious form of the issue helped summarize in an acute way the sickness that had eaten away at the foundations of Graeco-Roman society, and now threatens our own. That religious form of the problem was: if new converts to the Church are required to pass the test of Gentile cultural attainment, then, Paul insists, what distinguishes that from the test the Jerusalem Church for its part applied to Gentile converts themselves?[53] In other words, does not the relative value of culture remain the *same* even when, and especially since, the circumstances are *different*? And should not Christians advocate cultural *differences* where at the same time they are committed to theological *consistency*? That, it seems, is the only way to uphold *contingency* alongside *consistency*, or the *general* with the *specific*.

Paul's insight on this issue is to my mind decisive for all subsequent engagement with the question. He formulated pluralism as the necessary outworking of the religion he believed Jesus preached. This pluralism was rooted for Paul in the *Gentile breakthrough*. Paul's view is that God does not absolutize any culture, whatever the esteem of that culture. Furthermore, Paul believed that all cultures have cast upon them the breath of God's favour, thus cleansing them of all stigma of inferiority and

52. This idea brings to mind the words of the contemporary song: 'We are the forest of ten thousand seeds in shades of green that hold the sun. With mingled roots our limbs together lean; We are the many and the one.' Words by Caroline McDade.

53. Galatians 2: 11–14.

untouchability. These two ideas constitute what we may regard as the incipient 'radical pluralism' of Pauline thought. When he stressed faith over against works, Paul was intending to enunciate the inclusive principle of God's right and freedom to choose us without regard to our cultural trophies. Faith as the absolute gift of a loving, gracious God,[54] is the rule that unmasks culture. Western psychology and its theological variants have unjustifiably subjectivized the issue, pitting inward assurance against social engagement, with the tendency to reduce religion to what Flannery O'Connor has called 'sweet invention'.[55] In fact, Paul desired above all to safeguard the cultural particularity (not 'particularism') of Jew as Jew and Gentile as Gentile, while challenging both Jew and Gentile to find in Jesus Christ their respective true affirmation.

Paul's legacy to the Church includes this exacting vigilance over the double-sidedness of culture. Christian life is indelibly marked by the stamp of culture, while Christian sources also instruct a penultimate status for culture. In the final analysis the Church must utter the prophetic word in culture, and sometimes even against it. Paul could with justice be seen as a cultural iconoclast in his defiance of idolatrous tendencies in culture, but he cannot be regarded as a cultural cynic, for in his view God's purposes are mediated through the particularity of cultural streams.

Vernacular Languages and Cultures under the Gospel

With the modern missionary enterprise we come upon spectacular examples of cultural pluralism in the Church.[56] To begin with, vernacular translations of the Bible began with the adoption of

54. See the splendid and still relevant study of C. H. Dodd, *The Meaning of Paul for Today*, London: Fontana Books, 1964, 80. Also J. Christian Beker, *Paul the Apostle: The Triumph of God in Life and Thought*, Philadelphia: Fortress Press, 1980.
55. Flannery O'Connor, *The Habit of Being*, New York: Farrar, Straus, Giroux, 1979, 479.
56. In his summary of the cultural and linguistic impact of the Bible, Eric Fenn points out the indigenizing potential of Scriptural translation. Eric Fenn, 'The Bible and the Missionary', *The Cambridge History of the Bible, 1963, vol. iii: The West from the Reformation to the Present Day*, ed. S. L. Greenslade, Cambridge: Cambridge University Press, repr. 1988, 383–407.

indigenous terms, concepts, customs and idioms for the central categories of Christianity. Secondly, vernacular criteria began to determine what is or what is not a successful translation, with indigenous experts rapidly moving to challenge Western interpretations of Christianity.[57] Thirdly, the employment of the vernacular led to a proliferation of languages into which the Scriptures were translated.[58] Fourthly, in numerous significant cases missionary translations were the first attempt to write down the language. Where this was the case Christian translators have had to produce vernacular alphabets, grammars, dictionaries and vocabularies of the language, supplementing these with compilations of proverbs, idioms, axioms, ethnographic materials and accounts of local religions, customary practice and law, history and political institutions. Such a detailed and scrupulous inventory of the vernacular culture triggered unimaginable consequences in the wider society, resulting almost everywhere in arousing deep loyalties towards the indigenous cause. Often that was the seedbed of nationalism. It is impossible to overestimate the revolutionary impact of Christian translation on hitherto illiterate societies and their now new encounter with the West. In addition, to bring this list to its final stage, there was a theological truth implicit in all this enterprise, and that concerns God's prevenient grace which preceded the missionary and by which missionaries themselves proceeded to adopt existing forms and usage *as if God was their hidden life*. Thus could Newbigin say:

> In almost all cases where the Bible has been translated into the languages of the non-Christian peoples of the world, the New Testament word *Theos* has been rendered by the name given by the non-Christian peoples to the one whom they worship as Supreme Being. It is under this name, therefore, that the Christians who now use these languages worship the God and Father of Jesus Christ . . . The name of the God revealed in Jesus Christ can only be

57. A recent example of this shift of interpretation is given in Vincent Donovan, *Christianity Rediscovered*, Maryknoll, New York: Orbis Books, 1978.

58. In 1984 more than 1800 languages were involved in some form of Bible translating. In Africa alone some 522 languages were involved, with complete Bibles available in over 100 languages. *Scriptures of the World*, London, New York & Stuttgart: United Bible Societies, 1984.

> known by using those names for God which have been developed within the non-Christian systems of belief and worship. It is therefore impossible to claim that there is a total discontinuity between the two.[59]

Behind (and before) all that consecrated labour lies the precious jewel of God's impartiality towards all peoples and cultures, a truth dearer and closer in spirit to the meek and lowly than to the high and mighty.

It is clear that missionary translators saw a natural congruence between indigenous cultures and the gospel, with the diversity and plurality of those cultures justifying commitment to the particularity and specificity of cultural materials. Not only individual languages, but also minute dialectical differences were noted and preserved in translations.[60] Mission seems to press to its logical conclusion the premise of the admissibility of all cultures in the general sweep of God's 'plan of salvation', eager to witness to God in the words and names of other people's choosing.

Concerning the role of language, it is important to hold in our mind that in traditional societies language and culture are closely intertwined, and that in religion both are promoted in an integrated, dynamic way. Therefore missionary translations appealed to the very roots of these societies, touching the springs of life and imagination in real, enduring ways. Perhaps it was to this phenomenon that Pliny the Younger referred in his letter to the Emperor Trajan, namely, that Christian renewal also transforms while stimulating older habits and attitudes. Whatever the case, it would be appropriate to conclude this section of our discussion with a closer clarification of the vernacular issue in Christian missionary translation, and do this in two interconnected stages. The first concerns the 'instrumental' view of culture, and, in particular, the question of language and its relationship to religion and culture in traditional societies. The second has to do with the question of the particular and the universal, of the general and the specific, of truth as 'one' and of

59. Newbigin, *The Open Secret*, 192.

60. In the Chinese translations, for example, some 47 versions were employed by missionaries, with eight additional ones for Taiwan. *Scriptures of the World*, map 15. A similar detailed attention was given to Arabic and its local variants.

culture as 'many' in its diverse manifestations and contingencies, and how in the final analysis that impinges on the theme of gospel and culture.

With vernacular translation, missionaries introduced a new level of complexity into Christian usage. In the multilingual setting of tribal societies, concepts of God resonated with ancient usage, with refinements taking place in incidents of ritual observance and customary practice. Often it is not the jealous God of Calvinistic clericalism that translators had adopted, or thought they were adopting, for the vernacular Scriptures, but the polyonymous deity of the tribe, resplendent with theophorous titles. Furthermore, the very pluralism in vernacular translation created increased local awareness and forced practical comparisons across tribal boundaries, showing how the 'God and Father of the Lord Jesus Christ' of apostolic preaching came to be invested with a plurality of names, none of which excludes the others. This theological inclusiveness had its counterpart in the social sphere where in many places interethnic encounter became possible for the first time outside the constraints of tribal blood feud and fratricidal grudge.[61]

In turning to the second part of our analysis I should like to recapitulate at the same time the problem of the 'one' and the 'many', of the particular and the universal. It is clear that in employing vernacular languages for translation, missionaries saw these languages as more than arbitrary devices. On the contrary, they saw them as endowed with divine significance, so that they may substitute completely for the language of revelation. The fact that all languages are, for the purposes of Christian translation, interchangeable, makes them 'instrumental', so that in their very differences they all serve an identical purpose. A certain general view came to undergird and persist in the plurality of languages, with the important point that vernacular particularity is compatible, rather than in conflict, with such a general idea. Languages were seen as the 'many' contingent refractions in which believers testified to the 'one' God, so that particular cultural descriptions of God might convey in concrete terms the

61. I have described aspects of social and theological inclusiveness in my article, 'Christian Missions and the Western Guilt Complex', *Christian Century*, 8 April, 1987.

truth of God without that in any way excluding other cultural descriptions.[62]

The question then arises as to whether what is said in any language totally exhausts the meaning of God, or whether languages, any or some languages, have to be augmented to improve their intrinsic capacity. As an alternative view, it may be maintained that language, indeed all languages are inherently inadequate and that religious truth ultimately, if not immediately, transcends human words. This view has respectable advocates in many sections of Christianity, although the question for us is its implication for the culture that is thus transcended. Whatever the case, so far as the history of mission is concerned, such a transcendent view of religious truth does not seem to have induced in missionaries an indifference to culture. In that sense we are back to the question regarding the intrinsic adequacy of language. The missionary view was that all languages may be regarded as complete autonomous sytems, and that where it was possible to determine, purer forms of the language, however puzzling and unfamiliar, served best the purposes of translation. So linguistic investigations were mounted to erect as authentic an indigenous system through which God might be mediated with all the nuances and specificity of cultural originality.

A working principle of language and culture was implied in this procedure. Missionaries were confident that once they made a successful link between the linguistic symbol and what it brings to mind, the religious process could commence meaningfully, and we can say that much of what has been said against missionaries overlooks this vernacular confidence of theirs.

62. In his Introduction to Troeltsch's *The Absoluteness of Christianity*, James Luther Adams says of Troeltsch that he maintained 'a tension within his mind, asserting on the one hand that "the divine life is not one but many" and on the other that "to apprehend the One in the many constitutes the special character of love". This paradox was for him "the icon of God". Troeltsch, *The Absoluteness of Christianity*, 1971, 19. This is not so much a tension in Troeltsch as a lack of analytic consistency, resulting from a tendency to contrast and then to identify the *one* with the *many*. Even in his otherwise brilliant exploration of the religious phenomenon, John Oman views particularity as the *many* tending to obscure the true apprehension of 'the unity of an undifferentiated awe of one sacred reality'. Oman, 386. Particularity in this scheme casts a shadow over the 'promise of a shining temple of unity' which has made 'religion to appear at times the supreme mother-complex of humanity'. Oman, 387.

Three theoretical notions may be identified in their operational view of language and culture. The first is that the language furnishes 'elliptical' statements which enable people to define instrumental relationships, and in religious language elliptical statements refer to those things in which God reveals Himself, especially as effects.

The second is that language enables people to make 'symbolical' statements to the effect that what in itself is not God but represents God to certain persons is in fact God for those persons in those contexts. That is to say, such language or symbols achieve the end of directing attention to the symbolic character of an object to the exclusion of whatever other qualities language or symbols may possess in another context. Two brief examples may suffice. Kissing the crucifix was considered an act of reverence by early Catholic missionaries, whereas in certain parts of Africa kissing as such was considered an act of difilement, repugnant to the instinct of the people. To take a second example, for a mystical religious group the bat is considered a symbol of initiation and divine wisdom and occurs as such on the coronation robe of King Roger of Sicily. Yet in the different context of popular Western culture the bat is a symbol of ill omen. The two contexts share a recognition of the categories of divine wisdom and ill omen, but they employ constrasting cultural symbols to *signify* this.

The third is when language encourages the use of 'figures of identity' so that a close enough relationship is conceived between the thing spoken of with what it is said to be, with the result that virtual metamorphosis, a symbolic mutation, takes place. This clearly happens in most cultures: the sound and tones of Hebrew, Arabic and Sanskrit, for example, are in their respective religious contexts the embodiment of the divine or ultimate reality, while in certain sections of Christianity the bread and wine of the Communion are the transubstantiated body and blood of Jesus Christ. Among the Yoruba of West Africa the *orita*, the auspicious crossroad, is a symbol of power, while for the Nuer, rain, thunder, lightning, sun and moon, as well as consecrated cattle, are not God exactly, but *gaat Kwoth*, 'children of God', and so on. However, a missionary tradition like Christianity has to face the challenge of recasting symbols in terms meaningful to target audiences, and thus of rejecting literalness. Bread and wine in China or Japan,[63] for example, would have a vastly different understanding, if they have any at all, while the Good Shepherd theme would confound rather than enlighten an Eskimo congregation, or, as Nida and Reyburn have suggested, the pig-keeping communities of Polynesia.[64] Furthermore, a missionary Christianity would have to make room for new cultural symbols, such as the Peace Pipe of the Lakota Indians,[65] the Wisdom Fire of the Cherokee Indians,[66] the communal medicine and riverain oracles of African religions,[67] or the avatars of Hindu religion. Making room for these new cultural materials also requires relativizing them so they do not become new sources of ideology themselves.[68]

It is this incredible complexity that Christianity encountered, and in fact promoted, in its non-Western expansion. The specificity of vernacular usage was reflected in indigenous names for God and in idiomatic forms grounded in local life and experience. Missionary translators tried to get at authentic local

63. For a detailed account of this issue in Japan see Masao Takenaka, *God is Rice: Asian Culture & Christian Faith*, Geneva: World Council of Churches Risk Book Series, 1986, and for China, George Minamiki, S.J., *The Chinese Rites Controversy: From Its Beginning to Modern Times*, Chicago: Loyola University Press, 1985.

64. Eugene A. Nida and William D. Reyburn, *Meaning Across Cultures*, Maryknoll, N.Y.: Orbis Books, 1981.

65. See Paul B. Steinmetz, S.J., *Pipe, Bible and Peyote among the Ogala Lakota*, Stockholm Studies in Comparative Religion, Stockholm: University of Stockholm, 1980.

66. Dhyani Ywahoo, *Voices of our Ancestors: Cherokee Teachings from the Wisdom Fire*, Boston & London: Shambhala Publications, 1987.

67. E. E. Evans-Pritchard, *Witchcraft, Oracles and Magic Among the Azande*, Oxford: Clarendon Press, 1937, revised abridged edition, New York: Oxford University Press, 1976.

68. Commenting on this matter, Gordon Kaufman affirms: 'If indigenization were to mean that the idea of God became so completely adapted to the concepts and norms and practices of a new culture that it no longer could serve as a radical standard of criticism for that culture . . . full indigenization of the idea of God would be its destruction. For the concept of One who is at once truly absolute and truly human is never completely "at home" in the relativities and imperfections . . . of, any culture . . .' Gordon D. Kaufman, 'Theological Method and Indigenization: Six Theses', in Samuel Amirtham, ed., *A Vision for Man: Essays on Faith, Theology and Society*, Madras: Christian Literature Society, 1978, 59.

forms and in the process documented the result of their investigations, giving meticulous accounts of procedures and principles of research which went far beyond the narrow issue of Bible use. Such a detailed attention to indigenous particularity fostered unprecedented cultural pluralism within the general scheme of world Christianity. For example, indigenous hymns, prayers and invocations, laden with older religious attitudes, sentiments and ideas, were now transcribed and incorporated into Christian use where ecumenical interest gave them international range.

It turns out, then, that missionary translation expanded and enriched Christian religious repertoire, and it did this by eschewing uniformity as its norm. The operational view of language in Christian translation assumed a close relationship between language and the God spoken of, so that in any cultural representation God can be detached in the mind from the things said to be Him, even if these peculiar cultural forms, be they the Peace Pipe, the bread and wine, the Wisdom Fire, the *orita*, cannot in those specific situations be so easily detached from the idea of God as such. This gave culture and language a penultimate character, allowing them to be viewed in their 'instrumental' particularity.[69] In insisting on particularity, for example, Christian missionaries did not wish to imply that God is other than what He is, but that in particular cultural contexts and circumstances God has definite, particular qualities and attributes which do not belong to Him in other contexts and circumstances. It is not that these qualities and attributes are incompatible with God generally defined, but that something more, in respect to the pool of qualities and attributes, is added by each particular context.[70]

69. A kindred theme is treated in Aubrey R. Johnson, *The One and the Many in the Israelite Conception of God*, Cardiff: University of Wales Press, 1961, 14, 15–16, etc. Johnson is inclined to conceive a dialectical opposition between the One and the Many as between monotheism and polytheism.

70. Something like this idea may offer an escape hatch for Hocking who writes wistfully in this regard about the bewildering religious pluralism in Protestant Christianity. 'My own feeling about the multiplicity of sects,' he confesses,: 'is that most of them that have become a factor in contemporary society have had some reason for existence; most "reforms" have been needed. But that function of reform should be a function provided for within the church, not calling for schism, but for self-searching and reconception, in the persuasion that variety of expression which is not hostile to the essence may contribute to the life of the church.' Hocking, *World Civilization*, 134.

Those qualities and attributes become the modes and individual ways in which God becomes real for particular people in particular situations and circumstances even though those situations and circumstances by their nature do not repeat themselves for everyone anywhere else or to the same degree. The Psalmist may declare that God is a shield or a rock, or Luther that God is a mighty fortress and bulwark, or a Western existential liberal that God is the God of motivation without any of them excluding other descriptions of God, such as the dewy-nosed One of a cattle-owning culture, the One of the sacred stake of a pig-herding people, the nimble-footed One of the sacred dance, and the long-necked One of a hunting group. Furthermore, this rule makes it possible not only to approach God as the 'One' and the 'Many', but allows for indefinite polarities in descriptions of God. As such, apparently contradictory things may equally validly be said of God, such as that God gives life and that God takes life, that God creates and that He destroys, guides and leads astray, fills us with abundance and afflicts us with adversity at the same time, brings terrifying judgment upon us and also surrounds us with tender care and love, strikes us blind but also unseals the eyes of understanding, and so on.[71] So the Nuer speak of God being in the new moon and in the hurricane.[72] In this way the totality and range of human experience can be postulated of God's infinite manifestations, refractions and visitations without courting the awkward rationalist nemesis of admitting God on the explicable but not the inexplicable side of life.

On the cultural level a similar plurality and polarity is possible from this approach. The context of Western mission provides as good an example as any. Between Europeans and native populations on the one hand, and on the other, among tribal groupings themselves, there are differences on the cultural and linguistic level. These differences are unique and particular even though all these *many* groups represent the *one* idea of humanity. What unites them, however, is more than a question of species but their common *relationship* in respect to God. For this reason the cultural signs and symbols which *differentiate* them in their

71. See, for example, Isaiah 9: 21; Rev. 2: 8ff; Deut. 29: 1–5.
72. Evans-Pritchard deals with this subject in his book, *Nuer Religion*, New York: Oxford University Press, 1956.

respective particularities *unite* them in relation to God. It is God as this third term who thus normatively unites what cultural forms descriptively differentiate. Now it seems to me an important matter not to confuse *differentiating* and *unifying*, by treating the first, because it is nearer, as the source of the second, because that is farther, which is to say, by boiling down 'cultural signs and symbols' into a warm, genial teleology of the idea of 'God'. It is this difficulty, I suggested, that Christian realism can help resolve. Consequently, Christian commitment to this God has necessarily involved commitment also to cultural forms in their essentially radical pluralism.

In conclusion, no discussion of this topic is complete without mentioning H. Richard Niebuhr whose work more than a generation ago set the pace for us.[73] Niebuhr cuts through the liberal cultural transformation of Christianity into an enlightened, humanizing but essentially this-worldly philosophy, with social belief and action replacing human sinfulness, spiritual reality and eternal judgment. In taking up cudgels on behalf of a threatened and waning orthodoxy, Niebuhr was responding to particular cultural pressures of his day. Thus, neither in his methodology and language nor in his general conclusions did Niebuhr propose something which his contemporaries would not have recognized as natural developments from the stock and branch of Western culture, especially the form neoorthodoxy might take as the analogue of cultural respectability and intellectual sobriety – cool, rational, moderate and eminently

73. H. Richard Niebuhr, *Christ and Culture*, New York: Harper Colophon Books, 1951, repr. 1975. Compare also the same author's *Radical Monotheism and Western Culture*, the Montgomery Lectures, 1957, New York: Harper & Brothers, 1960. In *Radical Monotheism* Niebuhr argues that the central conflict in Western culture is between monotheist faith and henotheism, especially henotheist nationalism.

He distinguishes between monotheist faith and henotheism, saying the faith present in religious loyalty is the same as that present in other forms of faith commitment in the secular sphere. The conflict arises between the two types of faith, Niebuhr argues, because henotheism makes a finite society the object of trust and loyalty. In a different connection, but still related to the issue of radical pluralism and religious integrity, Gordon Kaufman has written about the radical effects of the principle of God's absoluteness. 'God is the great relativizer of all false absolutes', he writes. Kaufman, 'Theological Method and Indigenization,' 58.

affordable. Its songs would be robust, its hymns intrepid and its prayers hard-nosed. And that made him a powerfully effective voice for his time and circumstance. Nevertheless, Niebuhr was not concerned with the worldwide phenomenon of Christian cultural practices where he would have seen the outlines of fresh permutations and new combinations emerging under explicit Christian aegis. It is reasonable to speculate that such evidence might have affected his work about the Western religious crisis in a different direction.

Lesslie Newbigin was saying something like that when he paid tribute to Niebuhr for his *Christ and Culture*, and went on to say both Niebuhr and theologians like him 'had not had the experience of the cultural frontier, of seeking to transmit the gospel from one culture to a radically different one.'[74] In other words, even when we think we are free of the constraints of culture, we are still in unsuspecting ways chained down by countless minute links, hooks and clasps, including the terms in which we express our formal autonomy.

At any rate Niebuhr's concern for not reducing Christ into a mere cultural protagonist is a valid one, although in this chapter I have tried to advance *different* grounds for making the *same* distinction. The conclusion I have reached, therefore, is a slightly modified version of his own formulations. I am concerned not only to safeguard the authority of Christ but the authenticity of culture as well. The connection between Christ and culture, to stick to the Niebuhrian formulation, is much closer than either what Niebuhr calls the 'conversionist' or the 'dualist' position, and more susceptible to cultural manipulation than the liberals might think. It is thus pertinent to observe that it is not only religious sensibility which leads Christians to distinguish between Christ and culture, it is sensibility also for what promotes authentic culture. When we conceive the matter in these terms, it is obvious that the 'One' gospel becomes meaningfully mediated through the 'Many' refractions of culture and historical contingency, as well as through the many and diverse channels that constitute our individual and collective gifts and talents. It would

74. Lesslie Newbigin, *Foolishness to the Greeks: The Gospel and Western Culture*, Geneva: World Council of Churches, 1, 1986; also the same writer's *The Open Secret*, 164.

be well to remember that Plato made the 'many' incompatible with his design of the ideal city state in which occupational specialization in terms of 'one man one job' would operate to enable 'the whole city to be one and not many'.[75] Compared to that, Paul seems to represent a breakthrough, with abiding significance for all projects of multiculturalism. The Apostle's view of gospel and culture blunts considerably any sharp dualist notion. The incipient 'radical pluralism' we have identified in Paul helps us to moderate any endemic conflict between gospel and culture. For instance, when he admonishes the believers not to allow the rules of food to destroy the work of God,[76] Paul is not proposing that eating and praying are in conflict, or even that the one is done from a lower motive and the other from a higher one, but that God and food in any exclusivist combination nourish neither spirit nor body. It is the worst form of addiction, and it is not only Christians, but especially Christians, who deserve better. So Christian pluralism in its uncompromising, rigorous form, is not only a committed state of mind with regard to God's *Oneness* in sovereignty and power but a committed style of living with respect to the *many*-sidedness of culture. In that convergence we may find strength for the critical relationship between the gospel and the contending cultural ideologies of our time. The question we raised at the outset about the cultural captivity of the gospel at one end, and, at the other, its cultural emasculation, remains a formidable one for Christianity as a translated and translatable religion. However, something of real substance and merit is lost if, from within its own integrity, religion cannot repudiate the twin ideologies of cultural absolutism and pious escapism. Religion emptied of cultural concreteness would be an intellectual conceit, though if it were limited to such concreteness

75. Plato, *Republic*, Bk. IV, #423, in *The Collected Dialogues*, eds. Edith Hamilton & Huntington Cairns, New York: Pantheon Books for Bollingen Foundation, 1961, p. 665. Also *The Laws*, Bk. VIII, #846f, *Collected Dialogues*, pp. 1410f. Cf. John Stuart Mill, *Essays on Philosophy & the Classics*, Toronto: University of Toronto Press, *Collected Works of John Stuart Mill*, vol. XI, 1978, 94–95. There is more than a hint of Plato's civic ethics in Paul's conception of the ideal fellowship in Romans 12 and I Cor., though Plato's functional exclusivism is undercut by Paul's understanding of one body made real in its many members and their multiple functions.
76. Romans 14: 15, 20.

only it would incite ethnic jingoism, the Chosen People myth that has wrought more than its share of mischief in human affairs. In the next chapter we shall extend this theological inquiry by looking into what critical light cross-cultural missionary experience might shed on the Western encounter with non-Western populations primarily, but also in terms of the West itself being confronted with the claims of the gospel.

4

Religious Insiders and Cultural Outsiders, or Religious Outsiders and Cultural Insiders? The Intercultural Critique

Introduction

One of the most sensitive issues facing Westerners is whether they have any right to enter other cultures given the West's centuries-old history of slavery and colonialism and its continuing domination of Third World peoples. Christian missions in particular have come in for more than their share of criticism in this regard. However, let us be quite clear about what I propose to do in this chapter, namely, to describe how, as religious agents, Western missionaries provided some of the most important categories for understanding intercultural encounter, whether or not such encounter conformed to their motives and intentions or in other ways was to their credit. Such an approach is straightforward enough, but I suggest it has deeper implications for the subject. By shifting attention to the highly fluid and complex nature of missionary encounter with non-Western cultures, and by taking stock in the feedback of how missionary experience rebounds to critique Western culture, I try to show how the historic connection between Christianity and Western culture came under strain and how that led missionaries, or else justified local believers, to conceive an alternative non-Western cultural scheme for the religion.

The logic of my approach is as follows. When missionaries sought to transmit the message through the mother tongue of Africans, they committed themselves to operating in a medium in which Africans had the first and last advantage. Advancing the project of mission in the mother tongue requires a corresponding advance in penetrating the culture. Doubtless Africans learnt enormously from the encounter, but so did missionaries, as we can see in the degree to which their sombre assessment of Western cultural failures hardened with field exposure. Perhaps it can be said that missionaries fell for cross-cultural acclimatization because they committed themselves to translating the message before they knew where it would lead.

In any case, we may wonder how they came to hoist themselves on the horns of such a dilemma and marvel that any of them should succeed in a venture in which they were playing to their greatest weakness. The negative side of this is all too familiar, that is to say, of missionaries who bungled the job of transmitting the message or else committed serious mistakes, with or without malice towards Africans. Our task would be much simpler if that negative picture told the whole story, for in that case we could roll out the dreadful catalogue and move on to more uplifting matters. However, as we have seen, the picture is more complicated.

A striking paradox confronts us about missionary agency in that as 'insiders' or custodians of the religion they brought, missionaries viewed their foreign status in Africa as a serious limitation, yet as they learnt the vernacular, and in other ways succeeded in entering the culture, they became peripheral to the indigenous claims on Christianity and were forced gradually to relinquish control into local hands. In the numerous instances of cultural breakthrough, either of missionaries themselves or, no less momentously, of Africans with regard to missionary intentions and ambitions, and still more remarkably, in examples of mutual discovery, there is active interchange between 'outsiders' and 'insiders', two otherwise stable categories now framed by fluid, dynamic boundaries. In the vast and impressive output of religious and theological literature by Africans, for instance, we find evidence that contact of an enduring kind had taken place, however ambivalent the writers might be. Consequently in protest and criticism, in exegetical texts, in sermons, hymns, songs, prayers and invocations, there is evidence that local populations have engaged the most fundamental categories of a religion supposed to be completely foreign.

The Nationalist Critique

One representative African writer who makes this point eloquently is Jomo Kenyatta in his book *Facing Mount Kenya*, an impassioned nationalist work that launched Kenyatta into the front ranks of African political independence. He became in 1964 the founding president of his country, Kenya. In the book, Kenyatta speaks of European missionary presumptuousness towards African religion and culture. He charges that missionaries regarded the African 'as a clean slate on which anything could be written. He was supposed to take wholeheartedly all religious dogmas of the white man and keep them sacred and unchallenged, no matter how alien to the African mode of life. The Europeans based their assumption on the conviction that everything the African did or thought was evil.'[1] Kenyatta further alleges that missionaries thought of Africans as depraved souls to be rescued from the 'eternal fire', and consequently 'they set out to uproot the African, body and soul, from his old customs and beliefs, and put him in a class by himself, with all his tribal customs shattered and his institutions trampled upon. The African, after having been detached from his family and tribe, was expected to follow the white man's religion without questioning whether it was suited for his condition of life or not.'[2] Some of the examples Kenyatta gives of cultural violation by missionaries include the African's sense of community and the place that political and moral authority occupies in that. Kenyatta says missionaries imposed their religion of individualism on the African, and that this wrought havoc on Africa. Thus did the missionaries compound the nature of foreign domination in Africa, sharpening the lines of attack and occupation that colonialists had marshalled and extended on the political and military front.

As a reaction to such wholesale missionary attack, Kenyatta continues, Africans organized an intellectual resistance that focused on trying to regain the religious initiative. Thus was founded a new religious movement called, Watu wa Mngu ('People of God', sometimes also known as Arathi ('Prophets or

1. Jomo Kenyatta, N.D., *Facing Mount Kenya*, with an Introduction by B. Malinowski, New York: Vintage Books, Division of Random House, 259. The London edition was first published in 1938.
2. ibid., 259–60.

seers'). It was founded in 1929 in part response to the measures the Church of Scotland Mission Gikuyu adopted against clitoridectomy, but soon afterwards the movement went on to embrace a much wider range of religio-cultural issues.[3]

Kenyatta's detailed account of the Watu wa Mngu shows how Africans took the offensive against missionary interference, and he extols the virtues of the movement for that reason. Yet precisely the strengths Kenyatta identifies for the movement offer an astonishing demonstration of the significance of missionary translations for projects of African religious and cultural renewal, not to say the basis for resisting foreign values. Some examples make this clear. Kenyatta writes that 'The African, faced with these problems and seeing how his institutions have been shattered, looked again in the Book of Books'[4] where he found copious evidence in defence of his culture. This 'Book of Books' was in fact the Gikuyu Bible, the *Ibuka ria Ngai*, that missionaries had translated. The Gikuyu Bible was the breath of life for the Watu wa Mngu, particularly the stories told in it of those individuals who were favoured by God and rewarded with prophetic powers. This God, called in the *Ibuka ria Ngai* Mwene-Nyaga, was now resolved to deal as favourably and efficaciously with the Gikuyu as He had with the prophets of old. In preparation for such a time of God's favour, the members of the movement adopted a radical communal life, giving up private ownership of property, including their homes, banding together and setting out on an itinerant, footloose existence. They composed prayers that blended Gikuyu with biblical material, performing their rituals 'standing in a picturesque manner. In their prayer to Mwene-Nyaga they hold up their arms to the sky facing Mount Kenya; and in this position they recite their prayers, and in doing so they imitate the cries of wild beasts of prey, such as lion and leopard, and at the same time they tremble violently. The trembling, they say, is the sign of the Holy Ghost, *Roho Motheru*, entering in them. While thus possessed with the spirit, they are transformed from ordinary beings and are in

3. See Jocelyn Murray, 'The Kikuyu Spirit Churches', *Journal of Religion in Africa*, vol.5, no.3, 1974, 198–234, for a detailed examination of the Watu wa Mngu.
4. Kenyatta, *Facing Mount Kenya*, 262.

communion with Mwene-Nyaga.'[5] From the Bible they discover a venerable pedigree in Israel and promptly claim it for themselves. This God of Israel is, they urge, the God of the Gikuyu, and vice versa. The old prayers and hymns of the land, including communion with the ancestors as the patriarchs of the Bible, the principle of chosenness by which God calls obscure minorities to fulfil a historic enterprise, and the charismatic gifts with which God seals the elect and thus overrides worldly attainments, all find sanction in the very Scriptures missionaries introduced in the mother tongue. One prayer speaks to this new sense of spiritual liberation:

O Lord, your power is greater than all powers.
Under your leadership we cannot fear anything.
It is you who has given us prophetical power and has enabled us to foresee and interpret everything.
We know no other leader but you alone.
We beseech you to protect us in all trials and torments.
We know that you are with us, just as you were with our ancient ancestors.
Under your protection there is nothing that we cannot overcome.
Peace, praise ye Ngai, peace, peace, peace be with us.[6]

Such confident sentiments, supported by practices contrary to established convention, would be the recipe for direct administrative action, as proved to be the case. Very soon the movement's heady and impetuous path collided with the inflexible lines the authorities had laid down, and in 1934 they were involved in bloody clashes with the police, with the government claiming the movement was bent on fomenting a general insurrection.[7]

What remains relevant to the issue in the material Kenyatta has furnished on this question is not his spirited defence of customs such as clitoridectomy, performed, he says, 'with the dexterity of a Harley Street surgeon',[8] but the sources he utilizes to make the case he wishes to make. In that regard it is a fact

5. ibid., 264. 6. ibid., 267–8. 7. ibid., 268. 8. ibid., 140.

that the Watu wa Mngu have organized themselves on lines they felt to be entirely in harmony with the *Ibuka ria Ngai*, the objections of missionaries and colonial administrators notwithstanding. For the movement, the indigenous genie was out of the bottle, highly amenable to the conjuring power of the elect and initiated.

Let us, however, return to Kenyatta by another route. Organized resistance by Africans continued to be necessary in the face of relentless European pressure to break their resolve. Kenyatta's point is valid, that Europeans, sometimes with premeditated plans, sought to dismantle the communities that Africans conceived as indispensable to their life. Such communities would now inevitably have to adjust to new historical experiences, but they would still promote essentially African values and maintain meaningful continuity with a sense of the African past. At their heart communities were a fusion of the social, political and the religious, and the European policy of compartmentalizing these great centres of life was tantamount to declaring war on the most crucial and sensitive nerve in African society.

Africa's response to its encounter with Europe could not merely be restricted to the instrumental, two-dimensional level of administrative efficiency and conformity, of barricading tribes within stable administrative jurisdictions and documenting their goings and comings. It was not cultural obtuseness that prevented Africans from realizing the benefit of railways, the telegraph, the tractor, the school, the clinic and modern sanitation, but a holistic awareness that made them suspicious that Europeans would not accomplish their goals in Africa without attacking the very fount of life enshrined in community solidarity. That is to say, their protestations to the contrary, even Europeans could recover sufficiently from the alienating effects of their own cognitive dissonance to appreciate the integrative force of religion in the whole of life. Hence their use of missions. Consequently, the Africans' response correctly raised the encounter to the religious level, because at that point they could confront the comprehensive intellectual nature of the assault on their customs and traditions. God is not an item we are at liberty to include or exclude in our organized list of options, lodged in a remote niche on the crowded tribal reservation, competing there with diminishing returns with other commitments and requirements, as Europeans insisted. Rather Ngai is the fountainhead from which the living receive life and strength, and the dead their rest. Those who know Mwene-Nyaga's companionship, even though they be chased from their houses, are not homeless; they may be stripped of their land but they are not without a heritage.

Just as Kenyatta described it, Africans appreciated quickly enough that missionary preaching brought Europe's confrontation to the deepest level of the peoples' self-understanding. Europe intends not just technological mastery, for what is the transcendent value of metal that will rust, and literacy that cannot displace native accent or first language reflex? Rather, Europe intends spiritual mastery, to bring home to the dark races the lessons of a superior white moral dispensation. It is to their credit that Africans would not be misled by European insistence that the rules of political control they wished to impose involved no interference with the allegedly separate realm of religion, so that just as colonialists recruited missionaries on their side, Africans would also invoke Ngai and his masses of foot soldiers and thus demonstrate that they were equally capable of cultural consistency without, however, professing something different. Which might explain why those missionaries who could make a similar conjunction of religion, society and politics received spontaneous recognition from Africans.

There remains, however, the possibility of Europeans being able to detach an amenable group of Africans from the venerable stem of tribal solidarity, transplant them within the secure boundaries of supervised enclaves, trim and prune them in mission school and blunt their effectiveness by rewarding them as the secular successor class. Such an elite, torn from its religious roots, would perpetuate Europe's assault on Africa's hallowed memory, sowing seeds of doubt about the value of its past so that Africa may the more willingly consign its future into the hands of foreign technocrats or their native clones. That this strategy failed to carry all Africa before it, that it unravelled in the numerous instances of the disintegration of the doctrinaire national secular state, may be due to the revenge the ancient spirits exacted for being slighted or otherwise provoked. Christianity may not have introduced the idea of Satan or evil in Africa, but in slighting the old customs and traditions and ranging itself against them as evil, it furnished a metaphysical and eschatological scale for interpreting the West's own violent intrusion in African societies and its debilitating consequences. Some of that damage, in human cost as well as in scale, can never be repaired: the tens of millions lost or maimed in the trans-Atlantic slave trade and in resistance struggles against white supremacy, the hundreds of millions that felt possessed by Europe's evil spirits, their dark skins unable to deny or hide what Western conditioning would want them to disown. Injustice and misfortune became assimilated into the wretchedness, giving rise to social agitation and eradication cults and Europe's bogey loomed large in them.

The Missionary Critique

The next question is whether missionaries were capable of sympathizing with the African condition generally and with the motives of the Watu wa Mngu in particular, if not there and then, perhaps elsewhere and at other times. Kenyatta was adamant in the view that by the very nature of the religion they professed, missionaries were opposed to African culture and could not do their work except by assuming in African culture and religion a Satanic enemy. This is the subject we must proceed to examine.

One missionary whose work and life were profoundly affected by exposure to Africa was Vincent Donovan who records his experiences in his book, *Christianity Rediscovered*. Donovan was a Holy Ghost Catholic missionary among the Masai of Tanzania, a people for whose language and culture he came to have a high regard. In the process he was forced to re-examine many of the assumptions he made as a Western missionary, assumptions that he felt were in conflict with the African destiny of the gospel he came to preach. His problem that he could not so easily divest himself of his own cultural presuppositions as the necessary historical framework for Christianity, and that African culture, in being strange and unfamiliar to him, might nevertheless be no more and no less auspicious for the religion than Western culture, was essentially a contextual one, requiring as a solution the need to 'relativize' Western cultural forms in preparation for the fresh African transformation. If he was going to be the agent of such a transformation, Donovan felt, he would have to be a prime target of the accompanying stripping down.

His own words attest to that. He began with a stringent assessment of the history of Christian missions in Africa, with an implicit acknowledgement of the criticisms people like Kenyatta levelled at missions. 'There is no mistaking the fact,' he admits, 'that missionary work is in a shambles. Born to slavery, disoriented by the school system, startled by independence, and smothered in nation building – mission in East Africa has never had the chance to be true to itself.' Consequently, to 'make any sense out of mission, out of the meaning and purpose of missionary work, one has to start all over again – at the beginning.'[9] After struggling with trying to make headway with the catechetical outline he wished to introduce among the Masai, Donovan confessed: 'I became discouraged in a way it would be hard to describe . . . I suppose you could call it a crisis of faith, a loss of faith. I had begun to doubt the very message of Christianity.'[10]

Donovan then goes on to say that the missionary must willingly undergo a radical cultural conditioning in which he sheds the baggage with which he came even before he knows with what to replace it. 'The missionary facing an alien pagan culture, to be an efficient instrument of the gospel, has to have the courage to cast off the idols of the tribe, of the tribe he came from. There are many idols,' he charges, 'but two which, I believe, particularly mesmerize the Western church, are individualism on the one hand, and the love of organization on the other.'[11] Given the heavy cultural baggage with which the missionary is saddled, Donovan says we must contemplate a radical step for the true missionary. He continues: 'a missionary is essentially a *social martyr*, cut off from his roots, his stock, his blood, his land, his background, his culture. He is destined to walk forever a stranger in a strange land. He must be stripped naked as a human being can be, down to the very texture of his being.'[12] Many of the obstacles Africans encountered in Christianity, Donovan observes,

9. Donovan, *Christianity Rediscovered*, Maryknoll, N.Y.: Orbis Books, 12–13.
10. ibid., 62. 11. ibid., 89. 12. ibid., 193.

are there not because of Scripture but largely on account of 'the history of a church imbedded in a single culture, with its own ideas, coming from that culture, as to what is required of Africans.'[13]

Donovan takes one step in seeking to define Christianity that amounts to a breakthrough. He speaks of cultures, all cultures, as essentially equal in their potential, or lack of it, for receiving the gospel. 'It is surely here,' he affirms, 'in the midst of the cultures of the world, and not in the church, that the ordinary way of salvation must lie, the ordinary means of salvation, the very possibility of salvation for most of the human race. Or else it is a very strange God we have . . . As I began to ponder the evangelization of the Masai, I had to realize that God enables a people, any people, to reach salvation through their culture and tribal, racial customs and traditions. In this realization would have to rest my whole approach to the evangelization of the Masai.'[14] Ultimately, whatever Christianity emerged among the Masai would have to involve a radical recasting of Western religious categories such as the priesthood (153ff), community (84), organized religion (89), the creed (92,200), prayer (131ff), the church (93), and notions of justice (99,124).

Donovan admits that he had come among the Masai convinced that he knew what he wanted to bring, but discovered that he had much more to learn. He said he told the Masai of Abraham and the search for faith, and about how Masai culture had trapped God, made Him their cultural champion as they despoiled neighbouring tribes, and so on. To all of this the Masai listened politely and attentively. Then came the bombshell. 'This story of Abraham,' he was asked, 'does it speak only to Masai? Or does it speak also to you? Has your tribe found the High God? Have you known him?'[15]

Donovan says he was about to give a brash answer when he caught himself and thought of Joan of Arc and the many examples of European nations who sequestered God in their quest for national glory. When finally he answered, it was not what he came prepared to say. 'No, *we have not* found the High God. My tribe has not known him. For us, too, he is the unknown

13. ibid., 122. 14. ibid., 30. 15. ibid., 45.

God. But we are searching for him. I have come a long, long distance to invite you to search for him with us. Let us search for him together. Maybe, together, we will find him.'[16] Thus was gone the cockiness of unchallenged presuppositions.

The Intercultural Critique

Now it is the case that many such missionaries on returning to the West come back with fresh eyes and a new perspective on the religious condition of their compatriots. For many of them, this re-entry can be a painful experience, leading to a feeling of abandonment, and even of betrayal and alienation, a culture shock from which some may not completely recover. Clearly, some of this sense of alienation may stem from loss of power and influence in the mission field, but often it has little to do with that, particularly in the modern period when missionaries were normally the employees of local churches, hospitals, and technical institutions or otherwise the subordinates of local leaders. Often it stems from a genuine crisis of identity, for having made the transition to another culture, having assimilated into local styles of speech, dress, greeting, food, music and the smells and sounds that will always remind them of a second wind, these returning missionaries may adopt withdrawal as the line of least resistance, making do with what lies to hand or else maintaining a self-imposed silence out of fear of sounding unrecognized and unappreciated.

However, there are some who resettle back in the West on terms negotiated halfway between withdrawal and defiance, especially in the gaps where missionary experience can fill in. This is where we should consider the work of Lesslie Newbigin formerly of the Church of South India and for many years subsequently a leader in the World Council of Churches.

There is no doubt of the enormous influence of Newbigin and his significance for a cross-cultural critique of the West. He has broken wide open the shell of Western cultural exclusiveness by insisting that from the religious point of view Western societies are to be confronted with the gospel no less relentlessly than

16. ibid., 46.

Third World societies, the only difference being that the West may be a 'darker continent' for having reneged on its religious heritage. The decline of the missionary impulse in the West means not simply that people are unwilling to give but especially that they are unable to receive the gospel, so effective have been the competitive alternatives to religious faith. And so Newbigin poses his central question: 'What would it mean if, instead of trying to explain the gospel in terms of our modern scientific culture, we tried to explain our culture in terms of the gospel?'[17]

Newbigin brings a comparative missionary perspective to bear on the situation in the West. He contrasts the mission field with the West in this way. In the missionary context both the Bible and the community that responds to it form primary religious categories. The Bible as sacred Scripture is received by a community that is itself steeped in a religious way of life and knowing, and together Scripture and community come to reinforce an articulated, coherent worldview. By contrast, in the West, the Bible is simply a book among other books to which the critical historian brings tools of analysis and comprehension largely independent of religious values, and addressing an audience comprised of rational individuals whose allegiance is a matter of personal persuasion and preference. For such people the Bible might be a toolkit, a cookbook manual, serviceable in this or that respect, but always in an intellectual framework where the appetite is fed by wants and needs. The scientific viewpoint strips the Bible of its religious autonomy while technology gives us the categories of strategy and technique in which pragmatic goals replace faith. Consequently, it is a pressing duty to know how to communicate with our generation of religiously impaired people.

With great force of intellect and moral courage, and grounded in cross-cultural understanding, Newbigin has forced upon the churches and upon Christians generally an issue they cannot now ignore even if they do not agree with the terms in which he frames the debate. An important intellectual ferment is going on in

17. Lesslie Newbigin, *Foolishness to the Greeks: The Gospel and Western Culture*, Geneva: World Council of Churches,; Grand Rapids, Michigan: Wm. B. Eerdmans Publishers, 1986, 41

numerous circles on both sides of the Atlantic, thanks largely to his initiative and leadership. The issue is whether Christianity has any role to play in Western culture, and if so how it can do that outside the narrow walls of its Western captivity. Newbigin is thus important for us in the way he helps to focus the issue of religion and culture as rival contenders for the soul of Western society, and, cast in that form, we should see immediately how intercultural breakthroughs on missionary frontiers continue to be highly relevant.

In his *The Gospel in a Pluralist Society*, Newbigin develops the theme first broached in his *Honest Religion for Secular Man* and repeated in *Foolishness to the Greeks*, that is to say, how we might extricate ourselves from the modern intellectual heresy of science as objective truth and religion as subjective opinion, the one fit for public display and credence and the other suitable only as a matter for private adoption and individual inclination. While by no means saying the last word on the subject, Newbigin's *The Gospel in a Pluralist Society* represents a bold and major step forward in the debate on pluralism and Western self-understanding. It should, consequently, be welcomed as a precise formulation of problems that continue to perplex and trouble the West. Nobody can emerge from the pages of this book completely unaffected by the argument, a tribute to Newbigin's sharp and incisive mind and spirit.

The book has twenty chapters of uneven length and is divided into two main parts. In the first Newbigin undertakes the critical task of examining the intellectual roots of contemporary Western society, paying special attention to Western epistemology and phenomenology. Here the focus is on the epistemic dichotomy between 'knowledge' of so-called objective facts and 'belief' in so-called subjective values, a dichotomy Newbigin maintains is rationally indefensible. Nevertheless, having taken the step of assuming the validity of that kind of distinction, the modern West has put in place a 'plausibility structure' that justifies and promotes the distinction. In time, Western culture, founded on the distinction of knowledge and belief, facts and values, object and subject, public and private, and so on, stumbled badly in the challenge to take Christianity seriously.

The second part of the book deals with the constructive project of defending religious belief, and Christianity in particular, as a cogent 'plausibility structure' in its own right, with concluding remarks on congregational life and witness. Religious claims, in this regard, are a series of propositions that are coherent within their own terms and generate a historical tradition in which believers struggle to reconcile their understanding of truth claims with the pressures of life and experience. Believers thus take faith 'acritically' as in theology, and with strings attached, as in mission.

Religion and 'Plausibility Structures'

This constructive side of the book commands Newbigin's major interest, and is, consequently, not split off from the first stage in any formal or organized way, but instead pervades the entire book. The principle that holds the whole structure of the book in place is what Newbigin calls 'plausibility structures', borrowing the idea from Peter Berger, the sociologist, and linking it to the idea of knowledge as personal commitment à la Michael Polanyi. Berger and Polanyi thus are the two sides of the sandwich between which Newbigin attempts to insert the stuff of Christianity. This approach has both merit and drawbacks, although, for his purposes, Newbigin can insist that any project in communication has to begin with a particular standpoint rather than with an abstraction. In fact, it may turn out to be one of the great merits of the book that it calls us to a rigorous understanding of the nature of epistemological particularity, especially where it carries with it 'universal intent', i.e., the intention to commend faith and knowledge to the reasonable consideration and acceptance of others.

Newbigin seems concerned to establish the intrinsic particularity of modern Western epistemology, a procedure that would confirm both that the notion of objective factualness of scientific enquiry and of the great axioms on which they are based are rooted in particularity, that is to say, in a given plausibility structure. The danger that particularity might lead to unmitigated subjectivism is met by Newbigin's view that scientific knowledge as a particular worldview is legitimized by 'universal intent', namely, the enterprise of making public a claim and demonstrating its right to command credence. Thus, when we have stripped scientific knowledge to its barest essentials, we are left with its particularity and universal intent, a step that correspondingly would require us to modify any rigid distinction between the objective and subjective poles, or between knowledge and belief. This step is so critical to Newbigin's argument that grasping it enables the rest of the book to follow, although I am not certain the whole of the gospel that follows is equal to the sum of the rational parts that precedes. In other words, I am a little uneasy about the parallel lines drawn for science and religion, for, however helpful, rather different vehicles proceed by them, the one being a triumph of instrumental contrivance and the other the ark of the religious covenant.

There are hints in several places that Newbigin is aware of the difficulty. The difference between Kepler the scientist and an Old Testament prophet, we are told, is the difference between the former saying, 'I have brought it to light', and the latter declaring, 'God spoke to me', (or 'Thus saith the Lord'). In the one case we have a discovery and in the other a revelation. Yet in clarifying the distinction between discovery and revelation, Newbigin appropriates the norms of scientific discovery to expound what might be involved in revelation, saying 'both are inconceivable apart from their rationality'.[18]

My uneasiness with this way of formulating the issue becomes clear when we set Newbigin's claim for rationality alongside the remarks of Einstein to the effect that, 'the mechanics of discovery are neither logical nor intellectual. It's a sudden illumination, almost a rapture. Later, to be sure, intelligence and analysis and experiment confirm (or invalidate) the intuition. But initially there is a a great leap of imagination.'[19] Here Einstein the scientist is less exercised, though no less consistent, about the question of rationality than Newbigin the theologian, a role reversal that is instructive about Newbigin's Enlightenment roots. It also illustrates my unease about whether the rational analogy has not assumed too large a role in Newbigin's apologetics, so large as to become the rule by which faith acquits itself, leaving aside how a reasonable faith might bring us to submission before a sovereign

18. Newbigin, *The Gospel*, 60.
19. ibid., 31.

God. If Christianity proceeds by the path laid for it by reason, turning it into a look-alike or surrogate rationality, then it is more or less a coincidence that it had its origins in the higher elevations of Sinai and Calvary, a point with which Newbigin would not seriously disagree. Perhaps the point here is that through the channel of reason we may be brought face to face with the claims of God in such a way that an authentic response becomes the logical outcome, and at that point God's claims become the 'super reason' our broken reasoning comprehended not except in short, finite snatches. Newbigin speaks elsewhere of the fact that as long as religion is something 'already accounted for in our culture . . . and we know where to place it . . . how can it challenge us?'[20] 'Shall the axe vaunt itself over him who hews with it, or the saw magnify itself against him who wields it?' (Isaiah 10:15 RSV)

At any rate the point of departure from which we arrive at this rational transposition of Christianity is a necessary and important one, and that has to do with Newbigin's contention, with which I wholeheartedly agree, that 'a standpoint outside the real human situation of knowing subjects' is not available to us, and consequently Christianity is always received and transmitted within existing particular structures of life and thought, as is also the case with the tradition of scientific rationality. In both the religious and scientific case, we find also claims initially refracted through culture having universal intent flowing from them. Those two facts, of religion and science sharing identity in being culturally schematized and in rising to the level of universal intent, make the case for Newbigin of treating science and religion as also identical in form, so much so that we may, he argues, speak of purpose in machines and in eschatological faith as ultimately the same.[21] Such a bold idea, however, needs qualifying, which Newbigin does by reminding us of a God who acts in history to reveal and effect the higher purpose,[22] although such acting conforms to the structure of rational norms.

A report in the *New York Times* makes an observation that is germane to this point, and is, consequently, worth quoting at some length.

20. ibid., 43. 21. ibid., 16ff, 46. 22. ibid., 50–51.

> It is increasingly recognized that the validity of both scientific theory and religious conviction is not demonstrated by any one decisive 'proof'. Although scientific hypotheses may be confirmed or confuted by controlled experiments or systematic examination of evidence, the results are often ambiguous or approximate. Particular findings can usually be fitted, with sufficient pushing and shoving, into different theories. And there is almost always some obstinate data that a given theory cannot account for, just as the shortcomings of equipment and experimenters frequently introduce a margin of error. Whichever theory proves superior will be an overall judgment by the scientific community, working with certain standards that it has inherited. Like a jury, it will reach its conclusions on the preponderance of the evidence, presented according to the rules of the court and not as a matter of clean-cut mathematical demonstration. Science turns out to be more of an 'art', and more a matter of community judgment, than had generally been thought – more, in other words, like religion.[23]

It is, however, the case that such a parallel analogy can be taken too far, with the argument running away from people who press the view that faith and obedience have profound affinities with the nature and procedures of scientific hypothesis and empirical verification. For his part, Newbigin would avoid the trap with his observation that Jesus teaches about the reversal of expectations, or of religious knowledge being of the I-Thou rather than of the I-It kind.[24] Even so, the temptation remains very acute as when scholastic theology seeks in abstract reason the full measure of God's sovereign greatness. Some of the most illustrious figures in this scholastic tradition include Gregory of Nyssa and St Anselm for the West, and al-Farábí and Averroës for the East. Thus the scholastics would want to defend Anselm's dictum of 'faith in search of understanding', with the mind as 'understanding' rather

23. Peter Steinfels, 'The Big Bang, and why few theologians view it as a vindication of biblical accounts', *New York Times*, Saturday, August 29, 1992
24. Newbigin, *The Gospel*, 60.

than Scripture providing the grammar and the proof. Carried to its extreme, scholasticism reduced God to a syllogistic system where speculative thought ends up rewarding itself with the cultivated sensibility characteristic of the Romantics. In that system God as pure Being is deemed approachable only by pure thought, and with that a radical rejection of the incarnational principle of the human and material worlds marked by divine action, with the unsavoury social implication that only the elite few could have access to God. Indeed, Western academic theology continued this scholastic tradition of religion stripped of lived social reality, 'liberal' in the sense of a Bultmanian supernatural agnosticism, and 'radical' in the sense of religion as a historically conditional relative tradition. Such academic theology is typically uncertain of its centre, and with the centre so detached, the wings fly off in different directions, one flank yielding to atheism on the left, the other flank turning to Socinianism on the right, and the torso latching itself onto a timeless advaitic inclusiveness.

Newbigin's procedure, we may observe, does not, and, indeed, is committed not to produce this kind of intellectual fragmentation. He begins, for example, with trying to extract from reason a concession to religious faith and commitment. In this regard, he argues that scientific knowledge is not objective or factual enough to dispense with personal commitment. That is to say, in the very act of testing a hypothesis or gathering evidence, it is not possible to doubt or distrust the enterprise itself. This leads to the view that there is no knowing without believing and that believing is the way of knowing.[25] The converse of this is equally true, namely, that one can doubt only because there are things one takes as true without doubting. It is, he maintains, impossible to doubt all one's beliefs.[26] He elaborates: 'It is impossible at the same time to doubt both the statement, and the beliefs on the basis of which the statement is doubted.'[27]

If this is true, as on one level I am sure it is, then Newbigin has nevertheless left us with an acute dilemma about the way he sets out his case. For example, citing the story of the empty tomb, Newbigin says that the reigning plausibility structures of the

25. ibid., 33. 26. ibid., 42. 27. ibid., 19.

West turn around the account by explaining it as visions created in the minds of the disciples because of their predisposition to believe, whereas the Christian tradition would prefer to see it as 'a boundary event' that brought the disciples to a new way of seeing and thinking.[28] Yet Newbigin's own premise would force the conclusion that the disciples could not have known the empty tomb existed without a disposition to belief, since there is, according to him, no knowing without believing, and believing itself is a way of knowing. '*Credo ut intelligam*', says St Augustine ('I believe in order to understand'). There is a hint here that the sandwich may substitute for the meat, with religion becoming only a rationalist precursor with presumably troubling implications for its own integrity.

If one reads it in that light, the book offers some correctives. Religious people, for instance, sometimes think to oppose ideological scepticism only to find themselves being cast into its mirror image. Modern Western fundamentalism is one example where a conservative religious reaction ends up imitating the Cartesian scepticism it set out to combat. Descartes's quest for a form of knowledge about which no rational person could doubt, and from which one could proceed in verifiable logical steps, such as is allegedly provided by mathematics, spawned an intellectual gathering point where people sought knowledge without personal risk. Thus religious fundamentalism alighted on the principle of scriptural inerrancy (or ecclesiastical infallibility) in which believers would acquire automatic immunity to error and uncertainty.[29] It is a perceptive observation, its lesson being that Christian apologetics is always at risk from the ideas and systems it seeks to combat. We can easily become like the enemies we fight.

Science may claim the final word on truth and reality and still survive, though, according to Einstein, the propositions of mathematics are uncertain where they refer to reality and where they are certain they do not refer to reality.[30] However, religion can scarcely escape the damage to its reputation when it aligns

28. ibid., 11f. 29. ibid., 49.

30. ibid., 29. Einstein is quoted elsewhere as saying: 'Since . . . perception only gives information of this external world or of "physical reality" indirectly, we can only grasp the latter by speculative means. It follows from this that our

itself completely with any systems of finality, as millenarian movements illustrate. In a situation where the prevailing plausibility structures are millennial, institutional Christianity may appropriate aspects of those structures, and even commend the gospel as the eschatological hope in a pilgrim vocation, but woe betide Christians when they make the heavenly kingdom the synonym for the earthly estate.

World Christianity and Western Self-Understanding

This thought introduces the next stage of my exploration of pluralism and commitment. Newbigin is absolutely right in saying Christianity, or at any rate Christian mission and apologetics, is involved always in a pluralist tension, the tension between confidence in God and uncertainty about living out that truth in the world, between faith as God's gift and understanding as a form of growing discovery, between knowing who God is and seeking to bring that knowledge into situations of despair or resistance, not to say anything about the diversity and conflict of views among self-avowed Christians. Beyond that is the highly significant, although still flickering frontier of world Christianity now emerging beyond the West like a new universe bathed in dawn. There we have plausibility structures so inconceivable from our Western standpoint that we would confess to an extraterrestrial disbelief were it not for the fact that Jesus Christ is also their theme and burden. As Newbigin forcefully puts it:

> Only those who have had long training in the methods of thinking, of study and research, and of argument which have been developed in western Europe can share in its [the contemporary ecumenical movement] work. These ways of thinking have become so dominant throughout the world during the past two centuries that it is very difficult for those who have never known anything else to realize that they are only *one* of the [*many*] possible ways

---

notion of physical reality can never be final.' Cited in Northrop, *The Meeting of East and West*, 1946, repr. 1979, 292.

> in which men and women have found it possible to make sense of their experience . . . For those who have never lived in any other cultural world than that of the contemporary West it is very hard to see that theirs is only one of the tribal cultures of mankind . . . Anything else has to be translated into these forms before it can be seriously studied . . . '[31]

including the stories of non-Western Christians.

Elsewhere Newbigin identifies the peculiar character of Western science, saying, 'Science in the sense in which it has developed in our culture is not impossible, but it is unnecessary . . . The necessary precondition for the birth of science as we know it is, it would seem, the diffusion through society of the belief that the universe is both rational and contingent. Such a belief is the presupposition of modern science and cannot by any conceivable argument be a product of science. One has to ask: Upon what is this belief founded?'[32] Newbigin goes on to remind us that it is precisely the contingency of the universe as the basis for modern science that Indian metaphysics rejects while accepting the rationality of the universe, and thus removing itself from participation in the Western scientific thought infoormed by contingency. And contingency leaves the door open to a purposeful Creator, although modernist thought has rejected this completely.

The problem posed by the modernist rejection of God is at heart a cultural problem, that is to say, a problem concerning the claim for the superiority of Caucasian values in being able to explain, interpret and control the world, especially the world of non-white societies. It is easy to forget in that claim the role Christianity played in ridding the medieval West of its fatalist, determinist attitude towards nature, and producing in its place an attitude of taking charge of the created order in stewardship, as Francis Bacon and others urged. Given this cultural amnesia, the West seems unable to understand the double role Christianity

31. Newbigin, 1978, *The Open Secret*, Grand Rapids: Wm. B. Eerdmans, repr. 1981, 170–71. Emphasis added. See previous chapter for a discussion of the 'one' and the 'many'.

32. Newbigin, *Foolishness to the Greeks*, 71.

might play in Africa or elsewhere, on the one hand by speaking to traditional spiritual and intellectual needs, and on the other by furnishing people with the equipment needed to comprehend unprecedented change, just as the religion did in Europe.

At any rate how do we in North America, for instance, prepare ourselves for entry into the realm of world Christianity? The response has been varied, ranging from nervous apprehension, theological defensiveness, cultural withdrawal or evasiveness, cautious encouragement to missionary partnership and resource sharing. However we respond, we cannot deny the rise of world Christianity and its incredibly pluralist character.

The question for us is whether mainstream Western Christianity, in its Protestant, Orthodox and Catholic forms, as it emerges from its deep assimilation in the heritage of the Enlightenment, is capable of joining hands with a world Christianity framed by radically different 'plausibility structures'. Newbigin's own searching critique of Descartes and Kant, for example, suggests severe limitations in the way of exporting their legacy to the rest of the world. Consequently, other peoples and cultures are likely to come to their knowledge and understanding of Christianity outside the mediatory scheme of the Western Enlightenment or of the unitary advantage of a *corpus Christianum*,[33] though it would be rash to exclude the possibility of contact altogether.

The way forward lies through a radical shaking down of the reigning plausibility structures in the West combined with growing awareness of regions of Christianity lying beyond the borders of familiarity and congeniality. That shaking down has to affect certain basic cultural attitudes about science, philosophy and society and faith in national identity as a full and final substitute for religion. The second of these, that is, national identity, is, perhaps, the most obdurate force we have to contend with, though the first is also an issue of pervasive power.

To take the first, the new apostles of the philosophy of science have long argued in ways which signify a remarkable convergence of revelation and reason, and so broad is that consensus that theologians of various persuasions, from the right and the left, can be found making common cause with scientists. There

33. ibid., 115f, 130.

can be a rationalism of the left, resulting in religion as a historically conditioned cultural construct, and a rationalism of the right, resulting in religion as a propositional truth, with both appropriating science for their cause. Yet the reliance on science can prove costly, as when the norms of computation and enumeration are made the fundamental building blocks of reality and truth, leaving no room for God and the mystery of the mind, or for the nature of thought. In that scheme everything is an invention, a construction. Even if it is true, for instance, that the universe responds in certain of its processes to computer configurations, nevertheless the universe is not a linear projection of some mechanical device. Scientists concede as much by using the otherwise contradictory theories of quantum physics and relativity to study the universe, conscious that intelligence plays a crucial role beyond fitting neat pieces into place. Intelligence is conscious of theory and of the theorizing process as such, thus transcending the view that it is only a function of matter. As Gödel's theorem puts it, no algorithm, or computer program, that demonstrates a mathematical proof can also prove its own validity, a crucial indispensable link between machines and minds.

It is, therefore, necessary to indicate, as Newbigin has tried to do, that reason finds its own reason in doing homage to the Source of light and truth, the Author and finisher of faith. Two steps bring us close to the religious position on reason. First, that reason is not alien to the nature of the universe which responds in more or less precise and predictable ways to reason's probes; and, second, that reason is not the product of a biological process, for that would make the product merely a passive end result rather than what reason patently is, a superior principle capable of ordering and understanding nature. The snow-capped Kilimanjaro is an awesome sight and an anomaly in the tropical setting of East Africa, but it does not produce a logical scale of its own elevation. It is left to humans to subdue its pride and offer it as a homage to Ngai, the God of the Mountain. Mount Kenya is not just a tribal antediluvian relic that the flood could not wash away. It is the ark belonging to Mwene-Nyaga; the mountain is Mwene-Nyaga's from which He lifts the light of His countenance upon us.

Historical Purpose and the Nation State

When we come to consider the situation with regard to claims for an all-comprehending national state, however, we find much less interest in the corpus of liberal theological literature, though it is a relevant issue in terms of Western self-understanding. Newbigin, for example, claims that from Augustine to the eighteenth century, 'history in Europe was written in the belief that divine providence was the key to understanding events',[34] but that thenceforth history was mainly the history of nations, so that when Hegel proposed to write a universal history it only culminated in the Prussian state.

It could, in fact, be argued that one of the most significant paradigm shifts has been the move from a religious metaphysic to a political metaphysic and the messianic state it fosters. All of us in the past two centuries or so have been conditioned to believe that historical and social events will bring about the ultimacy of the national state which can then afford to allow religion to wither on the vine. Certainly in the West the transition has been accompanied by an emphatic ethical transformation: to die for one's religion is considered a fanatical act, whereas to die for one's country is considered an act of heroism. Thus the pledge before the flag becomes more potent than any religious mantra, though the henotheist faith it relies on competes in the same arena as religious faith. We continue to uphold the sanctity of life, but it is a notion now derived from the idea of the sacredness of citizenship rather than of religion.

The Witness of Reason

A similar imaginative leap is necessary with regard to the chain of causation to which the West has committed itself. To preserve the plausibility structure of that chain, when we are challenged with conflicting evidence, we respond that 'accidents', or 'unknown causes', do occur and leave the matter there. It would be difficult to practise our kind of science and medicine without the stable boundaries given us by cause and effect. The larger question, as to whether our kind of science and medicine deals adequately

34. Newbigin, *The Gospel*, 71.

enough with the intricate fabric of phenomena and persons, can only be raised when we confront a society and culture radically different from ours. From the standpoint of another culture, Descartes's confident assertion that 'I think, therefore I am' ('*Cogito ergo sum*') might sound like utter folly. From such a standpoint a more secure foundation for knowledge might instead be, 'I am related, therefore I am' ('*Cognatus ergo sum*'). For after all, we might ask, why should Descartes make his declaration unless there are others of whom he is conscious and whom he wished to persuade? From the relational perspective, then, even the most abstract theory presumes a social reality, and all sound knowledge, including great science is grounded in relational truths.

Newbigin himself expresses something of the same idea when he speaks of several kinds of knowledge, the computational kind that may be committed to retrieval systems, the idealistic kind marked by withdrawal into pure subjectivity, and another kind that he describes thus: 'The language of the Bible introduces us to yet a third view of knowledge. The central use of the verb "to know" in the Old Testament is its use in respect of the mutual knowledge of persons. It expresses a relationship in which much more is involved than knowledge of facts, of concepts, or of mathematical or logical operations . . . I believe that this understanding of knowledge helps us to understand that the knowledge of God is not unrelated to all our other kinds of knowledge, including that which can be stored in a computer.'[35]

'Plausibility structures' as a concept may not, however, deal well enough with the deeper aspects of religious claims, including this relational dimension. Something may sound entirely plausible without its demanding a searching openness, and I could go on conceding a structure or many structures as having a plausibility while never quite trusting them in certain critical situations where instinct, practice or simple trust take over. We all can recall occasions when an 'accidental' wrong turn in the road, a delayed or early arrival at the airport, setting out for a spot on impulse or a gut-level reaction in an emergency saved the day. And then, in retrospect, the pieces fall into place and we 'see'

35. Lesslie Newbigin, *Honest Religion for Secular Man*, London: SCM, 1966, 79–80.

a purpose and a bigger picture in it all. Meanwhile we are conscious of little emotional stirring or rational engagement in all of this, and yet the cumulative effect of instances of such 'seeing' might add up to faith and trust in a power wiser, greater and nobler than anyone we know, or, at any rate, it might prompt that sort of awakening, causing us to ask for a transcendent self-disclosure that is unlike anything remotely resembling self-aggrandizement. It would constitute a fresh capacity for 'receiving the message' that God was in Christ. Its outcome would be the recognition of a new relationship of faith, obedience and guidance. There might be a plausibility factor in that self-disclosure and the relationship it creates, but if so it would be like a trickle beside the mighty Zambezi.

At this stage it would be appropriate to invoke the idea of 'universal intent' that Newbigin talks about, for religious encounter of the kind I have just described will require commitment to truth and to the task of witness. The river exists for nothing else if it does not flow towards the sea, and faith points beyond itself.

As we saw earlier (chap. 1), C.S. Lewis brilliantly demonstrates how the laws of the universe, pulsating with the force of reason, harmonize with the faculty of faith, pointing to God as creator and redeemer. In that essay, 'De Futilitate', Lewis wishes to lay to rest the old standby that science is objective while human thought and reasoning are subjective. In one penetrating statement, Lewis observes that science and religion find in thought a common starting point, with matter as the inferred thing, the mystery. This idea we may join to another, namely, that antireligious ideologies present us with the mutilated or expurgated text of a book we already possess in the original manuscript. That is to say, the attack on religion by denying there could be a god of goodness and purpose, is actually a backhanded way of holding the universe to an inviolate moral standard the source of which is other than the universe we are in the act of challenging. The choice is either to conform to a purposeless universe, in which case we cease to practise any sort of moral criticism, including modern science as we know it, or else to submit to the fount of all goodness and wisdom, and with it to the view of a meaningful universe. The modern scientific view about the nature of the universe is rooted in space and time as actions of a transcendent Wisdom, so that the ripples of wispy clouds of matter that waft and glow ever so dimly at the edge of the universe fifty-nine billion trillion miles away are the primordial seeds planted by the Creator out of which stars and galaxies in symmetrical order eventually sprang some fifteen billion years ago.

The task of fully exploring the immense human and theological challenges and opportunities in such projects of heart and mind is beyond most of us, for it is difficult to disengage from the idiom of our own operative intellectual and social world, to worlds that often only remotely touch the theme of our common universal destiny. Yet it is clear if we are going to question the idioms of the omnicompetent state and the chain of causation, for example, we must see the wholly 'Other' as someone with whom we as well as others have to do in order to take serious stock of movements and ideas breaking out beyond our own borders. As Archimedes puts it, 'Give me somewhere to stand, and I will move the earth.'

Retreat from Mission

Christian mission has long learnt to do this, although, given the stern perspective of the critics, we have failed to understand the movement in its non-Western field setting. Instead we see mission in the telling Shaker metaphor as going through a tunnel that grows narrower and more distorted as it rapidly recedes from us. From that negative perspective it has not been easy to appreciate how missionaries had their 'reigning plausibility structures' dismantled at the hinges as they appropriated indigenous idioms for their work, and by so doing reaching into cultural regions the bare existence of which had scarcely entered into our dimmest imagination. But that missionaries pioneered in that way, and on an astonishing scale, is indubitable, as the example of Vincent Donovan shows.

Hence the irony today that mainstream churches have taken the sideline on mission, and instead turned to development projects as an expiatory offering for past sins. In that sense, mission as the spread of the gospel has given way to mission as an instrument of national policy, with diplomatic missions overseeing the implementation of foreign policy, and it is an important development that Western liberalism perceived the state as the final arbiter of human destiny, an attitude that fosters the sense of civic activism. Consequently, both official and voluntary organizations are prominent in promoting national and cultural values, with people encouraged to indicate their approval of affirmations rooted in the national purpose. There is probably more pietistic fervour in civil ceremonies than at a typical Protestant Sunday morning service, and people are more likely to feel solidarity with fellow nationals of a different religion than with coreligionists of a different nationality, as if national identity is prior to religious identity. The willingness of the churches then to offer development projects as a substitute for witness reinforces the shift from religion to national identity and obligation as forms of ultimate loyalty. Since development projects also rightly respond to searing need abroad, they may unwittingly conceal from us cultural and national values that unavoidably accompany them. Thus the churches become the religious equivalent of good citizenship.

Cross-Cultural Dimensions

The West is perplexed and troubled most about the cross-cultural ramifications of religious witness, feeling that if Christianity is good enough for us then we should call it there and desist from trying to convert others. By the same token, if Christianity is not good enough for us, then that clinches the argument that we should not expend any effort to extend what has served its usefulness. Besides, we are urged, how do we know others are not satisfied with their own religions? From a mixture of powerful motives, including genuine conviction or remorse, guilt, uncertainty, agnosticism, cultural exclusiveness, fear of criticism, disenchantment, mission has acquired a bad reputation in Church and society. The paradox, of course, is that through mission the West came upon some of the most searching and sustained critique of its reigning 'plausibility structures'. By undertaking to learn the languages of others and to communicate in their idioms, missionaries became their own first converts, providing an example of what might be involved when prospective believers saw their idioms had also become the idioms of outsiders. It is a remarkable fact that mission as the historical searching out of God's universal purpose became distinguished by its scrupulous development of vernacular particularity. That is to say, in their vernacular work, missions appropriated numerous plausibility structures with which to express the gospel. This action pluralized while simultaneously relativizing the notion of plausibility structures vis-à-vis the single theme of God's redemptive purpose in history. Newbigin refers to this theme by pointing out that Tamil Christians, for example, have come to their knowledge of Christianity outside the framework of the modern post-Enlightenment West.

> Anyone who has lived within the Tamil churches knows that there are rich resources of living Christian faith and experience embodied in the continuing stream of Tamil Christian lyrical poetry, a stream which has flowed for a century and a half and is still flowing strongly. The people who write and read and sing these lyrics do not take any part in the work of the ecumenical movement. Their lyrics cannot be translated into a European language without losing their power and beauty. The world of thought, the concepts through which they capture and express the deepest Christian experiences are not those which appear in the documents of ecumenical meetings. Only those Tamil Christians who have undergone a long and rigorous training in Western methods of study, argument and experiment can participate in these meetings. It is almost impossible for them to communicate in these meetings what is most vital and powerful in the life of the churches from which they come.[36]

Newbigin speaks too of 'the scandal of particularity', as when out of all the nations of the world the Jews are chosen to represent God's purposes in history, whenceforth God came among us in Jesus Christ, 'the Son of God'.[37] Traditional Western theology treats particularity as a problem in divine providence, or even as an issue in divine election: why should God's knowledge and

36. Newbigin, *The Open Secret*, 170–71.
37. Newbigin, *The Gospel*, 72ff.

mission be restricted to particular segments of human history? There is, needless to say, much in that approach to instruct and restrain, but I wonder whether another approach, building on cross-cultural insights, might help shed further light on the subject. We could say that when missionaries adopted the specificity of vernacular languages and cultures as mediatory vehicles for the gospel, they were extending the principle of Jewish ethnic particularity, the paradigm by which God has chosen to instruct the world in righteousness. Thus would all nations receive bountifully from Israel's cup of consolation. It was an insight that animated the Watu wa Mngu, as we saw.

It goes without saying that missions have produced many changes, both intended and unintended, though I remain unsure of the usefulness of judging missions by whether or not they extended the influence of the West in the socieites affected. That way of looking at the history of missions adopts a Eurocentric view of Christianity in which the sending rather than the *receiving* takes centre stage, accounting for everything in terms of how they square with the Western worldview. It is a view that does not reckon fully with the complex 'insider/outsider' role of missionaries: acculturated aliens abroad and alienated citizens at home. Perhaps it is this Eurocentric view that leads Newbigin to claim that Christian missions have created a revolution of expectations in the relevant societies, giving the people for the first time a sense of history.[38] In view of that, 'mission is a history-making force'.[39]

I think it is true missions were a historical force of incalculable importance, and here Newbigin speaks from experience, but we have to reckon within that fact that the changes included a radical

38. ibid., 129ff.

39. ibid., 131. In a review of Francis Fukuyama, *The End of History and the Last Man*, New York: The Free Press, a Division of Macmillan, 1992, Newbigin argues that the gospel as historical narrative views history not as linear or cyclical but rather as U-shaped. For Newbigin this means taking life 'from the source of all being, down into the depths of hell, and back to the glory of the new creation,' a pattern that marks all authentic human life. Newbigin, 'The End of History', *The Gospel and Our Culture*, Newsletter no. 13, Summer, 1992. One could argue in light of that how a similar dynamic operated for subject races when recovery from defeat allowed a recovery and renewal of selfhood. Whether or not it is what he intended with his remarks, Newbigin's comments about the end of history actually fit well into the idea of progress, and thus constitute a rejection of the existential claim for 'timelessness' and its fatalist ideology.

critique of Western political and cultural imperialism. Indeed, the force of those historical changes derived from the strength of the nationalist sentiment which the vernacular translations of missions did far more to excite and guide than any other single fact. It is to that source rather than in acquiescence to Western norms that we have to trace the roots of historical consciousness, for history does not rise from acquiescence. By not pursuing that historical theme to the field setting of missions, Newbigin unwittingly plays into the hands of his critics who see in missions proof of Western cultural insensitivity.

Pluralism and Christian Uniqueness

Contemporary theology is marked by a lively debate about the call to abandon any claim to Christian uniqueness, a claim viewed as offensive and outmoded in a religiously plural world. Newbigin addresses this question in two chapters, 'No Other Name' and 'The Gospel and the Religions'. He is right to note that the debate is inclined to be vitiated by what he calls cultural collapse in the West, a collapse eloquently described by Robert Bellah et al. The arguments in this debate tend to be rather repetitive, but they come down to one issue, namely, the contention by advocates of pluralism that the claims of Muslims, Hindus, Buddhists and others require a dissolution of the historic claims of Christianity. It is a one-sidedness in which the particularity of others is mobilized to block that of Christianity. It comes pretty close to what Tolstoy said of historians of his generation, that they were like deaf men answering questions which no one put to them. Thus it by no means follows that unilaterally abandoning historic Christian claims would lead others to do likewise, though even if they did that would be no less damaging to the prospects of pluralism.

It may turn out to be the Achilles heel of Western liberalism that its proposing to strip Christianity would alienate it from religions that reject the advice of the West. The idea that there is a pluralist essence pervading the particular claims of religions is, of course, not a new one, having been tried before. For example, Akbar the Great, the Mogul emperor, promulgated a decree in 1580 establishing the syncretist system of Dìn-i-Ilàhi, 'the divine faith', to channel the truth in all religions into one reservoir with boundaries that would be coterminous with Akbar's jurisdiction. Although the effect of such eclecticism was to underwrite the emperor's enlightened policy of equal treatment for Hindus and Muslims in his realm, that project of reasonable religion suffered the fate of its royal sponsor with whose fluctuating fortunes it was tied, in spite of the fact that learned Brahmins, Persian Sufis, Zoroastrian refugees and Jesuit missionaries inscribed it with the politically correct lexicon of open-minded pluralism.

In the final analysis, then, both pluralism and the integrity of religious faith are damaged by the adoption of a soap-and-water Christianity that Western liberal defensiveness seems to prescribe for us. Newbigin's answer and the insights of Donovan, in trying to clarify the grounds for a reasonable Christianity and in challenging Western cultural captivity of the religion, should help recover the initiative, thus advancing through Christian particularity and cross-cultural exchange the frontiers of authentic religiosity.

5

Religious Agnostics and Cultural Believers: Comparative Soundings on the Lost Trails of Christendom

Introduction

Contemporary Western culture, not excepting America, carries at its heart a moral relativism that discounts Christianity's transcendent claims, and resists the religion, or any religion for that matter, as a valid source of truth and guidance. Our practice of separating Church and State has allowed religious attitudes on such matters to survive into the modern world by being consigned to the subjective, private sphere, while the public realm is given over to the objective business of demonstrable facts. The roots of this cultural revolution go back to the Enlightenment, as we noted in Chapter 1, and its manifestations include postmodernist projects of deconstruction and the unravelling of inherited narrative threads connecting us to the past. With the collapse of canonical boundaries, many institutions, and especially the Church, have become exposed to criticism and to the attack of truth and vocation, and that has struck at the root of the Church's confidence in the continuity of the heritage. To amend Tocqueville, religious nations are most beholden to the heritage of moral responsibility that the rhetoric of individual freedom is least equipped to enunciate, and more at risk as the condition of equality becomes more widespread. When we have tried to account for religion after its historic role in Christendom as territorial orthodoxy, we have switched terms and in an instrumental way made the nation rather than the Church the bearer of cultural faith which, in its liberal form becomes moral relativism. Thus liberals dissipate religious genius into the commonplace by dividing it equally among all cultures, while conservatives suffocate it by restricting it to their own.

I would like in this chapter to examine the historical sources and religious consequences of Christendom's territorial meltdown with particular regard to mainline Protestantism and its resulting identity crisis. I would like to look at the ambiguity of Christian non-territoriality, to see how, on one side, the religion would function as transformative power on mainstream values, and, how, on the other, as licit society, it could, and often is, promoted as constitutional entitlement. I should especially like to examine the religious case for non-territoriality or the separation of Church and State, and suggest that religion may be valid as public truth without creating or exacerbating differences, and thus the case for religion assisting in protecting rights, especially those of minorities. Such a religious case, with special regard to its historical and interreligious dimensions, would be relevant in the face of efforts to being back territoriality. Our confidence in this matter, then, need not be at the expense of a sense of realism about past record or present potential.

The Church and its Territorial Shell

With that in mind, we should note that the Christian heritage in the world is becoming increasingly a non-Western phenomenon, with over sixty per cent of those continuing to call themselves Christian living outside Europe and North America. This massive shift has happened only very recently, since about 1960, but the forces that have created this extraordinary religious expansion abroad and its counterpart of religious recession in the West have been active for a very long time. At the heart of it is the dissolution of Christendom, the shattering of the territorial European shell of religious identity. The idea of Christendom was given us by the Holy Roman Empire, a process begun by Constantine who created the New Rome, Constantinople, to be 'the wholly Christian capital of a prince devoted to the faith',[1] and carried to

1. Charles Norris Cochrane, *Christianity and Classical Culture*, Oxford, 1957, 209.

its logical conclusion by Charlemagne. Constantine has become a potent personal symbol even though he was not Christendom's founder, for he was too preoccupied with his personal rule in a diverse, multicultural empire to think about a cohesive, unitary institution like Christendom. Rather, it was the Carolingians, as Pirenne suggests,[2] who made territoriality a rule of religious life and made the principle of political organization the 'unrestricted adhesion of the Western Church to the Empire'.[3]

The Empire was the scaffolding of 'the higher unity of Western Christendom', as Pirenne put it.[4] However, since the break-up of the empire and well before the coming of the Enlightenment, the notion of territory ceased to carry enduring or stable religious meaning or analogue, and therefore the title Christian stopped having any unified or unifocal national and cultural meaning. One of the last gasps of the Christendom idea was at the battle of Lepanto in 1571 when Christian forces routed those of the Muslim Turks – a short-lived triumph as it turned out – for a few years later the triumphalist-minded King Sebastian of Portugal suffered in 1578 a humiliating defeat at the hands of the Muslims at the land battle of Qaṣr al-Kabír. That defeat stunted Portugal's power. The rise of Protestantism and national states created, or else reinforced, the move towards the radical secularization of life. Consequently, the individual's identity became a matter of what country he or she belonged to and what language they spoke, not what Church or confession they claimed. Protestant leaders continued to flirt with the Christendom idea, leaders such as Calvin in Geneva, Luther in Germany, Zwingli in Sweden or John Knox in Scotland. In North America, the Puritan colonies for a season strove to establish the model Christian society, and even today, the Puritan offspring such as the Christian Reconstructionists based in California and the southern states have continued to be fascinated by the idea of Christendom. However, it remains only a dream and a fascination, not the workable arrangement it once was.

2. Henri Pirenne, *Mohammed and Charlemagne*, London: Unwin University Books, 1968.
3. Pirenne, *Mohammed*, 211.
4. ibid., 235.

The Voluntary Realm

We should be clear that 'Christendom' as an idea and institution was different from our modern notions of Christian fundamentalism which stresses the personal salvation of individuals rather than the territorial expression of religion, and from nineteenth-century classical theories of European imperialism, which sought control of other lands and peoples without responsibility to them, an imperialism to which America by general consent (if not illusion) was the virtuous exception. However, when America acquired the Philippines by treaty in 1898, Mark Twain felt America had become 'kin in sin' with European imperialism of which he wrote in derision: 'I bring you the stately matron called CHRISTENDOM – returning bedraggled, besmirched and dishonored from pirate raids in Kiaochow, Manchuria, South Africa and the Philippines; with her soul full of meanness, her pocket full of boodle and her mouth full of pious hypocrisies. Give her soap and a towel, but hide the looking-glass.'[5] However, under Christendom political membership implied membership in the Church, and vice versa.

Even though mainline Protestantism had identified itself with colonialism, it had little in common with it, because in the colonial territories Church and State were sundered in root and branch. The central principle of Christendom had been not so much the converting of individuals as having a stem in a pious emperor or ruler from whom official society draws its orthodox sap. It was such an idea that sustained the medieval world in its belief that the hero of the Grail was the same as the expected head of the Holy Roman Empire, the same figure who would become, in Julius Evola's phrase, 'an image and a manifestation of the "King of the World"', with the 'invisible emperor [becoming] the visible one'.[6] Mainline Protestants were as far removed from that world as the Western governments they chose as allies.

A few more words on this are necessary. Christian society from

5. 'Mark Twain on American Imperialism', *The Atlantic*, vol. 269, no. 4, 1992, 46–65, 49.

6. Julius Evola, *Il Mistero del Graal*, Rome: Edizioni Mediterranee, 1983, chap. 23. Umberto Eco makes extensive allegorical use of this idea in his novel, *Foucault's Pendulum*, New York: Ballantine Books, 1990, 119ff.

our medieval heritage was a *Respublica Christiana*, a Church and a State fused wherein morality and legality shared an indivisible, even invisible boundary. Temporal power vested in a civil magistrate was a limited liability under divine ordinance, with the Church as its appointed legatee. The classical Christian notion of dyarchy was first promulgated by Pope Gelasius I (492–96), and for him the two ends of the divine and the temporal are held in equilibrium, with the State and the Church 'each equal to the other when acting in its own sphere, and each equally dependent on the other when acting in the sphere of the other'. This notion was absorbed in *Respublica Christiana*. Law, justice, common morality, the protection and preservation of life and educational work were matters of responsibility equally for the Church as for the State.

One predictable effect of such a unitary conception of authority, with a *regalis potestas* merged with a *divina potestas*, was to thrust the clergy into the political arena. For example, the clergy thought themselves competent to deal just as well with the administration of just prices or the observance of treaties as with the sacraments. Perfect systems, as Mary Macarthy once said, evoke their contraries, and the Universal Church's far-reaching claims provoked an appropriate response from territorial kingship whose motto was: *rex in regno suo est imperator regni sui* ('each territorial king is the emperor of his kingdom'). Thus Philip IV of France challenged with effect the authority of Boniface VIII whose bull of 1302, *Unam Sanctam Ecclesiam*, was the triumphant consecration of the *lex divina* principle.

Unlike modern voluntary views of Christianity, religion under Christendom was not a matter of personal choice but of birth and soil, with the consequence of Christians, for example, encountering Jews and Muslims as foreigners and aliens even though they lived within common borders and submitted to the rule of the prince. Christendom consecrated the idea of a divinely designated race and Church. As such Christendom survivals persisted in Russian Eastern orthodoxy and, in its day, behind the Iron Curtain.

This Christendom idea in time underwent a radical shift, or perhaps series of shifts, none more ominous than the eventual bourgeois transformation in which prayer served the ends of profit and prudence – what Harvey Cox has called 'the gelding of God'.[7] Christianity as organized religion turned increasingly voluntary, becoming divested of much of its worldly status, while Islam by contrast continued to promote a temporal destiny for itself. To compensate for its loss of worldly status, Christianity in its organized counsels turned inside to its rituals and to personal piety, or else sought shelter as a subsidiary of the national security State, especially the State as the carrier of the doctrine of birth and soil. In that form the Church was content to go voluntary, since the State would do duty for biological and territorial loyalty. However, the price paid was religion being driven from the public square and made personal and subjective. The State learnt to get on without religion and to feel, when it was not useful or irrelevant, that religion was a mischief. Under these circumstances State autonomy was the obverse of religious decline, the one condition requiring the other. In a full-scale secular world there would be the least religious influence, in which case the State could tolerate it as harmless diversion. All this left the public realm without a shred of accountability towards religion. That in turn provoked a religious reaction with conservative fundamentalist political projects and agendas. Thus disinherited, believers indulged a fond, illusory nostalgia for a Christendom in which kings and rulers had been sacred messengers, with Christian society predicated on a model political head cast in the profile of Constantine on the principle of *cuius regio eius religio*. That notion had been so deeply inscribed in the collective Christian memory that believers deluded themselves by finding common cause with jingoist national policies.

In the post-Reformation world, the national State became the public guarantor of the Church, the principal stockholder of religion in its organized and applied forms. However, our meeting with other religions, and with Islam in particular, has made our religious Achilles conscious of his heel. But we would do well to remember that the retrieval projects of Christendom have never fared well. Consider, for example, the various concordats between the Vatican and national governments, especially with Catholic Portugal, Spain and Italy, Lutheranism in Germany and the Scandinavian countries, the Orthodox Church in Greece, Russia

7. Harvey Cox, *Religion in the Secular City*, New York: Simon and Schuster, 1984, 201.

and the former East European countries, Anglicanism in England, and, for a time, in colonial Virginia, Presbyterianism in Scotland, and so on. For Western Europe the peace dividend that people felt entitled to was achieved not by the ecclesiastical Peace of Augsburg of 1555 but by the political Treaty of Westphalia of 1648.

One might thus say that the early modern Catholic missions to Africa and New Spain were attempts to make bricks with Christendom's straw: looking for an ideal chief or king whose instructed piety would permeate society, in return for which his right to govern absolutely, long conceded by the Church, would provide an authoritative framework for religious work and life. The king's subjects, in the meantime, would forfeit all their natural claims and accede only to those rights conferred on them by virtue of their dual adhesion to Church and realm. In the Iberian Peninsula in particular, the politics of colonization were equated with the rationale for evangelization, just as the Kingdom of Christ was equated with its earthly counterpart in the kingdom of Spain and Portugal.[8] However, since power was virtually a monopoly of the new desacralized structures of the imperial national state, the Church was reduced, or had itself reduced, to seeking alliance with the new mobile mercantile classes whose utilitarian worldview supplanted its own prophetic ethic. In the words of current protagonists of liberation theology, the Church girded its loins to anoint the comforted and to postpone the day of reckoning for the high and mighty. Thus the use of national and social criteria to define religion involved this fundamental shift from the territorial public claims of Christendom in which the Church and government offered sanction and legitimacy, and sometimes mutally disquieting challenges to each other, to one where the secular magistrate could untie the moral knot that bound the Church to higher counsels.

Mission and the Separation of Church and State

Let me turn to the Christian missionary movement, the effects of which we have still to comprehend, let alone assimilate, and

8. For an acute analysis of this subject see Harvey Cox, *Religion in the Secular City*, 1984, and *The Silencing of Leonardo Boff*, 1988. For the relevant historical sources see H. McKennie Goodpasture, ed., *Cross and Sword: An Eyewitness History of Christianity in Latin America*, Maryknoll, N.Y.: Orbis Books, 1989

suggest that, in spite of what R. Pierce Beaver has written, it was born in this new context of the loss of Christendom, reinforced by the principle of the separation of Church and State. Even where missions were organized on the lines of a diplomatic embassy, or where the colonial venture was dressed in ecclesiastic garb, no sooner had they arrived on the ground than the two came into conflict with missionaries and local political officers locking horns. Consequently, we could say the Christian missionary movement was the funeral of the great myth of Christendom, because mission took abroad the successful separation of Church and State, of religion and territoriality. For mission religion was a matter for individual persuasion and choice. The missionary movement proved that religion could be separated from its Western territorial identity and succeed, if not in the hearts of the transmitters, in those of the receivers.

Mainline Protestant churches in the United States, veterans of religious toleration, were startled into contemplating what its practical implications might be for religious pluralism with the publication in 1932 of the Laymen's Report, *Rethinking Missions*, written by William Ernest Hocking. This report questioned the rationale of Christian missions, and indicated a willingness to embrace religious pluralism and the corollary of the downplaying of Christian distinctiveness. Thus the report pressed the view with the device of a rhetorical interrogation:

> It is through such reflections that those in the mission field who now face toward tolerance and association[sic.] have their qualms. They feel, and their critics feel still more keenly, that the presentiment of impending re-orientation introduces an element of uncertainty or hesitation into the whole enterprise. If we fraternize or accept the fellowship of the alien faith, what becomes of the original hope that Christianity will bring the world under its undivided sway? If that objective is surrendered, has not the nerve of the mission motive itself been cut?[9]

9. William Ernest Hocking, Chairman, the Commission of Appraisal, *Rethinking Missions: A Laymen's Inquiry after One Hundred Years*, New York & London: Harper & Brothers Publishers, 1932, 36.

Such words fed a powerful motive for Western Christian revulsion at World War I, with believers withdrawing into citadels of subjective isolationism to ponder why the God whom they would faithfully serve abroad was absent when war struck at home. Some of the most significant responses to the Hocking Report came from people like Pearl S. Buck, the wife of a Presbyterian missionary and a novelist whose *The Good Earth* became a national bestseller. She welcomed the Report. Notwithstanding, the serious theological questions it raised were answered in Europe where Hendrik Kraemer produced in response his influential work, *The Christian Message in a Non-Christian World* (1938). However, in the United States, certainly among mainline churches, *Rethinking Missions* struck a chord, however delayed or mixed the response, for the 1920s and 1930s had seen the dramatic fall in numbers in the Student Volunteer Movement that had been such a force in organizing and leading the missionary effort. *Rethinking Missions* could assume that from the splintered ranks of the SVM and their much sobered leaders would come a huge sigh of relief that the slogan, 'the evangelization of the world in this generation' could be abandoned to respectable applause, for already numerous leaders, including Sherwood Eddy, had sounded the note of compromise and retreat.

It cannot be emphasized enough that for missionary leaders of the period, for example, John R. Mott and Robert E. Speer, foreign missions were the extended frontier of the home front, and conversely, the home front was the nearer spectacle of its distant counterpart. As such did the American Board of Commissioners for Foreign Mission have its analogue in the American Home Missionary Society. On the whole, mainline Protestant churches had come to a common mind about mission, as expressed by Robert E. Speer, who wrote that 'the supreme and controlling aim of foreign missions is to make Jesus Christ known to all men as their Divine Savior and Lord and to persuade them to become his disciples', and to organize converts into 'self-governing, self-supporting and self-propagating churches'.[10] The doctrinal core of mission at the time remained Christocentric. Much of this core was soon to be abandoned.

10. Robert E. Speer, *Are Foreign Missions Done For?*, New York: Board of Foreign Missions in the Presbyterian Church in the U.S.A., 1928, 56.

The flywheel of the American missionary movement was the voluntary association: lay-led, market-researched, popularly supported, self-assured, self-funded, task-oriented, goal-driven, individually motivated, close-monitored and self-documented. This voluntary association rubbed off on the old denominational structures, paring away at brand-name loyalty and softening denominational lines between the churches. The institutional structure of the churches had to take notice of such implications of free and open membership that the missionary movement was pioneering, including the principle of ecumenical sharing and cooperation. Individual Christians became more demanding, retaining or transferring their membership according to what was or was not being offered. The missionary movement also blended youth and experience into a success formula, so that expansion abroad arose from the same impulse as the pioneer energy that opened and occupied the frontier. The organization of religion was only the setting out of specific goals and the instruments for achieving them, what my boyhood American friend, Douglas MacKinnon, called 'flexible planning', with organizational technique designed for optimal response on the pattern of individually modelled financial portfolios that Douglas was in business designing. The same principle of machinery, of tool-making, of religion as a marketable commodity, applied as much to frontier evangelism on the home front as it did to mission in foreign parts. The whole enterprise separately and jointly rested on confidence in proven methods and achievable goals.

Similarly, the American missionary movement pushed an egalitarian ethic of personal freedom and choice, and judged conversions in that light. The instinct of separation blinded many of the missionaries as to whether the collective, community ethos of Asian and African societies had any providential place in God's economy, and whether, therefore, conversion should, and would, occur within inherited cultural paradigms. Instead, most missionaries assumed that America's republican heritage of the separation of Church and State, sublimated by faith in the individual efficacy of the Cross, had automatic universal application. Those who had marched to the robust rhythms of the 'Battle Hymn of the Republic' found they could also keep in step with 'Onward, Christian Soldiers'. From the short end of the cultural telescope distant societies were viewed and assimilated as predicates of home-based ideas and institutions. The doctrine of formal separation allowed such quasi-Establishment cultural sentiments to persist unobserved.

However, in spite of all that, momentous changes were afoot. For example, as early as 1911, some people were beginning to question the emphasis on individualism. Perhaps that was an indication that the identification of the gospel with American culture was not watertight, with questions still remaining in people's minds about the theological validity of the individualist cultural norm. At any rate, Joseph E. McAfee, a Presbyterian leader with experience in urban home missions, put his finger on the issue when he wrote: 'If the missionary maintains that the individualistic method is ultimate, and represents an individualistic scheme of salvation as final and complete, he runs counter to approved world tendencies and repudiates a social theory which schools of thought in all civilized lands are successfully establishing.'[11]

The consistency in strategy and approach between home and foreign missions propagated a potential weakness of the missionary movement, for initiatives in the field might be cluttered and frustrated by constraints at home, and conversely, the realities of the wider world might affect attitudes at home. 'Even the most conservative denominational home mission boards had to concede that poverty, ignorance and alienation posed problems with which rescue missions, revival campaigns, and Salvation Army methods could not cope . . . the home missions movement was the most significant route by which social Christianity penetrated the conservative evangelical consciousness,'[12] showing how missions helped to transform American domesticity of Christianity. Mott sensed that missions might indeed create forces abroad that would take on a life of their own, but he put that to the debit side of the nationalist reaction against missions, whereas nearly two generations earlier, Rufus Anderson of the American Board had argued differently for the national cause.

11. Joseph E. McAfee, *The Crisis of Missionary Method*, New York, 1911, 37. Cited also in Sydney E. Ahlstrom, *A Religious History of the American People*, New Haven: Yale University Press, 1972, 866.
12. Ahlstrom, 1972, 863.

The two World Wars had a sobering effect on the ebullient mood that had infused the nature and character of Christianity, including its missionary dimension, and nowhere was this sobering process more conspicuous than on the matter of individualism as a religious subject. After all, the wars were between nations, not individuals, showing why Christians who wished to convert the world could not afford to ignore the life of nations and similar social aggregates. Voices began to be raised about a new definition of mission in which the focus would be entirely different, to the effect, as Robert Speer was made to recognize, that 'the most powerful restatement of the gospel message that could be made to the non-Christian people [of the world] would be that the Christian nations practice it themselves.'[13]

We would be right to suspect that this was the beginning of a massive loss of confidence, an internal corrosive doubt about the power of the gospel to change the world or the lives of those who controlled the world. Keen observers were quick to notice that the Christian concentration on presenting the gospel to the individual had proved inadequate in the face of German nationalism. Furthermore, Germany had been evangelized in the fullest sense of the term, and had been a country where the Church was already planted. 'In other words, Germany was a country that was evangelized as fully as our ambitions for the evangelization of lands now non-Christian would require. Nevertheless Germany was the cause of a great world tragedy.'[14]

Such reflections became more and more insistent, and they accompanied a seismic shift in attitudes towards mission. As Henry P. Van Dusen, student at Princeton and future president of Union Theological Seminary, acknowledged in 1924, in the aftermath of the Great War the deeper foundations of Christian spirituality had begun to rot away. A report in *The Student Volunteer Movement Bulletin*[15] admitted that students of that generation were more conscious of the shortcomings of Christianity and the example it set to other nations, and were as a

13. Cited in Nathan Showalter, *The End of a Crusade: The Student Volunteer Movement For Foreign Missions and the Great War*, unpublished Th.D. dissertation, Harvard Divinity School, Cambridge, Mass., 1990, p. 108.
14. ibid. 15. Vol. 5, no. 2, February, 1924, 121.

consequence unwilling to entertain the notion of 'the evangelization of the world in this generation', or that 'Jesus is the way.'

Two powerful currents surged forth from the ranks of committed Christians, and although these currents in a less disagreeable mood might have merged into a common, wider channel of mutual encouragement enlivened by evidence of genuine international Christian conversation, in those bitter times when little was forgiven or forgotten they collided in blocking the path to renewal of faith. One was the ambition to reform at home, with the emphasis on church activities rather than on mission and evangelism, and the other was a sense of the new internationalism on the rise in Africa and Asia and whose object lesson was the cessation of foreign political and religious interference and the promotion of autonomous national churches, culminating in the 1970s in the moratorium on missions. Thus the challenge on the home front combined with the indigenous challenge abroad to block the reassertion of the Church's public claims.

Even as early as the 1920s and 1930s, there were signs of change. Thus, at one of its conventions, the SVM heard from a black delegate whose reporter identified the two themes of domestic reform and international forces. He said there was an American delegate who denounced American imperialism, the KKK, race prejudice 'and our institutions that make for war. There was the Chinese deploring our lack of knowledge of things Oriental, and of the need for harmonic vibrations of purer tones; the African telling of the new Africa, and of the spirit of unrest throughout the continent; the Hindu asking for America's help without Americanization; the South American asking for help to create a more enlightened people; the American Negro denouncing segregation, jimcrowism, lynching, and the other forms of social and economic barriers which keep him from developing himself to the fullest, and asking for the chance to drink from the head of the fountain of knowledge, unimpeded.'[16] Thus people who had been the target of missions had found their own voices and wished to be heard. It is the alleged contradiction between the goals of mission and the independence of such new-

16. Cited in Showalter, 158.

found voices that seems curious, for the logic of America's own faith expressed in the channels of an American-adapted Christianity should have elicited sympathy for parallel developments elsewhere.

The Hocking Report appealed on somewhat similar lines for the need for positive acceptance of others on their own terms, although it was inclined to impute a priori motives to missionaries' failure to do so. The report said that when missionaries refused to consider evidence of the self-testimony of other religions, then they gave witness to the illegitimacy of their own operating premise, a position that led them to be false to others. 'We have in mind a missionary who defines the God of Islam as a God of power, whereas the Christian God is a God of love. He is accordingly disturbed when he finds a Moslem teaching that the compassion of Allah is the same as the love of God: he inclines to cry plagiarism! and to warn all Moslems that the idea of God as loving Father is Christian and private property!'[17] Mission under those circumstances was unworthy of those in whose names it was undertaken.

One seasoned Presbyterian missionary had a few years earlier given eloquent testimony to the fact that similarities between a faction-ridden American Christianity and an identical phenomenon in other religions justified, not the unilateral advantage for mission Christians claimed, but the sombre truth that people of other faiths are no better off by becoming Christian. They would merely be exchanging one form of imperfection for another. In the particular case of Islam, the missionary pointed out that the centuries-long Muslim repulse of Christianity cannot be reconciled with the command to win all nations to Christ. 'The spectacle of an irresistible force being effectively repulsed for thirteen centuries is one so utterly incongruous that Christians should be startled into heart-searching thoughtfulness . . . The question comes nearer home and must be faced more courageously. Either Christ has failed or we have failed Christ!'[18]

17. Hocking, 43.

18. R.C. Hutchison, 'Islam and Christianity', *The Atlantic Monthly*, November, 1926. A Roman Catholic theologian, writing in the 1960s, echoed these sentiments when he invoked the words of Gamaliel (Acts 5:38–39) in defence of religious pluralism, saying if God had intended other religions to exist, then our

The relatively recent experience of World War I lay at the roots of that crisis of confidence. 'Thinking Moslems are not so shallow as to blame that disaster on Christianity; but they see clearly that during the World War Christianity stood for nothing better than Islam, for the Christian Church throughout the carnage put the stamp of divine approval on every campaign of every army.'[19] So-called Christian nations might more suitably be a lesson for less ravaged societies on the wages of sin than on the virtues of love.

These dark musings raise a more probing question about whether the European tradition of placing the heavenly business of religion in a subordinate private sphere under the power of the sovereign national state has tempted the state with visions of earthly glory and left it without a sense of ethical accountability. If we have created and sustained a Church that has been largely disabled in wordly affairs, how can we also blame it for not averting the catastrophic exploits of morally impaired national states? Have we then not looked to the consequence rather than to the cause, like cutting down the tree to abate the storm? The deeper issue might be whether Christians have been too naïve to relinquish responsibility for the public realm to the State,[20] whether they have been at all wise to allow the national power State such wide latitude in providing the framework within which human beings pursue moral ends that the State, unprovoked, presumed on the authority to define what is moral. I am prepared to allow that Christians may have conceded too much to be blameless, but unsure whether they must also be held accountable for what they have not conceded. If Caesar takes what belongs to God,

---

denouncing them could unenviably pit us against God. Ronan Hoffman, 'Are Conversion Missions Outmoded? Yes!' in Donald McGavran, ed., *The Conciliar-Evangelical Debate: The Crucial Documents, 1964–76*, Pasadena: Wm. Carey Library, 69–86, 81f.

19. ibid.

20. W. Douglas MacKenzie, president of the Hartford Seminary Foundation, argued in his book, *Christian Ethics in the World War*, 1918, that, in spite of its inherent moral limitations, the nation state, though a human institution, rests 'on a divine basis' and has the moral right to employ force to restrain selfish and vicious men. The moral limitations of the nation state would in time be remedied by new international arrangements, such as the League of Nations, rather than by any eschatological consummation beyond history.

we might with reason complain about Caesar's presumptuousness rather than about God's forbearance in holding back from the final judgment, unless we wished to repeat the folly and make God in the image of Caesar.[21]

In any case the attention of the churches closed in on pressing domestic issues with the Crash and the Depression. These upheavals left their mark on the fabric of national life and occupied the best innovative thinking in theological circles, opening the way for the eventual triumph of Christian liberalism. The agenda for the churches was identical with the agenda for the nation, and that was increasingly dominated by the new secular forces of urban concentration, with the great majority of Americans living in cities, changes in agriculture, a new social activism among the lay, especially women who led the Temperance Movement, and an enlarged role for government symbolized by the New Deal. The postwar reconstruction had produced a mood of social optimism and reinforced liberal faith in human institutions and man's perfectibility, the active milieu in which theology came to be acclimatized. Both the pacifist and jingoist strands of Christian activism shared this faith in religion as a human potential. Consequently Douglas Clyde Macintosh (1877–1948), a Canadian pacifist who came to Yale, and Benson Y. Landis, a Congregational leader, to name but two, conceived of religion in programmatic terms. They would sympathize with James Dennis, a Presbyterian leader of an earlier generation, who described missions as 'a sociological force, with a beneficent trend in the direction of elevating human society, modifying traditional evils, and introducing reformatory ideals.'[22] Macintosh and Landis would demur only if Dennis was not programmatic enough. For his part, Landis, for example, had little doubt where the Federal Government under FDR had got its ideas on alleviating social distress and ushering in economic recovery.[23] Those churches that opposed the New Deal, such as

21. Walter Rauschenbusch had declared in 1917 that 'the ultimate cause of the war was the same lust for easy and unearned gain which had created the internal social evils under which every nation has suffered. The social problem and war problem are fundamentally one problem.' Cited in Ahlstrom, 1972, 888.
22. James S. Dennis, *Christian Missions and Social Progress*, 2 vols., New York: Revell, 1897, i, 23.
23. Benson Y. Landis, *The Third American Revolution*, New York: Association Press, 1933, 128–33.

the National Council of Methodist Youth, did so further along the left-wing spectrum by raising the stakes of dialectical ideology, because they viewed the New Deal as a capitalist tool that blurred the line between socialism and capitalism, not by staking out a theological position.[24]

The religious reaction, when it amounted to anything, came from different quarters. Michael Harrington (d. 1989) may or may not be right in his assessment about the lack of hospitableness of America for the socialist cause, putting this down essentially to the weakness of class lines and the potential for absorption into the economic mainstream. But it is a fact that the initiative for theological leadership on both the left and right lay with those grounded in the Bible. Biblical studies, for example, provided intellectual armoury for both the left and the right, with Princeton Seminary producing a powerful rejoinder to the threatened liberal avalanche. J. Gresham Machen (1881–1937) wrote for this purpose his influential *Christianity and Liberalism*, described as 'the chief theological ornament of American Fundamentalism'.[25] Yet even Machen's fluid and lively pen could not staunch the tidal assault on propositional orthodoxy, although when the seminary was reorganized in 1929, a conservative breakaway rump attempted a salvage job with the residue of orthodox pietism. Thus were spawned several separatist movements, including the establishing of an independent foreign missions board, movements whose energy and pace depended on their narrowness and numerical abstemiousness rather than on reconstructing and revitalizing the mainstream.

Mainstream Northern Presbyterians, meanwhile, had decided to take head on the crying social issues of the day, including questions about whether classical capitalist economics was an effective machinery for achieving general prosperity, a prosperity that the churches had come more and more to assume as the material embodiment of salvation. Thus did the interwar theological critique anticipate the radical manoeuvres of liberation theology in the 1960s and 1970s, although few saw the wider or deeper connections then.

24. Ahlstrom, 1972, 922. 25. ibid., 912.

Neo-orthodoxy and Counterculture

The liberal tide gave few signs of ebbing when a countermove with neo-orthodox Barthianism was staged on its own ground, a countermove that might, indeed, be considered liberalism in continuity with its rational antecedents, although Karl Barth, its eponymous originator, intended something rather different. In North America, its rising apostles included Reinhold Niebuhr and William Sloane Coffin and its rallying call was moral action in an immoral world. Neo-orthodoxy as an intellectual movement carried into academic theology the sharp reflex of a Bultmannian metaphysical agnosticism, the same sort of religious stripping textual scholars had used in demythologizing the Bible. This stripping was taken into numerous kindred fields: in the theory of the Church not as the repository of unchanging truths but as the focus of prophetic witness; a doctrine of hope not as the facile optimism in inevitable historical progress but as the new realism about human tragedy and its final resolution in a cosmic Christ rather than in a historical Jesus; an emphasis on moral accountability not in terms of inherited codes but in a love ethic that dissolved the old rigidities; a fresh historical seriousness concerning the radical relative complexity of the human and natural enterprise vis-à-vis the absolute realm of divine providence. All of this led to a sharp cultural critique, a prophetic warning against unremitting faith in human schemes and solutions.

Thus did neo-orthodoxy give men 'a more realistic awareness of institutional power, social structures, and human depravity. It made men at once more biblical in their standpoint and less utopian in their advocacy. Most important, perhaps, it built bridges that opened communications not only with modernists who had all but decided that Christianity was obsolete, but also with conservatives who had all but decided that true Christians must repudiate modern modes of thought and action.'[26] All of which amounts to saying that neo-orthodoxy remained eminently sensible: sober-minded in things of reason, even-tempered in its sentiments, restrained in its emotions, worldly-minded in its

26. Ahlstrom, 1972, 948.

judgments, its will tempered for action and its courage staked unwaveringly between commonsense faith and practical self-help. It embraced messianic faith for its restive activism and its iconoclasm, but rejected its other-worldly outlook. It eschewed enthusiasm in religion and gave a dignified, measured account of whatever things are worth thinking about.

Neo-orthodoxy, then, may be said to be the social derivative of liberal philosophical idealism, with its criticism of politics and society based on dialectical assumptions about change, with an underdog morality of the marketplace. In the academy neo-orthodoxy assimilated into the world of historical and linguistic science. It was the middle-class way of taking the unexciting in religion and making it respectable, which might explain why *Rethinking Missions* made such an impact with its appeal to cultured respectfulness as a principle of interreligious relationship. At any rate, while Enlightenment thinkers might see ideas and theories as exceeding the measure of sense data, just so neo-orthodoxy saw in the events of lived social reality, or rather, reality as projected by science, 'the essential raw material of God's revelation of himself',[27] as a piece of theological axe-grinding puts it. In neo-orthodoxy a cruel, suffering world proves, and demands an activist God, a God who is necessary to the defence and affirmation of human promise and fulfilment and is moral legitimizer of social concerns. These theologians were even willing to go as far as saying that the gaps in our knowledge of the physical universe should require a downsizing of the idea of an All-knowing deity, a deity whose aggressive sovereignty science had effectively tamed with cumulative authority.

Whatever its considerable achievements as an intellectual movement, then, and however much it might be credited for ushering in a new theological dispensation, neo-orthodoxy made eschatological faith, together with mission, unfashionable, if not unrespectable,[28] so determined was it to bring religion into line

27. Hugh Searle, 'Choice between restoration and rebirth', *Church Times*, 10 July, 1992.

28. However, Emil Brunner,unflatteringly dubbed the 'poor man's Barth', stressed what he called 'missionary action' as necessary for the Church to be the Church. In his famous phrase, he said, 'the Church exists by mission, just as fire exists by burning.' Emil Brunner, *The Word and the World*, 2nd ed. London, 1932, 108. Some scholars take Brunner to mean by 'missionary action' the effort

with the prevailing cultural ethos of a socially transposed post-Enlightenment rationality and domestic self-preoccupation.

In the era of Eisenhower, this domestic self-preoccupation was one of ebullience and optimism that the West, and America in particular, knows the solutions to the world's problems, and a conviction that the free world represented the cause of righteousness vis-à-vis the Communist world. It was the facile optimism in 'the power of positive thinking' and trust in the beneficence of free enterprise that Christian neo-orthodoxy attacked, and it is hard to overestimate the success of neo-orthodoxy as a counter- cultural movement. In the churches there was put in place a solid deposit of distrust of all causes, including mission, a smouldering scepticism about the possibility of virtue and truth except in social projects, with religion as action charter. Eisenhower's decision to commit American forces to Vietnam after the French defeat at Dien Bien Phu in 1954 was to open a trail that would bring the nation to one of its most traumatic crises. A decade later the nation was in the grip of an anti-Vietnam furore, and even Nixon who ended the war in 1973 came to be identified with Watergate, reinforcing the mood of self-preoccupation and doubt that neo-orthodoxy had done so much to foster. In his trenchant reflections on what happened to America in Vietnam, Conor Cruise O'Brien spoke of 'a loss of confidence in a millennial or quasi-millennial future for America. More than any other great culture, America has been moved by what the late Mayor Richard Daley of Chicago – underestimated as a thinker – once called "nostalgia for the future" . . . It is not a question of the future only. The faith in innocence itself is weakened. That innocence had been a somehow self-evident goodness *of feeling*, detachable from the historical record of action.'[29] However, all that was to change. 'My Lai, Watergate, the revelations of the Church Committee about the homicidal Keystone Kops of the CIA – these and other grisly

---

by Christians to help the adherents of other religions to become better adherents, not to become converts to Christianity. Such an interpretation of mission adheres to the terms of *Rethinking Mission*.

29. Conor Cruise O'Brien, 'Innocent nation, wicked world', *Harper's Magazine*, April, 1980, 32–34.

apparitions have left the image of a special American innocence tattered, bedraggled, though not, I think, either dead or dying.'[30]

O'Brien, following Ernest Lee Tuveson,[31] identifies two forms of millennialism in America, one active, outgoing and interventionist, and the other quiescent and isolationist. Woodrow Wilson described the first, active type when he spoke of America striving for 'nothing less than the liberation and salvation of the world', a trail whose traces go back to Puritan religious ideals and the Manifest Destiny of the nineteenth century, and one whose course John F. Kennedy widened beyond the Western hemisphere. The second, quiescent type stressed a virtuous millennium reserved only for America, a doctrine of American 'exceptionalism'. Such a special dispensation is intended to contrast favourably with Old World vices. Even in her pessimism, America is considered special, for her sense of what is wrong with the world does not rest on historical proofs but on 'the purity of heart' that Webster's Dictionary, though not Oxford, says is the definition of innocence. It explains why O'Brien could say of Herman Melville that he would characterize America as the scene 'of the ultimate failure of the human race, of man's squandered last inheritance',[32] or, as F. Scott Fitzgerald expressed it in *The Great Gatsby* (1925), America offered the spectacle that 'had once pandered in whispers to the last and greatest of human dreams; for a transitory enchanted moment man must have held his breath in the presence of this continent, compelled into an aesthetic contemplation he neither understood nor desired, face to face for the last time in history with something commensurate to his capacity for wonder.' O'Brien continues: 'There are many of us who, looking to the United States, feel that we are looking at ourselves in the process of becoming: ourselves as we might be and do, given the opportunity, for good or ill.' This mood of special pessimism was caught in Christopher Lasch's iconoclastic book, *The Culture of Narcissism: American Life in an Age of Diminishing Expectations*, a work whose wide acclaim, from both the left and right, made it a symbol of the national outlook.

30. ibid., 33.
31. In Tuveson's book, *Redeemer Nation: The Idea of America's Millennial Role*, Chicago: University of Chicago Press, 1968.
32. O'Brien, 1980, 34.

Yet it is a fact that by their inward-turning and confronting what they find ugly in themselves, Americans even in their quiescent millennialist 'disengagement' were more likely to change their condition than others. America's encounter with the world takes on a spiritual, intellectual flavour, for it must be judged by standards that, as O'Brien says, are 'detachable from the historical record of action', and fixed on faith in the ideals of freedom, justice, equality and tolerance, that is, faith in things hoped for, not in things seen. That was how, for example, President Woodrow Wilson conceived of the League Covenant to the Peace Conference in Paris, with America's spiritual leadership offering mankind the fruits of the peace nations yearned for but had not seen. Thus he spoke of the League Covenant as 'a practical and humane document . . . intended to purify, to rectify, to elevate'.[33] It is that positive reflex that the theological critique in its implacable thrust caused to atrophy, a reflex that makes America the moral experiment in nation-building that she has become, as the replica of the Statue of Liberty at Tiananmen Square in Beijing demonstrated. We might amend the words of Aristotle to the effect that 'American society exists for the sake of noble actions, and not of mere companionship', a vision of the nation that the Puritan offspring of the classical heritage understood as the 'New Atlantis' of their days.[34] In other words, America exists for a mission and holds herself accountable to noble goals lest she be no different from the nations of the Old World, nations conceived in the archaic bonds of blood kinship. Theirs would be the greatness of biology and nostalgia, whereas America's would be that of the moral and the optimistic.

The bitter strife of the Vietnam era showed America's instincts to be moral and renewable, with the stern test of open public discomfiture revealing its energetic, even confrontational character. In the religious sphere, however, leaders were distrustful of 'noble goals' or 'purity of heart' as practical guides for conduct,

33. Cited in Gene Smith, *When the Cheering Stopped: The Last Years of Woodrow Wilson*, New York: Time Reading Program special edition, 1964, xvi.

34. F.S.C. Northrop, *The Meeting of East and West: An Inquiry Concerning World Understanding*, New York: Collier Books, London: Collier-Macmillan, 1960, chapter viii.

and as 'tamed cynics' they bristled at talk of religious motives in the nature and pattern of Christian involvement in the world. Missions took a direct hit.

Colonialism, Christendom and Mission

The view has been widespread that missions under colonialism have sought by the back door to retrieve a failed Christendom by looking to the 'Dark Continents' of the non-Western world for the purpose. To the contrary, the idea of missions may have prompted the complementary thought that 'Dark Continents' existed on two entirely different levels: the lost 'continents' of Europe that may be reached in a few strides, even though ecclesiastically they be less easily possessed, and the unknown 'continents' of Africa and Asia that may be reached for the gospel though through great physical and cultural obstacles. Thus could George Sims say in 1889 of England: 'In these pages I propose to record the result of a journey into a region which lies at our own doors – into a dark continent within easy reach of the General Post Office.'[35]

Colonialism reinforced the same point by showing colonial officials ignoring or dismissing the religion of their subjects and still ruling over them. As it turned out, many senior colonial officials were anti-clerical and combated the Church with administrative measures, at times spiced with personal prejudice. Whatever the case, the fact remains that Christendom was irretrievable, and if missionaries fondly imagined they would retrieve it through collaborating and colonialism, they had only identified what would complete its ultimate demise. Under colonialism the exercise of government was removed from any religious support, something that the citizens of Christendom would not have comprehended. A rulership that is so detached from religion is one side of the coin the other side of which is religion detached from territory. This has been an irreversible process.[36]

35. Cited in Julian Pettifer and Richard Bradley, *Missionaries*, London: BBC Books, 1990, 215.

36. Newbigin concedes as much when he writes: 'The Christendom era has ended. It can no longer be expected that the church will have the power of the state and the influence of society on its side.' *Honest Religion*, 124.

Secularism: Left and Right

An important consequence of this revolution is our ceasing to associate the term 'Christian' with 'Christendom', so that in practice we may or may not carry the Christian name without much religious content, ready as we may be to settle for metaphysical agnosticism encased in cultural convictions, whether it be human rights and constitutional liberty among liberals or anticommunism and white Anglo-Saxon values among conservatives, in contrast to any notion of an all-embracing historical community of believers. Indeed, as pointed out by Adrian Hastings, modern people have believed that 'a devout agnosticism was . . . a logical progression beyond Liberal Protestantism as the latter was beyond Reformation Protestantism.'[37] By the 1950s and 1960s agnosticism acceded to the position of a new orthodoxy, turned conservative, 'Anti-romantic, anti-ideological, a dry man-of-the-world cynicism, as bored with left- wing enthusiams as with religious credulities . . . the safest core of a conservative Establishment.'[38] Even today all of us calling ourselves Christian still have in our eyes the mists of a complacent agnosticism, reinforced by the deterritorialization of religion and its consequences: none of us is looking for a new Eden or a new Jerusalem in the West, except, perhaps, as gnostic themes, for it is such quasi-gnosticism that has fed our brand of personal piety, as Harvey Cox has eloquently reminded us.[39] Trust in territorial safeguards for religion has its analogue in the obligations of national citizenship, while religion abides as romantic stimulus for optimism. Consequently religion has

37. Adrian Hastings, *A History of English Christianity: 1920–1985*, London: Fount Paperbacks, 1986, 227.

38. ibid., 496.

39. Harold Bloom, for his part, has argued, or overargued, that gnosticism is the most typical American religion, equated as it is with that freedom that puts the individual alone with God or Christ, the individual, to coin a phrase, as the 'pea-pod' self who hangs by a narrow, slender creed to its Maker, sealed in on itself, and resistant to interference from others. Bloom, *The American Religion: The Emergence of the Post-Christian Nation*, New York: Simon & Schuster, 1992. It is not clear how Bloom allows for such gnostic persons also adopting activist political agendas.

become relegated to a subcategory of private citizenship rather than being the necessary rule for universal human solidarity.[40]

Our primary unit of identity continues to be the State and its laws, and it is as citizens, loyal or not, and not as believers, that we die as heroes for country or race. If we laid down our lives for religion, then it would be as fanatics, not heroes. Our fundamental identity is narrowly set in Establishment or anti-Establishment loyalties: either we have enormous faith in government and the State as indispensable vehicles of the progressive and humanist agenda, or we see government and the State as obstacles or enemies of those goals. Whether in its positive or negative version, such a view of what constitutes our ultimate identity represents the triumph of the secular metaphysic over the religious, of government over the Church, with the rules of governance having priority over the habits of worship. We have nailed our colours to the instrumental mast, with method and machinery replacing truth and hope. Thus even the phenomenon of liberal bourgeois disenchantment with the State is just another version of the State as the unit of discourse, and evidence too that the bourgeois disenchantment is the obverse side of faith in machinery. The Church conforms to this secular discourse by accepting a secular rationale for its *raison d'être*. Whether or not this is a desirable development, we can scarcely deny that the shift from the religious to the instrumental norm is the grid proliferating and entangling all our actions and thoughts.

Contemporary Christians have as a result sought to make common cause with secular forces in order to demonstrate the usefulness of Christianity,[41] in other words, to transform Christianity into a secular establishment, as a recent report in the *Christian Century* makes clear. It said that the Presbyterian Church (USA), with 2.8 million members, has filed suit with the

40. On this matter Freud, at least in the works in which he explores cultural matters, takes a less sanguine view than Bloom on what gnostic individualism might imply for normative civilization. Freud writes: 'Thus civilization has to defend itself against the individual, and its regulations, institutions and commands are directed to that task.' *Future of an Illusion*, 6.

41. In the 1960s all the major denominations maintained a lobbying office in Washington, D.C., with the black civil rights movement providing a rallying point for Church involvement in public affairs.

State Surpreme Court of Kentucky challenging as unconstitutional the State's prohibition of homosexuality. James Andrews, the stated clerk of the Church, said the Church was entering a brief in the case in defence of First Amendment rights on privacy. Mr Andrews said moral or theological arguments were not relevant to the case, and concluded that there is a difference 'between moral persuasion within a voluntary religious community and sexual laws imposing criminal penalties that apply to anyone, regardless of religious belief.' The Church's concern in the matter, he said, was with infringements on 'personal privacy and liberty.'[42] His position is reminiscent of that taken by a predecessor of his, Eugene Carson Blake, who in the 1960s was similarly active during the civil rights movement, and who led a delegation of religious leaders in testimony before the Judiciary Committee of the US Congress.[43] However, Mr Andrews signals an important shift from the moral, religious rationale of Dr Blake's position to his own pragmatic civil libertarian argument, indicating that religion has become effectively sidelined in the public domain. If religion survives it would be as a question of free speech and right to privacy, and thus light years removed from 'Christendom'. However long or circuitous the trail, modern Christians have arrived at the point where they could now retain the prerogatives of prayer and worship only by cooing like a private dove or else flocking with the public hawk with their religious wings clipped.

In what is on its own grounds a valuable theological document, the Board of Social Ministry of the Lutheran Church of America nevertheless stated that 'religious liberty' is a political term and as such is not dependent upon Christian freedom.[44] The document

42. The *Christian Century*, August 21–28, 1991, p. 770.

43. Dr Blake testified on that occasion: 'The religious conscience of America condemns racism as blasphemy against God. It recognizes that the racial segregation and discrimination that flow from it are a denial of the worth which God has given to all persons . . . As churches, synagogues, and religious leaders, our concern is with the purpose of civil rights legislation and with the moral principles that indicate the necessity of enacting such legislation.' Cited in James Luther Adams, *The Growing Church Lobby in Washington*, Grand Rapids: Wm. B. Eerdmans, 1970, 11.

44. *Religious Liberty*, New York: Board of Social Ministry, Lutheran Church in America, 1968, p. 5.

makes protection of liberty under the Constitution a matter of individual rights even though that omits for Christians the matter of faith and obedience to a sovereign and transcendent God. Nothing, then, better illustrates the comprehensive collapse of the Christendom ideology than the pragmatic, politically correct trail that brings us expeditiously to the user-friendly argument that the Church may now discharge its high responsibility by looking no further than to the rights of privacy and personal freedom, with little pretence at following any theological guidelines or helping those believers still having theological scruples. The phrase 'regardless of religious belief' seems to define the last horizons of Christian responsibility, and it sits prominently on the brow of a defensive Christianity. It is overshadowed only by the professional euphemisms and the understated equivocations of the politically correct lexicon.

However, it was not always the case that Christians thought only in Establishment terms, whether religious or secular. In the 1970s, for example, some of the major public policy statements and actions of the churches demonstrated a willingness to relinquish Establishment control and exercise responsibility for a deterritorialized Christianity. In 1971 the United Presbyterian Church gave $10,000 for the defence of Angela Davis, the militant black activist who was on trial for murder in an attempted jail break. In 1975 the Division of Education of the United Methodist Church produced a study document in which it laid responsibility for the woes of the world's poorer nations at the door of Western capitalism in general and the US in particular. 'Profit, military might, and alliances with powerful interests in the world have made our nation the hub of a vast network of "economic plunder".'[45] In 1977 a Church delegation visited Cuba which it praised for a political revolution that was in process of 'creating a society without beggars, starvation, or illiteracy', and as such 'deserving of our respect and support'. The delegation put Cuba favourably not on the side of countries that perpetrate injustice and repress dissidents in the process (as in Chile and Brazil, for example), but on that of countries that try to

45. Else M. Adjali and Carolyn D. McIntyre, *Liberation as an aim of the church's educational work*, New York: Division of Education, United Methodist Church Board of Discipleship, 1975, 11.

remove injustice and in the process imprison those opposed to them.[46] In 1978 the Committee on Justice and Service of the World Council of Churches, under the chairmanship of Robert C. Campbell, executive secretary of the American Baptist Church, approved a grant of $85000 as humanitarian aid for the guerilla forces fighting for the overthrow of the minority white government of Mr Ian Smith of Rhodesia (now Zimbabwe). In 1979, during the American hostage crisis in Iran, the Methodist Bishop Dale White issued a statement in which he observed that we are all of us '"hostages" to a vast political economic system of the cruelty structures which are preordaining that the rich get richer and the poor get poorer.'[47] The Quaker organization, the American Friends Service Committee, produced a pamphlet written at about the same time by James Bristol who asserted that 'before we deplore "terrorism", it is essential to recognize clearly whose terrorism came first', going on to observe that to much of the world 'the United States is an outlaw nation.'[48] Russell Johnson, an official of the Friends Service Committee, wrote in a *Fellowship of Reconciliation* magazine that 'our nation today is the very fount of violence in many places in the Third World.'[49] The National Council of Churches fed the same mood when in 1979 it launched a stinging attack on the American legal system as being designed 'to suppress non-violent political dissent, to cope with social problems, and to provide cheap labour.'[50]

Such forays into political activism placed religion in the public domain, with believers transforming and renewing the mainstream, a sense that religion has not lost its savour or its moral credibility. It was telling evidence, too, of a growing global awareness and sensitivity, the genuine heritage of a deterritorialized, post-Christendom Christianity. For believers moral leader-

46. *Statement of Church Persons after Visiting Cuba*, United Methodist Church, dakotas Area, 1977.

47. *A Time for Candor: Mainline Churches and the Radical Social Witness*, Institute for Religion and Democracy, 1983, 41. Cited in A. James Reichley, *Religion in American Public Life*, Washington, D.C.: The Brookings Institution, 1985, 265.

48. Cited in Reichley, 265–66.

49. Reported in the *Wall Street Journal*, June 10, 1982, and cited in Reichley, 266.

50. Cited in Reichley, 264.

ship and civic loyalty combined in political action without requiring territorial conformity. A peculiar sword of distrust thus came between Church and State, and churches took up that sword, not always as *fait accompli* conscripts.[51]

It is such factors, whether of discouragement or encouragement, that have much exercised the minds of thoughtful people who feel Christianity should come out of its hold-all cultural assimilation. Tocqueville wrote that through religion Americans acquired a high sense of civic responsibility that did not turn idolatrous, and freedom that did not become destructive greed – though he might take some of that back had he been able to witness current scandals in religion, politics and business. Recent decisions by the US Supreme Court, however, have confronted people with a seemingly insoluble contradiction between the call to nurture civic virtues and the demand to reject the religious source of those virtues. This contradiction threatens a major moral upheaval, because to 'teach values as autonomously secular seems not only dishonest but ultimately destructive: by aggressively severing values from their religious roots, an exclusively secular values curriculum becomes, in effect, antagonistic to religion.'[52] In its more or less comprehensive cultural captivity, then, the Western Church finds itself reduced to a mock rehearsal of society's agenda, gaily adopting the language of rights and justice in place of truth and repentance, and perforce capitulating to the litigious ideology of individual preference and group conflict. It shows the Church unwilling to embrace with the right hand of fellowship the penitent, preferring instead with the militant left to receive those claiming to have been wronged. It is the position of an enclave Church whose teeth have been set on edge by the sour grapes its Christendom forebears consumed.

51. However, the churches in the Cold War sometimes acted and spoke in ways that cast them as tools of Moscow or of Washington, with ecclesiastical bodies and individuals inclined to think Marxist politics much closer to the Kingdom than Western capitalism, and vice versa. Either way, such a choice effectively converts Christianity into a political *fait accompli.*

52. Betty Mensch and Alan Freeman, 'Religion in the Schools; Should We Celebrate Church-State Separation?' *Tikkun*, a Bimonthly Jewish Critique of Politics, Culture and Society, March/April, 1992, 31–36, 31. The authors are professors of law at SUNY, Buffalo.

Cross-Cultural Encounter

Now the problem in our dealings with people of other cultures and religions is simply this: their equivalent of 'Christendom' is to some degree in place, as Hindus (in India), Buddhists (in Tibet, Sri Lanka or Thailand) Kodo or Jinja Shinto (in Japan), Jews (with reference to Israel), Confucians (in China) and Muslims (in the Arab world). I say, to some degree, because the forces that toppled our Christendom have entered many of these societies, or at any rate have entered them in ways that are subtly transforming relationships and habits of thought. Nevertheless, territorial orthodoxy rings far truer to the experience of, say, Muslims, Buddhists and Hindus than it does to that of Europeans and Americans, and the tragedy of religious minorities in these non-Western societies is that they live against the grain by representing the non-territoriality of religion while the wider society has still to make the shift. Such is the fate of Copts in Muslim Egypt, of Bahais and Zoroastrians in Shiite Iran, of Hindus in Muslim Pakistan, of Protestant and Catholic Christians in Buddhist or Shinto Japan, and so on. In such societies where the choice has been between 'misbelief' and correct belief, our modern Western notion of agnosticism or atheism as neither threatens the societies with a major upheaval.

In a great deal of the Western theology of religious pluralism and dialogue, nevertheless, we have promoted the idea that anyone calling himself or herself Christian has shared in the offences normally associated with Christendom and must do suitable penance by yielding the religious ground completely. Liberal theology, being rooted in national state jurisdiction, has had a hard time freeing itself of the territorial complex, so that it condemns to a territorial fate anyone defending any version of Christian truth. It is an attack that touches a sensitive nerve in us all, and we offer as restitution a worldly-wise religion in terms which demonstrate that we have suitably left the past behind. Religion is a powerful trigger of the Western guilt complex, so that we smother it with a nationalistic, cultural earnestness, forgetting it was religious doctrine no less that rescinded territoriality and replaced it with liberty and freedom of conscience as the linchpin of God's incarnate and redemptive purpose.[53] In any case the theologians' assumption of citizenship being primary to religious identity, creates a guilt trip of having us confess to sins that we have long ceased to have any power to commit even if we wanted to. Consequently, anyone calling himself or herself Christian today has to swallow a large dose of defensive or relativistic pride to do so. This is in sharp contrast to the cases of Buddhists, Hindus, Muslims, Jews and others, unless, that is, we have succeeded in putting them also on the defensive. One consequence of the loss of territoriality for us in the West is that religion ceased to be synonymous with territorial security and social standing, with persuasion and personal conviction replacing collective national affirmations. However, in situations where the Church continues to retain marks of territoriality, that is, where the Church is established, theology is secondary to social prestige and political influence. Consequently, theology schools in those situations have had to secure their *raison d'être* on academic rather than pastoral grounds.

All of which implies that Christendom did have its advantages, especially that of its turning the very ground on which we stood into a natural privilege. In effect, Christendom relieved us in things religious of the need for personal and individual choice or defence, and thus of lay responsibility for theology. Christendom gave us cumulative advantage, the advantage of territorial mass, so that believers in one corner could know that their religious forms and styles were the same as those in any other part. A common Latin Mass vested in an organized clergy did in the sacerdotal sphere precisely what territory did for rank and file believers. With the fall of the empire, therefore, this cumulative religious weight broke down, and religion began to acquire a more self-conscious theological nature, detached as Christianity became from European cultural roots, or else went adrift enough in the subsoil of Western culture that it required mental effort to reconnect at the surface level. Under Christendom the notion of 'unbelief' as atheism or agnosticism was almost unknown, since

53. 'The "Christendom Era" is not,' Newbigin challenges, 'normative for the church. It can be an exhilarating and liberating experience to be called to live as Christians in a situation nearer to that of the New Testament than to that of the nineteenth century.' *Honest Religion for Secular Man*, London: SCM, 1966, 124.

all peoples believed in something, the difference being between 'misbelief' or wrong belief, and true or correct belief. It may explain why heresy, contrasted with orthodoxy, came to lose its meaning for us today. It was only in the Enlightenment that this religious outlook underwent a profound change. Once Christendom went, Christianity yielded to the force of subjective scepticism in which religion became a function of thought, rather than the historical basis of life and community. While Christianity underwent this critical shift, no similar change in scale or degree has taken place in the other world religions.

This complicates our relations with Muslims as well as with other religious traditions. For one thing, being religious means different things in the two contexts. A person calling himself or herself Christian in Paris or New York, for example, is very different from someone bearing the Muslim name in Cairo, Kano or Karachi. The sentiment so forcefully expressed in Muslim sources that 'the [religious] law of the sultan is the law of the country', is remote from the experience of Western Christians. A similar sentiment is expressed by a nineteenth-century Muslim political tract, *Uṣúl al-Siyásah* (*On the Fundamentals of Government*) to the effect that rulers 'are like a spring of water, and the rest of the administrators of this world are like streams flowing out of it. If the spring is pure, the streams will have no impurity, but if the spring is foul, then the purity of the streams' will be affected.[54] Unlike Muslims, Westerners have in the main given up identifying land and territory with faith, so that many Christian Zionists, such as Paul van Buren, feel they can defend territory for Israel only by jettisoning religion in spite of its place in Jewish history. Van Buren writes that 'Israel was founded not by divine intervention from heaven or the sending of the messiah, but by Jewish guns and Jewish effort against seemingly insuperable numerical and material odds. Had the early pioneers,' he claims, 'the fugitives from the Holocaust or supporters of the project from the Diaspora waited upon a so-called act of God, they would in all likelihood be waiting still, those who were still alive.'[55]

54. B.G. Martin, 'A Muslim Political Tract from Northern Nigeria: Muhammad Bello's *Uṣúl al-Siyása*', in Daniel F. McCall and Norman R. Bennett, eds., *Aspects of West African Islam*, vol. 5, Boston: Boston University Press, 1971, 82–3.
55. Paul van Buren, *Discerning the Way*, New York, 1980.

Pax-Islamica as Territoriality

The territorial instinct is alive and well among Muslims even though the caliphate as the Muslim 'Holy Empire' has long ceased to exist. However this territorial instinct has sometimes threatened to derail the Muslim national state as when it opposes national state sovereignty to God's law: *lá hukm illá bi-lláhi* ('there is no judgment except under God'), that is to say, government as subject to God's law. It has thus come about that the machinery of the national state is being increasingly used as a catalytic force for Pan-Muslim solidarity, with several international organizations established for the purpose: the World Muslim League; the conference of Islamic Foreign Ministers; the Arab League; the organization of Islamic countries, and so on. As Ernest Gellner, the British sociologist, put it:

> For all the indisputable diversity, the remarkable thing is the extent to which Muslim societies resemble each other. Their traditional political systems, for instance, are much more of one kind than were those of pre-modern Christendom. At least in the bulk of Muslim societies, in the main Islamic bloc between Central Asia and the Atlantic shores of Africa, one has the feeling that the same and limited pack of cards has been dealt. The hands vary, but the pack is the same. This homogeneity, in as far as it obtains, is all the more puzzling in the theoretical absence of a Church, and hence of a central authority on Faith and Morals. There is no obvious agency which could have enforced this homegeneity.[56]

Kenneth Cragg has called attention to a similar phenomenon. He cautions:

> . . . in the circumstances of the contemporary world, the failure of the household of Islam to achieve any outward form of unity higher than a fragmentary nationalism need not be interpreted as implying any essential failure in the consciousness of Muslim singularity in the face of the non-Muslim world. Islam may have baptized to itself some

56. Ernest Gellner, 'Post-Traditional Forms of Islam: The Turf and Trade, and Voices and Peanuts', in the same author's book, *Muslim Society*, Cambridge: Cambridge University Press, 1983, 99–113.

> of the forms of political order which, in parts of the West, are associated with religious neutralism or indifference. But it has shown a steady capacity to harness those forms to its own world of ideas . . . even in Turkey, where, it may be said, the concept of a laic secular state made the greatest inroads into Muslim ideas of state and religion, in the five decades since Kemal Attaturk, Islam has shown a surprising resilience and power of continuity under change . . . there can be little doubt that, for all the political diversity of its existence today behind national frontiers, Islam is no less self-conscious and singular than it ever was. Dár al-Islám is still a meaningful concept and an abiding reality. And though the political and national forms of the present day seem to belie much of Islamic history, Islam itself has demonstrated its capacity to survive in the contemporary political order with no essential loss of identity. Perhaps we doubted it could be so only because we conceived of Islamic unity in terms of empires and caliphates. If these have departed, the community they once ruled remains.[57]

Nevertheless, one should observe that Muslims have also sensed something of what might be involved in the shift from territoriality to voluntarism, what one modernist Muslim scholar calls 'the positive sides' of postmodernity, 'like diversity, the freedom to explore, the breakdown of establishment structures, and the possibility to know and understand one another . . . an historic phase that holds the possibility of bringing diverse peoples and cultures closer together than ever before.'[58] Dr Akbar goes on to say, however, that postmodernism has not made much of an impression on Muslims, though a recent book attempts to prove otherwise.[59]

57. Kenneth Cragg, *The Call of the Minaret*, Maryknoll, N.Y.: Orbis Books, 1985, 176–77.
58. Akbar S. Ahmed, 'The Threat of the Western Media to Traditional Society: The Case of Islam', unpublished manuscript, 8–9, based on Akbar and Ernest Gellner, in press, *Postmodernism and Islam*, London: Routledge & Kegan Paul. See also Akbar Ahmed, *Discovering Islam: Making Sense of Muslim History and Society*, London: Routledge, 1988.
59. Michael M.J. Fischer and Mehdi Abedi, *Debating Muslims: Cultural Dialogues in Postmodernity and Tradition*, Madison, Wis.: University of Wisconsin Press, 1990.

Thus the mismatch in terms of cross-cultural attitudes in this sphere is quite striking: at the point where the Muslim effort rises to the surface with public affirmation of religion our Christian path of religious privatization falls away to obscure the point and place of our meeting. Dr Hasan Saab, the Lebanese Muslim intellectual, or Dr Rana Kabbani, the Syrian Muslim writer,[60] calls for Christian responsibility on behalf of Muslim political and territorial grievances, while Langdon Gilkey or Thomas Altizer is calling us to abandon all Christological language as the false myth of Christian uniqueness. Muslims expect that Christians would be able to respond to Muslim grievances whereas the reality of a Christendom lost in the sand trails of history has removed the very ramparts from which to meet Muslim expectations. It has still not entered the consciousness of Muslims forcibly enough that in the post-Christendom West the Church is subordinate to the State, not in the Erastrian sense merely of being a wholly owned subsidiary of the national security state, but of playing no organizational role in government, such, for example, as the Roman Catholic Church has had in Poland. It may be precisely because Muslims instinctively sense this that they have bypassed Christian religious institutions and gone directly to Western governments and civil organizations to secure concessions.

The following paragraph is worthy of a separate discussion.

It could be pointed out that US foreign policy has been beneficial to several Muslim countries: the seven billion dollars of Egypt's foreign debt that the US forgave; the massive support that over the years the US has given to Pakistan vis-à-vis India, and to Afghanistan, Pakistan's neighbour; the long-standing support for Muslim Indonesia and its forcible annexation of East Timor; the support for Iraq until August, 1990; the support for a Muslim Somalia against a Christian Ethiopia, and for a Muslim Sudan against its Christian minorities in southern Sudan; the alliance with a Muslim Turkey against a Christian Greece, and the support for a Muslim-dominated Nigerian Federal government against a Christian Biafra, the refusal of the White House and the Bush administration in March, 1992, to

60. Rana Kabbani, *Letter to Christendom*, London: Virago Press, 1989.

meet Salman Rushdie, author of the *Satanic Verses*, in deference to Muslim sensibilities, are some well-known examples. It is an irony that the conservative Christian support of various administrations in this country has thus helped to bolster Muslim fortunes abroad.

A good deal of the extensive Christian writings on religious pluralism misses this fact, and instead bulges with all the complexes of a Christendom more honoured in the breach than the observance, although, like long-domesticated farm animals, we continue in our post-Christendom world with our nest-making instincts to gnaw at the steel barriers of our exile as if they were nourishing hay.

Territoriality and Domestic Enclavement

Whatever religion may mean to us, I maintain, it does not any longer imply territorial expression, and the success abroad of Church and gospel suggests that world Christianity is maturing without Christendom's custodial protection. By contrast, Christians in the West are increasingly a 'moral' minority: it is not just our statistical decline that matters; it is our status as a religious enclave that is forced to secure its future as an appendage to mainstream culture that clinches our marginal, secondary role. To be a Christian in our society requires, among other things, our projecting religion as a constitutional by-product, with the stress on individual rights and the legal protections for them. America is not just a 'republic' in the political sense; it is a 'republic' in the market sense of choice and options carrying no privileged hierarchy or immunity. Consequently, as Lawrence Friedman expresses it[61] religion is a matter of choice and personal inclination. 'Today,' he says triumphantly, 'we have the right to pick our own *personal* supernatural.'[62]

How we sustain the dual loyalty of membership in Church and State and the corresponding mental habit of instrumental effectiveness in the public realm alongside moral integrity in the personal sphere, remains a vexing problem. It threatens to plunge

61. Lawrence Friedman, *The Republic of Choice*, Cambridge, Mass: Harvard University Press, 1990.
62. ibid., 118.

the Church into the next, most critical stage of its development, namely, as a society that is at the behest of the strategies of special interest groups, free-market pluralism and individual advantage. House fellowships have sprung up among both Catholics and Protestants to try to answer the need created by promoting religion as a function of market forces, or, as a front-page report in *The New York Times* characterizes it, 'Home Worship is an Intimate way to Reach God',[63] and although I myself have experienced the great value of these house fellowships, they remain symptoms of the problem, which is whether faithfulness must incur the penalty of going completely domestic and marsupial.

I recognize 'intimacy' to be a powerful motive for home fellowship groups, but I am unclear as to whether the perceived failure of the churches is one of size and scale or of kind and style: have the churches become too big and gone too public in a vain gambit to retrieve an illusory Christendom, leaving the faithful to grope after small-scale private assurance, or have they failed to provide real pastoral care grounded in Scripture and tradition, concentrating instead on therapeutic values and the activist agenda of a pragmatic society? In a notice in the *Christian Century*, for example, the ideal church is described by a professional pastoral counsellor as 'a well-organized psychiatric unit' marked by 'acceptance and tolerance; equality; commitment to honesty; meaningful rituals; and mutual helpfulness',[64] the kind of white middle-class massage parlour that mainstream Protestantism has been threatening to turn into. Maybe, heaven forbid! that is inevitable, in which case house groups would be a stage along that slippery route.

Our nest-making habits acquired in Christendom's protective shadow have been overlaid with the new realities of our domestication. We find we can afford to be deeply agnostic about religion because the cultural consensus serves as the ground of ultimate concern. We are cultural believers after we cease to be religious believers. In our cultural headiness, we ransack the

63. 'More People are Staying at Home to Worship', *Sunday New York Times*, December 1, 1991, pp. 1, 44. The report is by Ari L. Goldman, author of *In Search of God at Harvard*.

64. The *Christian Century*, November 20–27, 1991, pp. 1093–95.

inheritance of Jacob for material profit and influence. The energetic exertions of our theologians, their scramble to offer religious discount in the bid to make amends for past wilfulness, and their wish to plead guilty for all forms of Western commercial, political and military excesses abroad even though they lack the power to influence or control their government – all this indicates a potent Christendom aftertaste.

Nevertheless, what has replaced Christendom is less than reassuring. Religion in our new age has become the sacrificial lamb for cultural innocence, as the novels of Virginia Woolf make clear. Consequently we appear unable to cope with the implications of Christian expansion beyond our shores, especially since such a fact might suggest religion is not about to disappear in the rest of the world, as we thought it did with the fall of Christendom. We seem keen to hail the cultural speck in our neighbour's eye, though we are tone deaf to more conspicuous evidence of religion. Our new orthodoxies are now construed and validated as psychological uplift, self-esteem and other versions of emotional quick-fix, in the name of all of which we would make sacrifices that we would begrudge Church and fellowship.

The fundamental texts of authority have become issues and concerns staked on social status, life orientation and affiliation and mood nurturing, all of which are seen as the ark destined to take us into what professionals have darkly called 'cohesive' selfhood. Whatever that means, it seldom means coming to terms with the Church's heritage of faith, service and discipleship. So many seminary groups and Church conferences have now adopted the theme, 'Seeking Justice and Empowering Ourselves', or variations thereof. Our modern tendency to see the Church in terms of individual healthy-mindedness, as a selfhood that is vulnerable to bouts of low self-esteem, is light years removed from the Church as a fellowship of faithfulness to God's promises. Our idea of truth as a question of good feelings leaves us hoist with our own petard: either we contain our disappointment and feelings of betrayal and remain positive but disconnected, or else we give in to rage, depression and corrosive self-doubt and thus remain maladjusted. A parish then can become either a chronically ill 'self', or a synthetic lifestyle enclave, in either case a parish that does not know or want to know the heights and depths, the breadth and width of sin and grace. We seem to seek life in the very things that bring death. Opulent magazines, appealing to our emptiness and forlorn plight, continue to appear with titles that make lucrative traffic in the name of the 'preferential self' and the imperial 'I', icons of New Age affluence and sensibility.

One response to this state of affairs is to capitulate, to join in the stampede of pandering to the ego, and exhaust ourselves in the energetic promotion of personal wellbeing and fulfilment. In other words, to adopt contemporary affirmations as redemptive. Yet that response indulges the self in the grim deaths of infatuation, addiction and chronic partiality. Everyone with a whiff of sanity in his or her veins should have no traffic with that way. Another response is to confront the self more in pity than in flattery, to hold the self as ambiguous rather than as assured. The wrong love of the self destroys it, while the right kind heals and restores it. We should all be challenged to embrace that path.

I recognize that we are speaking from a North American vantage point, and consequently we cannot escape the pressure of the forces that have produced our kind of religion in our kind of society. We are both beneficiaries and victims of that heritage. Whether or not the massive retrenchment of religion in the West can be halted, whether, indeed, the dramatic fall in numbers and the ruthless process of secular alterations of the religious habit can be reversed, we should place ourselves in the dynamic context of world Christianity whose presuppositions are so vastly different from those of our Christendom with its exclusivist territorial scruples. For it is in this worldwide context that we see a remarkable efflorescence of Christian life without the shibboleths of Christendom, and a relentless challenge to the territorial instinct of Muslims and others – there are many communities that share a territorial boundary with Muslims but not necessarily a religious one. Such people as Arab Christians, Iranian Zoroastrians and Bahais, Pakistani Hindus, Chinese Malaysians, Moroccan Jews, and so on, are a reminder of the restricted value of territorial designations for religion. And qualitatively as well as quantitatively, the world is becoming more and more so. Can we as believers witness to faith without the coercive recourse implicit in religious territoriality or numerical preponderance? Can we embrace democratic freedoms, including the freedom of religion, as the necessary development of the religious spirit rather than as a hostile contender with religion?

Part of the reason for our contemporary malaise has to do, as I explained, with our defensive complex about Christendom, as Mark Twain's words bear testimony, and part with our predisposition to think difference with others is a threat and a danger to be met by politically prudent calculations or else by reducing it to handy formulas of self-reproach, or perhaps by a denial of the other.

Jon Levenson has identified what he sees as a problem in cultural moralization, especially as that was developed in National Socialism. For National Socialism, 'culture is determined mostly by biology, so that one ethnic group's acceptance of another's cultural legacy [i.e., northern Europe's adoption of a Jewish-influenced Christianity] is [deemed] unnatural and takes place only because of violence . . . If the cultural system is already implicit in the biological self [i.e., the body], then any large-scale cultural shift, such as the Christianization of northern Europe, must be altogether owing to domination and in no sense the result of the greater persuasiveness of the new order.'[65]

Our modern tendency to explain all human relations in terms of power relations assumes an absolute moral autonomy for human partiality, the fragmented particularities that constitute our differences, and sees encounters between groups essentially as forms of hostility. We are left with human relationships as basically non-negotiable lines of suspicion and antagonism. The 'hermeneutics of suspicion' is brought into forced union with that of alienation, giving us the warrant to name the 'other' as illegitimate. When forced into personal contact with others, whether at work, at school or college, in shopping malls, in church or religious gatherings, or as neighbours, we have as a last resort what Le Carré has called 'the safe bastion of infinite distrust' where unconditional love is excluded.

We should develop a cross-cultural understanding of the wider

65. Jon Levenson, 'The God of Abraham and the Enemies of "Eurocentrism"', *First Things*, October 15–21, 1991, p. 17.

religious world, to begin to equip us for a world we increasingly share with others, and a world in which the role of the West requires spiritual as well as economic leadership. The challenge for Christians is whether they will reckon, for example, what they perceive as Muslim Arab attacks and insults only in national political and military terms, or whether anywhere a Christian frame of reference might apply. In other words, if the religious name has any meaning beyond what nationality and citizenship involve, then we cannot be content, as Muslims insist we should not be, with the thought that the West as a political and economic entity is an adequate substitute for religious identity and moral obligation, with the military means to look after our interests. Instead, we have to seek a deeper responsibility for witness, tolerance and sharing on the basis of God's intention for human beings.

Christians have long felt challenged to play an active public role, to say something that goes beyond considerations of national and cultural interests, to speak not just of human rights and economic wellbeing, but of truth and commitment as distilled in their own distinctive religious stream. However, they have felt powerless and clueless in knowing how to do this. The only recourse seems to be to a nostalgic Christendom because that is the closest analogy to a public role for the Church. Since such a possibility of a return to Christendom no longer exists, our attitudes to the challenge for a public ethic have been at best ambivalent, leaving us vulnerable to those who hold the title deeds of our captivity.

Many of us have found grateful, if temporary refuge in civic organizations such as the Red Cross, Amnesty International, Greenpeace, Oxfam, Habitat for Humanity, Shelter, Christian Aid, Save the Children Fund, the many UN organizations, World Vision and numerous others where we can retreat to nurse some version of Christendom's avuncular care for the world while we put on hold any committed and open religious identity. Yet these gallant organizations can scarcely solve the problem of religious marginality and moral relativism that their very success reinforces. We continue to fear that the alternative to an ascendant Christendom is the intrareligious contentiousness and wrangling of religious divines that marked the epoch called the

Thirty Years' War (1618–48), that soon followed the demise of Christendom, and that is enough to drive many of us to seek less obstreperous company elsewhere. Nevertheless, such postponement of the religious task does not deal with the fundamental issue of the many idolatries of tribe, nation, power and success.

It is hard to see how we can move forward without taking account of the new realities of the global religious context, including that of world Christianity. We seem to feel we should compensate for all the wrongs committed in the name of Christendom by yielding not only the territorial ground but the religious ground too. Furthermore, we feel that missionary work should be repudiated for its territorial presumptions. Yet such accusations fly in the face of historical facts as well as being out of step with the dynamics of the worldwide Christian expansion. We may, therefore, hope that the encounter with Third World Christians as our coreligionists, and with Muslims and others as our neighbours would encourage us to find a successor to Christendom in a form of Christianity that does not continue to make compromising concessions to nationalistic claims, materialism and individualism. However, whether or not we recover a renewed Christian vision (and I devoutly pray we do), we should still understand how and why the twentieth century seems so auspicious for Muslim religious resurgence, if not insurgency, carrying with it the corollary of a downgrading of nationalist idols. The increasing presence of Muslims in the West requires critical reflection on the issue of religious territoriality, and on making citizenship definitive of human worth and moral obligation, indeed, on whether religion can vindicate itself and transcend the idolatry of nationhood, as Muslims believe and urge.

Issues

Among the great issues confronting us today three call for urgent attention. One is the danger of giving undue or overdue emphasis to secularism and of seeing it as a more or less formidable opponent than it is. It would require great religious statesmanship in us neither to reduce religion to the categories mandated by secularism nor, on the other hand, to overlook the positive role Christian thought has played in a maturing secularism. It would help our task if we grappled with these issues in the open and public arena rather than retreating behind our familiar specialized ramparts.

The second is the pressure society brings to bear by turning religion into a matter of private values, making religion a function of special interest agendas or of the supremacy of the individual. Early Christianity had met in Gnosticism a similar challenge, with the difference that in our age the gnostic subjectivizing of Christianity has the backing of the commanding authority of the political economy. In some cases the weight and prestige of the law are tilted against Christianity's public credibility, the very credibility that has been the source of much of our democratic heritage of public and open accountability.

The third issue is the reassertion of territoriality for religion just when Christians in the West have more or less got used to the idea of the separation of Church and State. With the drive in Muslim societies towards the establishment of religious states, for example, Christian minorities have been painfully exposed. Such Christians may preserve their identity as tolerated communities faced with two uneven choices, peaceful persuasion or forcible absorption by the religious state. In either case these minorities remain vulnerable to takeover.

On the side of the West we have witnessed since about the 1960s a substantial rise in the number and diversity of religious groups coming in to settle. These groups have sometimes demanded not just the rights of citizenship, but special laws and regulations granting them religious and political concessions, concessions which severally and together whittle away at the claims of absolute national sovereignty. That is the incendiary challenge compared to which legally enacted international structures and institutions are a blank charge, for such structures and institutions, unlike religious territoriality, seek the contraction of the nation state for purposes such as economic expansion and individual improvement that exceed the capacity of nation states in their presently constituted form. These structures and institutions would reward national mobilization with the fruits of economic enterprise, while religious territoriality would impose a stigma on national identity. The paradox is this: these religious groups have entered and flourished in the West precisely because territoriality there ceased to carry religious force, with citizenship implying no religious standing whatsoever. This allowed different religious groups to enter the West and flourish. Yet once in they demand legal and political concessions that are really demands to have a notion of religious territoriality restored for them. Can the West make this adjustment without abandoning the very ground that has made it hospitable to plural religious communities? Can the branches survive if the roots are exposed?

The debate that is raging in certain quarters in the West about mission and religious pluralism is an indication of how much out of step we are with the history of religious territoriality, and how on our side we continue to flounder in the cracks between a lost Christendom and the pressures of religious territoriality. Can we give with the tolerant right hand the religious freedom that would be taken away from us with the left hand of territoriality? In consequence, whatever the attractions of territoriality, the chief argument against it is not that it would be retrogressive, though that is true, but that it would attach a stigma to religious minorities and leave them in a pejorative situation. Under territoriality religious differences would carry the force of suppression.

We cannot deal with this problem or say anything meaningful about it without being convinced ourselves that territoriality carried too severe a handicap to be advantageous to religion, and that its abandonment by Christians from both the left wing Anabaptist tradition and the right wing quasi-Erastrian groups has proved beneficial to the cause of Christian renewal and witness. Without territoriality, for example, Christians have been forced to confront the idolatry of culture and nationalism, even though many Christians have fallen victim to those things. Any theology of religious pluralism would have to tackle territoriality as a problem for religion lest a one-sided calculation interpret any Christian response as a hankering after a 'Christendom' status, a position from which any concession would be illegitimate because it would be anachronistic. Which then leaves us with an acutely embarrassing methodological question, namely, whether to make it our mission and press for concessions from all those religions that still nurture the idea of territoriality as we once did in 'Christendom', or, in view of territorial survivals in religion, whether we should make territorial retrieval the goal for interreligious dialogue, with all the disadvantages for religious minorities that we have identified.

Two clear choices then stare us in the face: one is to retreat into a nostalgic Christendom and strive for territoriality, and the other is to remain a voluntary society that would be unable to make common cause with contemporary movements of religious territoriality. However, a Christendom retreat is inconceivable, while encounter with other religions striving for territoriality is an increasing reality. Small wonder, then, that Christians feel under siege and defensive in the circumstances, for the tradition of secular accommodation that has qualified their practice of religion is being progressively overhauled by the new forces of religious territoriality whose explicit agenda demands repudiating the principle of separating Church and State. Yet without that separation the West as the successor to Christendom would have been decidedly less propitious for the thriving pluralism of religion and culture that characterizes it today. This religious dilemma is aggravated by a moral dilemma of not wishing to judge other religions while being unwilling to concede – or confront – the judgments they bring against us. By keeping ahead of others in being the first to reject on our side any monopoly of truth, we find ourselves out of step with those whose view of truth necessarily excludes our qualified version and yet whose inclusion we saw as vindicating us. Whatever our final answer to this issue, it is obvious our great historical consensus of Church, State and Society is poised to undergo a fundamental recasting.

Conclusion

Some such painful sifting is necessary in order to respond creatively to the implications of Christianity as a non-territorial religion. Turning away from non-territoriality would place us in the acute position of having to replace alleged Christian unilateralism with the serial unilateralism of religious pluralism: one religion for one culture, and one culture for one religion, a kind of microterritoriality hatched to a pluralist formula. Yet this is not religious pluralism in any meaningful sense of the term, just religious exclusiveness under a new name. It preserves territoriality as a mutually exclusive multilateral prerogative, with the religious genius becoming only a multicultural convenience, what each culture has come to regard as useful and valuable for itself. It makes impossible interreligious or intercultural encounter. Those calling us to it are not offering a way forward, however sincere their intentions, nor does its antithesis of restricted exceptionalism represent any advance. Thus we cannot accept the left-wing or right-wing status quo without playing into the hands of commissars of the politically correct lexicon, and the fragmenting that comes from legitimizing the preferred prejudices of lifestyle enclaves. It calls to mind Plato's rule in *The Republic* (Bk. IV, #423) about occupational specialization in which no one may do the job of anyone else in order that the whole polis 'may be one and not many'.

The dogma of religious pluralism has tended to promote interreligious encounter in precisely such unilateral terms, with the universe of faiths yielding culturally defined boundaries that would exclude Christian, and by implication, mutual interest. Even so, religions as the subject of comparative syncretist study have been plundered and made to yield grand archetypal myths as the so-called 'religious essence' with which writers have proceeded to unravel the whole fabric of religious particularity. Thus we have inherited the implacable Enlightenment tradition of the efficacy of universal theories, and thus too, we have denied the historical character of religion, with truth reduced to abstract imaginative deconstruction. Yet prophetic religion cannot be content with such a postmodernist project of cultural deconstruction as the arbiter of truth, or with value engendering as definitive of vocation, even if in either case culture must schematize and mediate the gospel and values express its truth claims.

6

'The Garden of Eden without the Snake?' The Moral Sting in the Cultural Tale: Some Conclusions

Introduction: Western Encounter

The Western encounter with Africa, and with other non-Western societies, has produced an ambiguous legacy of modern development, including the establishing of national states and modern educational institutions, and of pressures on Africa's ancient customs and values. In general writers on the subject have taken a jaundiced view of the consequences of such Western encounter, particularly those stemming from the colonial and missionary legacies. In their view Africa was forcibly thrust in the path of Western domination and stripped of her *amour propre* by colonial oppression and missionary cultural subversion. The scholarly development of this grand theme has magnified Africa's victim image and promoted an idyllic picture of traditional societies, a delineation containing all the primeval force of the struggle between good and evil. In order to deal with Western injustice, scholars have proposed a radical cultural relativism of absolute equality among essentially autonomous cultural systems. Such equality would avoid invidious moral judgments and the privileging of one culture over another, although in this scheme great value continues to be set on cultural equality as a sounder basis for knowledge and understanding and, therefore, as the superior, and therefore, preferred moral approach. Obviously some moral judgment is unavoidably being made even here.

In any case, the theory of cultural relativism sought on one level to cope with the demise of the West's hegemony over the rest of the world and with the dispersal of power to the former colonized peoples, Africans included. The vehemence with which missionaries condemned traditional cultures, it is argued, was only the moral version of the material superiority that the West in its military and political projects established over non-white races. Thus religion consecrated the sentiments that stemmed from military and political control. Now that the West has lost the substance of its power, the argument proceeds, it can afford to forgo its moralizing posture, although paradoxically the West by its academic specialists remains the arbiter of cultural relativism.

What remains unclear in all this apparently fundamental intellectual shift is whether the Western encounter, by the mere fact of its being Western, must be, or was, an unmitigated disaster on the religious front as well, whether the premise of cultural relativism as a defence of non-Western cultures accomplishes its declared objective of removing the West from centre stage, and, whether, in the bargain, it provides an adequate safeguard for tolerance, equality, harmony and inclusiveness. We have argued, for instance, that modern Western Christian missions, which arose after the demise of territorial Christianity in Christendom, introduced, even in the colonial context, great complexity into the Western encounter with non-Western societies by translating the Scriptures into the mother tongue, and furthermore, such mother tongue translations advanced the prospects of pluralism with as yet unassimilated implications for theology.

We cannot, for reasons enunciated here, leave the subject of the rise and expansion of the West merely with its technological and economic aspects, or with its cultural triumph, for that would neglect the special role religion has played in the West's own formation. The trick is to know how to do this accounting without condoning the violent or uncharitable attack on the heritage of others, though in the transmission of the Christian Scriptures the heritage of others became the heritage of the West too. Perhaps the very success with which the religious insights of the Western Church have been assimilated by non-Western societies has overshadowed the less spectacular, though no less real, process of the quiet re-education and reorientation of the West itself.

In any event the very technological mastery which allowed non-Western societies to be swept into the unifying net of Western domination, and by that fact to become for the first time truly united, that technology has produced fruits of paradox, including moral ennui, precisely in those institutions set up to parade the West's triumph. The monuments to war and conquest, the museums of national glory that are dwarfed by cenotaphs to the lost and fallen, the weapons of strategic security whose stockpiles, and ultimate disposal, leave their possessors no less imperilled than their targets, the sprawling bureaucratic machinery that has stalked with lucid logic victims of discrimination and left a trail of ruthless efficiency and the human and environmental degradation that has accompanied industrial mastery – all these are signs of paradox and decay from within. One worthwhile exception is the moral legacy that non-Western societies have appropriated to avert a similar fate for themselves, a legacy that the West's own rise and culminating historical expansion brought providentially within range of the whole human race. Thanks to their encounter with the West, these societies have the possibility of transcending themselves in a way that the West in its unyielding cultural self-righteousness has shown signs of failing to do.

It is important, in view of such historical paradox, not to allow the claim to stand of non-Western cultures being prelapsarian specimens of primordial purity and innocence which a herpetoid West proceeded to despoil with projects of exploitation, subterfuge and subjugation, though we must oppose Western exploitation without supporting such primordial innocence. At any rate such a claim is unflattering to these cultures, for it leaves them stranded in romantic isolation. The claim also caricatures the West and removes it from any impartial historical scrutiny. Some such claim is the unspoken operative rationale of Western scholars who would rescind any well-worn intellectual category if it carries a whiff of Christian influence, though such scholars are less critical with non-Christian traditions. That approach dissolves Christian particularity. Besides, such a procedure, when applied, or anticipated, in other religions, would be unacceptable intrusion. Self-criticism must be distinguished from self-distrust which is harder to restrict in its effects of mutual suspicion. I would thus wish to avoid pitting Africa's alleged primordial innocence against an untrustworthy fallen West. Rather, we could still concede the West's violent intrusion in Africa without losing sight of the fact that in the religious sphere the encounter was less one-sided. I would press the view that the encounter proceeded along at least two distinct, and often inconsistent lines, the political and the religious, with the language projects of religion, for instance, contradicting the logic of colonial superiority. Thus the movements that arose from the West and came to reside in Africa as missions promoted, on the level of language development, the anti-Western ethos that fed a sense of indigenous nationalism, a nationalism that may be seen as the local analogue to the cultural criticism that attended the rise of Christianity in the West. On its positive side, the nationalism of mission-educated Africans was evidence of Christianity not eradicating sources of local criticism, though on its negative side nationalism might incite ethnic malice. Whether as positive or negative, however, nationalism would be inconsistent with the charge of missionary brainwashing. Some such ambiguity and cultural parallel most certainly belonged with the religious phase of Africa's response to the West.

Cultural Innocence

The related question about cultural innocence raises comparable complex issues of analysis and explanation. If we take an historical view, cultural innocence is an inaccurate, misleading understanding of human societies and an illegitimate concealing of the tendentious basis on which we promote the view. You do not have to be a sociobiological determinist to understand how the human spirit develops cumulatively through struggle and contest to reach higher forms of consciousness, and this in spite of material or physical circumstances. It is something that writers have testified to both from the experience of unrivalled physical stamina, as with Lawrence of Arabia, and from life-sapping infirmity, as with Robert Louis Stevenson on the eve of his death. Persons or societies are alike matured and seasoned through the *Sturm und Drang* of life's inevitable ebb and flow.

Ethnic minorities, for example, subject, or vulnerable, to more than their share of misfortune, are entitled to protective attention, with safeguards against absorption by domineering neighbours, but are not thereby immune to the capacity for good and evil or to the internal rhythms of pain and growth. The laudable goal, then, of defending them need not require the spurious absence of the knowledge of good and evil. Consequently we may criticize cultural innocence without rejecting the special claims we make on behalf of particular cultures, claims, it turns out, that promote some notion of intercultural mutual recognition, even understanding. In such circumstances it is not a hindrance to think of cultures, especially weaker ones, as being ethically worth, and responsible for, more than the sum of their physical parts, and thus as worthy of ethical scrutiny and interest. However, such a procedure breaks the rules of strict cultural relativism.

Cultural Mutuality, Moral Relativism

It would thus follow, in any unrestricted consideration of the evidence, that cultures are not ethically neutral, that even unprocessed cultural facts and the laws undergirding them carry at least a trace of moral and ethical recognition, and that stripped of the norms of ethical accountability cultures in their neutral form exclude each other or else make war on each other, for neutrality flourishes on indifference and hostility on exclusion. In our mutual silences we would refrain except from value judgments; we would exercise a silent embargo on each other. The fruits of cultural innocence, plucked from the no-man's-land of moral abdication, are far more deadly than the wages of sin for which we may repent and receive forgiveness. Consequently, intercultural communication is necessary in order to transcend the implicit ethnocentrism of superior cultural detachment, still the old unilateralism under which we propagated ideal or bestial images of each other. Cultural recognition can hardly be separated from qualitative appreciation and judgment. We 'see' because we compare and contrast, that is, we introduce into the stuff of perception certain normative comparative criteria: homelessness as defined by demographic statistics is short – and needful – of moral compassion for the less fortunate. Consequently, the rule that says that my culture is superior or inferior to yours is little different in reverse, and would not matter unless we intend to commend, or condemn, with it. Such commending or condemnation presumes the capacity for judgment, if not for discernment, and it would be much healthier to deal in the open with that fact than to pretend it is alien to culture and can be swept off the field by some objective momentum. In effect, we should grasp the ethical challenge implied in cross-cultural relationships and responsibility, approach human difference and diversity as a resource for truth-seeking and accept the possibility of mutual correction and instruction as profoundly consistent with the enterprise of being human. The space in which we may be true to ourselves would, by implication, be hospitable to mutual discovery and to the pursuit of interpersonal virtues like tolerance, equality, harmony and generosity. Tolerance of difference, equality in terms of our mutual inadequacies, harmony as a restraint on self-interest and generosity in preferring one another –these and more are the genuine currency of intercultural traffic and they invoke trust of a transcendent kind.

The situation, however, has been sadly different. We had thought to be able to promote cultural pluralism by deploying arguments of cultural relativism, but found we had created difficulties far worse than the defects we set out to remedy, for cultural relativism led us, unprepared, into moral relativism. The methods of cultural investigation are lamentably unsuited to the ends of moral reasoning,[1] so that using cultural description to condemn, or commend, the moral position produced mixed results for culture and for moral reasoning: cultural facts became absolutized as moral precepts and moral precepts became relativized as cultural precursors. Consequently, religion came to be viewed as a cultural anticlimax or flag of convenience, as a mystical fixation with cultural forms, with the Church as the religious chrome of vintage culture, all shine and no torque. Culture as religious false consciousness resulted in moral confusion, and incited ambitions that cultural systems were unable

1. Evans-Pritchard delicately raised a similar question for anthropology. He wrote that with regard to religion the method of the anthropologist is the phenomenological one. But, he said, many anthropologists went beyond that scope. He continued: 'It was precisely because so many anthropological writers did take up a theological position, albeit a negative and implicit one, that they felt an explanation of primitive religious phenomena in causal terms was required, going, it seems to me, beyond the legitimate bounds of the subject.' Evans-Pritchard, *Theories of Primitive Religion*, Oxford: Clarendon Press, 1965, 17.

to restrain or guide, having conceived them as value-free.

By contrast, the evidence as we know it, or can know it, supports a teleology to make it cohere and stand up, while teleology itself needs to be grounded in an 'epistemology of the concrete' to make it valid. Furthermore, there is support in the evidence for intercultural and crosscultural mutuality as the foundation of religious transmission, whatever the ambiguities of script, context and result, a point I should now like to expand.

Strict cultural neutrality, assuming it is possible, cannot by itself promote equality or harmony between cultures. On the contrary, if all cultures are equal, so that anything and everything we find in one culture we can find in another, then alienation and discord between cultures, what we have identified as serial ethnocentrism, are the only results we can expect. Absolute equality creates absolute hostility, since any sign of cross-cultural interest must be read as proof of unwarranted interference, one culture sticking its nose into another culture, thus violating the rule of cultural autonomy. In conditions of optimal equality, then, a singular lack of curiosity and interest in the other must arise to safeguard cultural autonomy and characterize intercultural relations, assuming, that is, such relations are any longer feasible. In a condition of absolute cultural equality, total ignorance of each other would turn out to be blissful virtue to be preferred to knowledge and informed interest in each other's affairs, and ignorance is fertile ground for caricature. It may be this situation that Ernest Gellner has in mind when he writes:

> . . . the imaginary universe of our hermeneutic relativist is symmetrical. It somewhat resembles the expanding universe of the physicists, in which discrete galaxies all recede from each other, and the universe as a whole looks much the same from any given vantage point. The important thing is, indeed, that there must be no privileged vantage point. This was the ideology of colonialism. The truth is that all cultures are equal, and no single one of them has the right to judge and interpret the others in its own terms, and, above all (the ultimate horror), it must not claim that the world is correctly described in its own terms. It is this fearful symmetry which is a total and disastrous travesty

> of the world we live in. Anyone who endorses it cannot even begin to understand the present human condition . . . The real and greatest objection to relativism is not that it proposes a false solution (though it does), but that it prevents us from even seeing and formulating our problem.[2]

Gellner speaks confidently of knowledge of the scientific and technological kind as being beyond culture and morality and controlling our world in a way that is outside our power to affect. This knowledge is culturally impartial and non-endorsing, and is not confined by place and time of origin, being available to any and all. However, it is not clear what room this leaves for cultural participation of the religious kind where reciprocity would occur even in the context of uneven technological resources. Thus, it may be said of Bible translation that the cultural renewal and improvement it made possible in the field was unrelated to any advantages it bestowed, or did not bestow, on the missionaries' own culture. It is impartial knowledge which is necessarily culturally endorsing at the point of reception, and sometimes also mutually transforming.

The translation work of missions was in this sense the diametric opposite of the blissful virtue of relativism, and for that reason became the target of criticism. Missionary translation represented precisely what was deemed wrong with cultural asymmetry, with the idea of one culture bringing something that another culture is assumed to lack. Such an idea of cross-cultural mission offends our sense of intercultural equality, although in Bible translation, at least, some level of cultural give-and-take was essential to the enterprise.

When we set out to clarify the African circumstances of a transmitted Christianity and its indigenous appropriation, we would, as a corollary, be embarking on exploring the form and meaning of mutual knowledge in cross-cultural communication, with a tacit recognition that such communication, when con-

2. Ernest Gellner, *Postmodernism, Reason and Religion*, London and New York: Routledge, 1992, 56–7, 62. Gellner in this work targets for stringent criticism the ideas of Clifford Geertz on relativism. See Geertz, 'Anti antirelativism', *American Anthropologist*, 1984, 263–278.

ducted in the mother tongue, is feasible only as a two-way, bilateral process. There is, thus, at least an implicit continuous dialogue between missionaries and Africans, just as inevitably as there is, according to C.S. Lewis, 'an implicit continuous commentary in translation'.

Tacit Language, Bible Translation

All cultural systems depend on what Michael Polanyi has called 'tacit language' for their inner vitality, and not simply on conscious, deliberate, focused acts of speech and reflection, those aspects of communication that form the unacknowledged background to the active foreground of formal discourse.[3] It is, for example, nearly impossible to try to recall all the cluttered items of marginalia compressed in the attic or garage before someone has disturbed the scene, when subliminal details surge to the surface. This is especially so with mother tongues that are undisturbed and 'underwhelmed' with written texts. In those tongues much of the most vital and statistically most preponderant forms of communication take place in the 'background', in what is half-said, half-unsaid, with gestures, signs, with periphrastic and interrupted conventions, things that frustrate and try the avatars of analytic discourse. Yet Polanyi is right that the discourse of deliberate analysis and consciousness is intelligible and fruitful because of the background afterglow which suffuses the formal landscape of discourse with evocative intimations, the light of effortless recollection by which we transmit and receive coded and decoded signals. Given the special merit of Polanyi's 'tacit language', it may be thought that the stiff, joyless posture of Bible translators would drain the indigenous reservoir of all spontaneity and subtlety, with the Bible as a scarecrow in a barren meadow. However, we would do well to remember the non-loquacious, non-aleatory narrative style of Scripture, those pearls of pithy, simple, economic wisdom that reek of earth, breeding and human intimacy, narrative themes that bespeak an Instructor long before schools appeared in the land. It is this implicit language that Bible translation has done so

3. Michael Polanyi, *The Tacit Dimension*, London, 1966.

much to promote, not just as a subtheme of textuality, but as its overt impulse and manifestation.

It is, I think, an identical point George Steiner has made about language, whatever his own complex attitudes on the matter, to the effect that: 'Languages codify immemorial reflexes and twists of feeling, remembrances of action that transcend individual recall, contours of communal experience as subtly decisive as the contours of sky and land in which a civilization ripens. An outsider', he challenges, 'can master a language as a rider masters his mount; he rarely becomes as one with its undefined, subterrenean motion,'[4] or as aware of the hidden throb and rhythm that power the outward action.

Bible translation in the field setting cultivated this great, native impulse, dusting off evocative films that have lain undisturbed over the storehouse of memory in order to make their implicit treasure compatible with the public truths of Scripture. In the people's tongue lay the jewel of great price. Such compatibility, unrehearsed and unanticipated, provided for mutual knowledge and encounter with the West, whether or not missionaries set out consciously with such an agenda. It is impossible in the field to embark on learning the mother tongue for the purpose of reproducing in it the greatest of texts without opening at the same time channels of mutual transformation in the deeper cultural hinterland of both recipient and transmitter. It would consequently be hard to indicate how anything else has done more to induce changes in the forms of Western Christianity itself than the feedback effects, the 'tacit dimension', of translating the Scriptures into non-Western languages. Such translating is marked by the sheer diversity and range of materials appropriated, the figures, colour, music, artistic styles, idioms and tones that are adopted and incorporated into regular usage, a process that in detail and combined effect has left its mark on the worldwide practice of Christianity, even though for its part Western theology may have been slow to respond.

Translation broadly considered demands a special case for Bible translation vis-à-vis the ethnographic projects of field anthropology. Godfrey Lienhardt thus described such ethno-

4. George Steiner, *Language and Silence: Essays on Language, Literature and the Inhuman*, New York: Atheneum, 1970, 125.

graphic projects when he wrote: 'The problem of describing to others how members of a remote tribe think . . . begins to appear largely as one of translation, of making the coherence primitive thought has in the language it really lives in, as clear as possible in our own . . . [It is a translation in which we] mediate between their habits of thought, which we have acquired with them, and those of our own society. In doing so, it is not finally some mysterious "primitive philosophy" that we are exploring but the farther potentialities of our own thought and language.'[5] For such ethnographic projects translation is a reflexive act in which the West can demonstrate its superior prowess and make the shift on the basis of an implicit idea of progress from the 'primitive tribe' to the modern West. Under colonial control such a shift was executed with tools of subjugation and order. Bible translating, on the other hand, required give-and-take.

Even so, it is true that in some cases at least, Bible translation, or better, Bible translators, aided and abetted this colonial process of control, turning over knowledge and skills gained in translation to the 'civilizing' mission of administrators. In general, however, Bible translation was far too ambiguous, too locally encrusted with tacit nuances and other unprocessed indigenous penumbra, to be of much predictable use to colonial rule, and was consequently often curbed or else quarantined to contain its effects. In many places, the policy of colonial administrations to stigmatize missionary language schemes was effective, cutting off any impartial interest, then or now, in the otherwise obvious achievements of such language work. As a result, a rich field continues to go unexplored, or underexplored.

Translation, Colonialism and Ethnology

Be that as it may, field ethnography as systematic inquiry looked to, or else tended to find in, colonialism an ally. Thus did Malinowski ally himself with Lord Lugard, the architect of Britain's tropical African empire, arguing that 'an important task of anthropology was to provide scientific recipes for facilitating

5. Godfrey Lienhardt, 'Modes of Thought', in *The Institutions of Primitive Society*, 96–7.

colonial control.'[6] It may be this kind of situation that led Jacques Derrida to complain that professional ethnographers, in particular Lévi-Straussian structuralists, are guilty of ethnocentrism. He challenges: 'To say that a people do not know how to write because one can translate the word which they use to designate the act of inscribing as "drawing lines", is that not as if one should refuse them "speech" by translating the equivalent word by "to cry", "to sing", "to sigh"? Indeed "to stammer" . . . And ought one to conclude that the Chinese are a people without writing because the word *wen* designates many things besides writing in the narrow sense?'[7] Derrida maintains that ethnology could emerge as a discipline only because the West itself had gone through a 'decentreing' when its own sense of the history of its metaphysics 'had been dislocated, driven from its locus, and forced to stop considering itself as the culture of reference.'[8] Yet, as Derrida concedes, ethnology as a European science assumes as operatively valid the premises of ethnocentrism that it has set itself up to denounce, which prepares the stage, among other things, for calling Lévi-Strauss to task.

The 'ethnocentrism' that Derrida criticizes has its roots in the Enlightenment humanism of Voltaire, Rousseau and Hegel, among others, writers for whom the snake of historical change has left the Garden of Eden. In his inaugural lecture at the Collège de France, for example, Lévi-Strauss considers all ethnology as an act of translation. He declared: 'When we consider some system of belief . . . the question which we ask ourselves is indeed, "what does all this mean or *signify*?", and to answer it we force ourselves to *translate* into our language rules originally stated in a different code.'[9] While this might appear to 'balance the books',

6. Cited in Obafume F. Onoge, 'The Counterrevolutionary Tradition in African Studies: The Case of Applied Anthropology', in Gerrit Huizer and Bruce Mannheim, eds., *The Politics of Anthropology*, The Hague: Mouton, 1979. See also Malinowski, 'The Rationalisation of Anthropology and Administration', *Africa*, vol. 3, no. 4, 1930.

7. Derrida, *Of Grammatology*, trans. Gayatri C. Spivak, Baltimore: Johns Hopkins University Press, 1976, 123.

8. Derrida, 'Structure, Sign, and Play in the Discourse of the Human Sciences', in *Writing and Difference*, trans. Alan Bass, Chicago: University of Chicago Press, 1978, 282.

9. Claude Lévi-Strauss, *The Scope of Anthropology*, trans. Sherry Ortner Paul and Robert A. Paul, London: Jonathan Cape, 1967, 80.

as it were, and to make for equal exchange, what George Steiner innocently terms 'exchange without loss',[10] in fact it reaps dividends for the West's own humanism, as Derrida argues, and as Lienhardt and Malinowski prove. The Western encounter with non-Western societies must on this basis alone constitute an embezzlement of other people's treasures, legitimated by the effective control Europe asserted over the heritage and destiny of the subject races.

The universalist categories of Western Enlightenment humanism have produced, beyond such practical ethnographic and political dividends, the theoretical intellectual format that makes little distinction between ethnographic 'translation' and Bible translation, both being dehistoricized and stabilized as timeless facets of 'primitive nature', and both denoted as transparent episodes of a hegemonic universalist process. Valentine Mudimbe may be right on target if it is this phenomenon he has in mind when he speaks of the West 'inventing Africa' and leaving no space for Africa's own contribution,[11] although, as I have argued, the picture is a lot more complex with missionary translations of the Scriptures. It is, nevertheless, a fact that the legacy of the Enlightenment, in predisposing us to look for universal unities and laws in languages, has exercised a griplock on our freedom to take in alternative readings from the deceptively similar activities of ethnographic translation and Bible translation.

In her stimulating study of translation and its colonial context, the Indian scholar, Tejaswini Niranjana, says ethnographic transcription adopted the convention of 'the complete effacement of the speaking or experiencing subject from the scientific texts of anthropology and its displacement into the genre of personal narrative.'[12] Such an approach tries to legitimize cultural encounter as a one-way traffic with double emphasis: imposing on the non-literate world the written technology of the West and

10. Steiner, *After Babel*, New York: Oxford University Press, 1975, 302.

11. V. Mudimbe, *The Invention of Africa*, Bloomington, Ind.: Indiana University Press, 1989.

12. Tejaswini Niranjana, *Siting Translation: History, Post-Structuralism, and the Colonial Context*, Berkeley & Los Angeles: University of California Press, 1992, 82.

containerizing non-literate gestures like feelings, intentions and figures of speech with comprehensive rules of exposition and interpretation, all of which says that actions of 'natives' speak not louder than our words. Everything in the ethnographic world *means and signifies* something which is in the power of the external observer to give or withhold. This is the opposite of the view of Walter Benjamin that certain (Western) works of art exist deliberately *not* to be translated, because 'any translation which intends to perform a transmitting function cannot transmit anything but information – hence, something inessential. This is the hallmark of bad translations.'[13] Another way of stating this is to say that certain works maintain their integrity by defying the intrusive efforts of outsiders, in which case the predominance of Western scholars in ethnography as empirical science demonstrates that ethnography lacks the power to repel the unsolicited attention of outsiders. Yet it is not clear why, for example, descriptive ethnography should represent a less objectionable native intrusion merely for not raising normative questions than religious inquiry, or why Africans should be less at risk of contamination thereby. Furthermore, what happens when, as with the Bible, you have a text that, by its very nature, is a *translated*, and therefore *translatable* text, a Bible whose transcendent status is almost everywhere a function of the interlayered, multitrack complexity of mother tongues that in an endless translation stream pour from, and into, its pages?

It is hardly consistent or adequate with regard to such a text to speak in the manner of Enlightenment humanism of an original, pure essential speech, the *reine Sprache*, that lies behind all words, to be located somewhere in the deep, unfathomable structure of language, in this instance Latin grammar. Thus did such proponents believe in a sort of afterlife in which they would resurrect from verbal mortality the sanctified unity of linguistic intention.[14] Benjamin held out such prospects before us when he

13. Walter Benjamin, 'The Task of the Translator', in *Illuminations*, ed. Hannah Arendt, trans. Harry Zohn, New York: Schocken Books, 1969, 69. Cited also in Niranjana, 1992, 113.

14. The idea recalls the words of George Steiner when he declares: 'I do not, therefore, believe that an answer . . . to the negating epistemology of the surd . . . can be found, if it can be found at all, within linguistic or literary theory . . . I want to ask whether a hermeneutics and a reflex of valuation – the encounter

spoke of a single intention underlying each language, an intention that is expressed in the striving towards a 'pure language', the *reine Sprache*, which Niranjana summarizes in the following way: 'Every translation, in taking the text further from its origins, raises it spiritually into a realm where it can approximate the *reine Sprache* more closely. Julian Roberts compares Benjamin's notion of translation to the Romantic concept of *Kritik*, which was supposed to 'raise the power' of a work by creating a fuller universe of meanings through intense contemplation. For Benjamin, suggests Roberts, *Kritik* could be a paradigm for intellectual activity other than that which is purely poetic.'[15] Conceivably, *Kritik* might also be a paradigm for intellectual activity that is spiritual, i.e. the 'intense contemplation' of spirit, James Joyce's 'epiphany' and Benjamin's 'aura', as Steiner observed.[16]

Benjamin is certainly flexible enough to be read in a multitude of ways, and one reading that may not be an illegitimate construction of his intention would be the theological implication of his work. This means we may extend his notion of 'pure speech' beyond meanings and verbal representation to a reality whose presence is signified, in Newman's phrase, by the 'testimony born to truth by the mind itself',[17] including the habits by which the heart learns to trust, a teleology vindicated in encounter of the personal kind. The Scriptures in the mother tongue were eminently predisposed to effect such an encounter, with the autobiographical testimony its visible proof and identity.

These considerations, taken together, constitute a compelling case for going beyond Frazer and Lévy-Bruhl, beyond the anti-

---

with meaning in the verbal sign, in the painting, in the musical composition, and the assessment of the quality of such meaning in respect of form – can be made intelligible, can be made answerable to the existential facts, if they do not imply, if they do not contain, a postulate of transcendence.' George Steiner, *Real Presences: Is there anything in what we say?* London: Faber & Faber, 1989, 133–34.

15. Niranjana, 1992, 116. See also Julian Roberts, *Walter Benjamin*, Atlantic Highlands, N.J.: Humanities Press, 1983.

16. Steiner, *Real Presences*, 112. We might amend Steiner to the effect that the fire of revelation contains the truth of which authentic language is testimony.

17. Ian Ker, *John Henry Newman*, Oxford, 1990, 646.

Aristotelian determinism of logical positivists or the Enlightenment doctrine of the primacy and adequacy of universal theories, beyond cultural reductionism and philosophical idealism, and, indeed, beyond the hostile polarization between authentic ethnography and the mother tongue work of Christian missions. A more adequate anthropology would have to embrace facets of material culture alongside the internal indigenous reflection that gives narrative coherence, dynamic sense and moral resonance to human existence. The human family is a unity and diversity not only of cultural forms but of intellectual endowment, and the development of that unity and diversity is as much a mutual task as it is self-directed. Consequently, religion and ethnography need not diverge or cancel each other out in their work of describing and elucidating this phenomenon, since any divergence between so-called scientific ethnography and religion as a normative code incurs the double jeopardy of cultural absolutization and moral vacuity. Religion emptied of cultural specificity is a worthless abstraction, just as ethnographic details cut off from judgment become an incoherent and meaningless miscellaneous jumble. Conversely, religion restricted to its material forms would paralyse the capacity for ethical action, and ethnography sublimated into moral advantage would create Chosen People excesses.

What is a danger in ethnographic science would be a peril in theological inquiry. Theological integrity requires the harmony of knowledge and practice, of theory and experience, of precept and example, and is at risk when we drive a wedge between what we know, or claim to know, about God, and what we do. As a medieval scholar put it, 'God's deceiving the servant is that He should provide him with knowledge which demands practice, and then deprive him of the practice.'[18] Such separation breeds an implacable dualism that strikes at the root of religious integrity and, as we saw in earlier chapters, results in infecting the sources of cultural renewal. That, plus the objective inquiries of scientific ethnography, would, so to speak, bring on the 'meadow blues' much sooner than the religious inquiry implicit in Bible translation. It is one of the reasons we should look to the field setting of

18. William C. Chittick, *Ibn al-'Arabi's Metaphysics of Imagination: The Súfi Path of Knowledge*, Albany: State University of New York Press, 1989, 151.

such translation, with its concrete context of mother tongue specificity, in order to find a realistic basis for making mutually instructive distinctions and connections as well as for engaging in responsible intercultural and cross-cultural encounter. The metaphor I have used in this context is the 'one' and the 'many' as a way of harmonizing the ideal and the real, faith and conduct, the universal and the particular, word and deed, concept and perception, idea and figure, norm and prescription, symbol and material form, unity and diversity, and so on.

On the matter of Christianity and cultural preservation, I have argued Bible translating to be a vehicle of enormous significance for indigenous cultures, that the process as such fosters change-in-continuity, familiarity-in-the-strange, mystery-in-knowledge, tacit-cultural-values-in-formal-discourse, etc. Some such unity-in-diversity was characteristic of the historical projects of missionary translations, and indicates a potentially positive mutual impact of world Christianity on world cultures.

A crucial operative premise in this aspect of the missionary enterprise is a valid religious history preceding, and complementing, the work of Bible translating, an assumption, in effect, of indigenous societies not being strangers to change, and of religious change itself as the reorientation of the intellectual and moral life being as valid for Africans as it was for the Western heirs to Archimedes and Zeno. Such religious history is part and parcel of the wider, more general human process of true self-discovery and enlarging the scope of mutual understanding and sympathy, and indicates an historical consciousness that is at variance with the doctrine of cultural innocence. Such a doctrine, however well motivated, represents a setback for mutual understanding and personal responsibility. From the nature of the evidence we have considered, the indications are that world Christianity has thrived, and continues to thrive, without the shibboleths of philosophical relativism, or, in the matter at hand, without promoting a false dehistoricized cultural innocence, and if that were so, then religion in that guise would be an important source for human potential and global awareness, in which case we should see the expansion of the one as conducive to the other, and vice versa.

Bibliography

1

Allen, Frederick Lewis, *Only Yesterday*, 1931, repr. New York: Bantam Books, 1959

Aristotle, *Nicomachean Ethics*, in *Introduction to Aristotle*, ed. Richard McKeon, New York: The Modern Library of Random House, 1947

Arnold, Matthew, 'Culture and Anarchy' in *Selected Prose*, ed. P.J. Keating, London: Penguin Classics, 1987

Averroës, *The Incoherence of the Incoherence* (Tahâfut al-Tahâfut) 2 vols., ed. and trans. Simon van den Bergh, London: Luzac & Co., 1954

Bacon, Francis, *Advancement of Learning*, 1605, ed. G.W. Kitchin, London: J.M. Dent & Sons, 1915

The Masculine Birth of Time, 1603; in *The Philosophy of Francis Bacon*, trans. and ed. B. Farrington, Chicago: University of Chicago Press, 1964

New Atlantis in *The Works of Francis Bacon* vol. III, eds. J. Spedding, R.L. Ellis and D.D. Heath, London, 1857

Barish, Evelyn, *Emerson: The Roots of Prophecy*, Princeton: Princeton University Press, 1989

Benedict, Ruth, *Patterns of Culture*, Boston: Houghton Mifflin Co., 1934, 1961, 1989

Bidney, David, 'The Concept of Value in Modern Anthropology' in J. Kroeber, ed., *Anthropology Today: An Encyclopedic Inventory*, Chicago: University of Chicago Press, 1953, 682–99

Bury, J.B., *A History of Freedom of Thought*, New York: Henry Holt & Co., 1913

Butler, Joseph, *Sermons*: London, 1862

Carey, John, *The Intellectuals and the Masses: Pride and Prejudice among the Literary Intelligentsia, 1880–1938*, London: Faber, 1992

Chesterton, G.K., *All Things Considered*, Philadelphia: Dufour Editions, 1908, 1969

Collingwood, R.G., *An Essay on Metaphysics*, Oxford: Oxford University Press, repr. Lanham, Md.: University Press of America, 1972

Emerson, Ralph Waldo, 'The American Scholar' in *Selections from Ralph Waldo Emerson*, ed. Stephen E. Whicher, Boston: Houghton Mifflin Co., 1960

Evans-Pritchard, Sir Edward, *A History of Anthropological Thought*, ed. André Singer, New York: Basic Books, 1981

Theories of Primitive Religion, Oxford: Clarendon Press, 1965

Freud, Sigmund, *The Future of an Illusion*, ed. & trans. James Strachey, New York: W.W. Norton, 1961

Introductory Lectures on Psycho-analysis, 4th edition, trans. Joan Riviere, London, 1933

Gillman, Peter and Leni, *Collar the Lot! How Britain Intervened and Expelled Wartime Refugees*, London and New York: Quartet Books, 1980

Glover, T.R., *The Conflict of Religions in the Early Roman Empire*, 3rd edition, London: Methuen, 1909. Repr. New York: Cooper Square Publishers, 1975

Grubb, Kenneth, review article, 'The Relations of Church and State' in *International Review of Missions*, vol. 36, no. 142, April, 1947

Hartman, Geoffrey H., 'Art and Consensus in the Era of Progressive Politics', in *The Yale Review*, vol. 80, no. 4, October 1992.

Hastings, Adrian, *A History of English Christianity: 1920–1985*, London & Glasgow: Collins Fount Paperbacks, 1987

Henson, Barbara, *A Straight-out Man: F. W. Albrecht and Central Australian Aborigines*, Melbourne: Melbourne University Press, 1992

Herskovits, Melville, *Man and His Works*, New York: Alfred A. Knopf, 1948

Hocking, William Ernest, *The Coming World Civilization*, London: George Allen & Unwin, 1956

Hourani, Albert, *Islam in European Thought*, Cambridge: Cambridge University Press, 1992

Johnson, Paul, review article, 'Eliminate the negative . . .' in *The Sunday Times Book Review*, 12 July, 1992

Kant, Immanuel, *Critique of Judgement*, trans. J.H. Bernard. New York: Hafner Press of Macmillan Publishing Co., 1951

Critique of Pure Reason, 1781, trans. N. Kemp Smith. London: Macmillan, 1929

Klaaren, Eugene M., *Religious Origins of Modern Science: Belief in Creation in Seventeenth-Century Thought*, Lanham, Md.: University Press of America, 1985

Lamb, Charles and Mary, *Tales from Shakespeare*, New York: Grosset & Dunlap, N.D.

Lawday, David, 'My Country, Right . . . or What?' in *The Atlantic*, vol. 268, no. 1

Levenson, Jon D., 'The God of Abraham and the Enemies of Eurocentrism' in *First Things*, Oct. 15–21, 1991

Lewis, C.S., *Christian Reflections*, Grand Rapids, Mich.: Wm. B. Eerdmans, 1967, and London: Fount Paperbacks

Miracles: A Preliminary Study, London and Glasgow: Fontana Books, 1963

'New Learning and New Ignorance' in *Oxford History of English Literature: English Literature in the Sixteenth Century*, London and New York: Oxford University Press, 1954

'The Vision of John Bunyan' in *Selected Literary Essays*, Cambridge: Cambridge University Press, 1979, 146–53

Medawar, Sir P., 'On the Effecting of All Things Possible' in *The Listener*, lxxxii.

Meyer, Ernest H., *Elizabethan Chamber Music: The History of a Great Art from the Middle Ages to Purcell*, London: Lawrence & Wishart, 1946

Mill, John Stuart, *Journals and Debating Speeches: Collected Works of John Stuart Mill* vol. xxvii, London: Routledge; Toronto: University of Toronto Press, 1988

Newbigin, Lesslie, *The Open Secret*, Grand Rapids, Mich.: Wm. B. Eerdmans, 1978, 1981

Oman, John, *The Natural and the Supernatural*, Cambridge: Cambridge University Press, 1931

Orwell, George, *A Collection of Essays*, New York: Harcourt Brace Jovanovich, 1953

Plato, *The Republic* in *The Collected Dialogues*, eds. Edith Hamilton and Huntington Cairns, New York: Pantheon Books for Bollingen Foundation, 1961

Rolleston, Thomas William, *Life of Gotthold Ephraim Lessing*, 1889

Ruskin, John, *The Art Criticism of John Ruskin*, ed. and abridged Robert L. Herbert, New York: Da Capo Press, 1964

Russell, Bertrand, *Autobiography*, London: Unwin Paperbacks, 1975, repr. 1989

Schiller, Friedrich, *Über naive und sentimentalische Dichtung*, 1796

Schlesinger, Arthur Jr, *The Disuniting of America*, New York: W.W. Norton & Co., 1992

'The Opening of the American Mind' in *The New York Times Book Review*, July 23, 1989

Schopenhauer, Arthur, *The World as Will and Representation* 2 vols., trans. E.F.J. Payne, New York: Dover, 1958, 1969

Steiner, George, *Real Presences: The Leslie Stephen Memorial Lecture*, Cambridge: Cambridge University Press, 1986

Strachey, Lytton, *Eminent Victorians*, New York: Modern Library, 1918.

Strolz, Walter, 'The Humanism (sic.) of the Other: On the Philosophy of Emmanuel Levinas' in *Studies in Interreligious Dialogue*, vol. 2., no. 1, 1992

Tawney, R.H., *The Radical Tradition: Twelve Essays on Politics, Education & Literature*, London: Penguin Books, 1966

Thomas, Keith, *Religion and the Decline of Magic*, New York: Charles Scribner's Sons, 1971

Tillich, Paul, *Theology of Culture*, New York: Oxford Galaxy Book, 1959, 1969

Toynbee, Arnold J., *Christianity Among the Religions of the World*, New York: Charles Scribner's Sons, 1957

Trevor-Roper, Hugh, 'The Paracelsian Movement' in *Renaissance Essays*, Chicago: Chicago University Press, 1985

Religion, the Reformation, and Social Change, London:

Macmillan, 1967
Troeltsch, Ernst, *Religion in History*, Minneapolis, Minn.: Fortress Press, 1991
Turgenev, Ivan, *Fathers and Children*, 1861
Walker, D.P., *Spiritual and Demonic Magic: From Ficino to Campanella*, London: The Warburg Institute, University of London, 1958
Wightman, W.P.D., *Science in a Renaissance Society*, London: Hutchinson University Library, 1972
Williams, Bernard, *Ethics and the Limits of Philosophy*, Cambridge, Mass.: Harvard University Press, 1985
Wilson, F. Paul, Letter to the editor in *New York Times Book Review*, Aug. 13, 1989
Winckelmann, *Werke*, Dresden, 1808–25

2

Amegatcher, Andrew W., 'Akropong: 150 Years Old' in *West Africa*, July 14, 1986
Austen, Ralph, 'Africans Speak; Colonialism Writes: The Transcription and Translation of Oral Literature Before World War II', Boston University Discussion Paper, *AH Number 8*, 1990
Belloc, Hilaire, *Cranmer, Archbishop of Canterbury, 1533–1556*, Philadelphia: J.P. Lippincott & Co., 1931
Bradley, Henry, *The Making of English*, New York and London: Macmillan, 1904
Christaller, J.G., *Dictionary of the Asante and Fante Language: Called Twi*, 1881, 2nd edition Basel: Basel Evangelical Missionary Society, 1933
Colenso, John W., *Bringing Forth Light: Five Tracts on Bishop Colenso's Zulu Mission*, Pietermaritzburg: University of Natal; Durban: Killie Campbell Africana Library, 1982
Comaroff, Jean and John, *Of Revelation and Revolution: Chrsitianity, Colonialism and Consciousness in South Africa*, Chicago: University of Chicago Press, 1991
Cronin, Vincent, *A Pearl to India: The Life of Robert de Nobili*, London: Rupert Hart Davis, 1959
Danquah, J.B., *The Akan Doctrine of God*, London: Lutterworth Press, 1944
Davis, Asa J., 'The Orthodoxy of the Ethiopian Church' in *Tarikh* vol. 2, no. 1
Debrunner, Hans W., *A History of Christianity in Ghana*, Accra, Ghana: Waterville Publishing House, 1967
Deissman, Adolf, *The New Testament in the Light of Modern Research*, The Haskell Lectures. New York: Doubleday, Doran & Co., 1929
Doke, Clement M., *The Phonetics of the Zulu Language*, a special publication of *Bantu Studies*, a journal devoted to the scientific study

of Bantu, Hottentot and Bushmen vol. II, July 1926. Johannesburg: University of Witwatersrand Press

'Scripture Translation into Bantu Languages' in *Contributions to the History of Bantu Linguistics*, eds. C.M. Doke and D.T. Cole, Johannesburg: University of Witwatersrand Press, 1961

Dvornik, Francis, *Byzantine Missions Among the Slavs: SS. Constantine-Cyril and Methodius*, New Brunswick, N.J.: Rutgers University Press, 1970

Erasmus, Desiderius, *Christian Humanism and the Reformation: Selected Writing* (with the life of Erasmus by Beatus Rhenanus), ed. John C. Olin, New York: Harper Torchbooks, 1965

Fabian, Johannes, *Language and Colonial Power: The Appropriation of Swahili in the Former Belgian Congo, 1880–1938*, Cambridge: Cambridge University Press, 1986

Fuze, Magema M., *The Black People: And Whence They Came*, Pietermaritzburg: University of Natal Press; Durban: Killie Campbell Africana Library, 1922, 1979

Gérard, Albert S., *Four African Literatures: Xhosa, Sotho, Zulu, Amharic*, Berkeley and Los Angeles: University of California Press, 1971

Guy, Jeff, *The Heretic: A Study of the Life of John William Colenso: 1814–1883*, Johannesburg: Ravan Press; Pietermaritzburg: University of Natal Press, 1983

Haile, Getatchew, 'A Christ for the Gentiles: The Case of the za-Krestos of Ethiopia' in *Journal of Religion in Africa* vol. 15, no. 2

Holmes, Oliver Wendell, *The Autocrat of the Breakfast Table*, 1858

The Influence of the English Bible upon the English Language and upon English and American Literatures, New York: American Bible Society, 1947

Latourette, Kenneth Scott, *A History of Christianity* 2 vols, Revised edition, New York: Harper & Row, 1953, 1975

Livingstone, David, *Missionary Researches and Travels in South Africa*, London: John Murray, 1857

Livingstone, David and Charles, *Narrative of an Expedition to the Zambesi and Its Tributaries and of the Discovery of the Lakes Shirwa and Nyassa: 1858–1864*, New York: Harper & Brothers, 1866

Metropolitan Dorotheos, 'The Influence of the Moravian Mission on the Orthodox Church in Czechslovakia, *International Review of Mission*, vol. 74, no. 294 (April) 1985

Nyembezi, C.L. Sibusiso, *A Review of Zulu Literature*, Pietermaritzburg: University of Natal Press, 1961

Paz, Octavio, 'Edith Piaf Among the Pygmies' in *New York Times Book Review*, Sept. 6, 1987

Pedersen, Holger, *The Discovery of Language: Linguistic Science in the Nineteenth Century* trans. John Webster Spargo, Bloomington, Ind.: Indiana University Press, 1959, 1962

Pettifer, Julian and Richard Bradley, *Missionaries*, London: BBC Books, 1990

Quiller-Couch, Arthur, *On the Art of Reading: Lectures Delivered in the University of Cambridge*, Cambridge: Cambridge University Press, 1920

Reindorf, Carl Christian, *The History of the Gold Coast and Asante*, Basel, 1889

Robinson, A.T., *Grammar of New Testament Greek*

Sanneh, Lamin, *Translating the Message: The Missionary Impact on Culture*, Maryknoll, N.Y.: Orbis Books, 1989, 1990

West African Christianity: The Religious Impact, Maryknoll, N.Y.: Orbis Books, 1983, 1990

'The Yogi and the Commissar: Christian Missions and the African Response' in *International Bulletin of Missionary Research*, January 1991

Smith, Edwin W., *The Golden Stool: Some Aspects of the Conflict of Cultures in Modern Africa*, London: Holborn Publishing House, 1926

In the Mother Tongue, London: British and Foreign Society, 1930

The Life and Times of Daniel Lindley (1801–80), London: The Epworth Press, 1949

Robert Moffat, One of God's Gardeners, London: Student Christian Movement, 1925

Stamoolis, James J., *Eastern Orthodox Mission Theology Today*, Maryknoll, N.Y.: Orbis Books, 1986

Tamrat, Taddesse, *Church and State in Ethiopia: 1270–1527*, Oxford: Clarendon Press, 1972

Ullendorf, Edward, *Ethiopia and the Bible*, London: Oxford University Press, 1988

Vilakazi, Absalom, *Zulu Transformations: A Study of the Dynamics of Social Change*, Pietermaritzburg: University of Natal Press, 1962

Wallace-Hadrill, John Michael, *The Frankish Church*, Oxford: Clarendon Press, 1983

Westermann, Diedrich, 'The Place and Function of the Vernacular in African Education' in *International Review of Missions*, January 1925

Whitman, Walt, *November Boughs*, 1988

Wolff, Kurt, ed. and tran, *The Sociology of Georg Simmel*, New York: The Free Press; London: Collier-Macmillan, 1950; paperback, 1964

Wright, Robert, 'Quest for the Mother Tongue: Is the Search for an Ancestor of All Modern Languages Sober Science or Simple Romanticism?' in *The Atlantic*, April 1991, 39–68

3

Adams, James Truslow, *History of the United States*

'Ancient Letter Discovered: The Seminary Crisis at Nicopolis' in *The Christian Century*, Feb. 5–12, 1992, 116–17

Augustine, *City of God*, New York: Penguin Books, 1972

Confessions, New York: Image Books, 1960

Beker, J. Christian, *Paul the Apostle: The Triumph of God in Life and Thought*, Philadelphia: Fortress Press, 1980

Black, Matthew, 'The Biblical Languages' in *The Cambridge History of the Bible: vol. i. From the Beginnings to Jerome*, eds. P.R. Ackroyd and C.F. Evans, Cambridge: Cambridge University Press, 1970, 1988, 1–29

Carr, E.H., *What Is History?* New York: Alfred A. Knopf, 1962, 1964

Chesterton, G.K., *The Everlasting Man*, London: Hodder & Stoughton, 1925

'The Priest of Spring' in *Stories, Essays and Poems*, London: Everyman's Library (No. 913), 1935, 1965

Collingwood, R.G., *The Idea of History*, London and New York: Oxford University Press, 1946, 1966

Dawson, Christopher, *Beyond Politics*, 1939

Religion and the Rise of Western Culture, London: Sheed and Ward, 1950

Deissmann, Adolf, *The New Testament in the Light of Modern Research*, The Haskell Lectures. Garden City, N.Y.: Doubleday, Doran & Co., 1929

Dodd, C.H., *The Meaning of Paul for Today*, London: Fontana Books, 1964

Dodds, Eric R., *Pagan and Christian in an Age of Anxiety*, New York: W.W. Norton, 1970

Donovan, Vincent, *Christianity Rediscovered*, Maryknoll, N.Y.: Orbis Books, 1978

Eliot, T.S., *Christianity and Culture: The Idea of a Christian Society and Notes Towards the Definition of Culture*, New York and London: Harcourt Brace Jovanovich, 1968

Elshtain, Jean Bethke, 'The American Battlefield' in *First Things*, No. 23 May 1992, 69–72

Elton, G.R., *Reformation Europe: 1517–1559*, Cleveland, Ohio: Meridian Histories of Modern Europe, 1964

Erasmus, Desiderius, *Christian Humanism and the Reformation: Selected Writing* (with the life of Erasmus by Beatus Rhenanus), ed. John C. Olin. New York: Harper Torchbooks, 1965

Evans-Pritchard, Sir Edward, *A History of Anthropological Thought*, ed. André Singer, New York: Basic Books 1981

Nuer Religion, New York: Oxford University Press, 1956

Witchcraft, Oracles and Magic Among the Azande, Oxford: Clarendon Press, 1937, revised abridged edition, New York: Oxford University Press, 1976

Fenn, Eric, 'The Bible and the Missionary' in *The Cambridge History of the Bible Vol. iii, The West from the Reformation to the Present Day*, ed. S.L. Greenslade, Cambridge: Cambridge University Press, 1963, 1988

Frazer, James, *The Golden Bough: Part IV, Adonis, Attis, Osiris: Studies in the History of Oriental Religion*, 3rd edition London: Macmillan & Co., 1914

Frend, W.H., *The Rise of Christianity*, Philadelphia: Fortress Press, 1984

Geertz, Clifford, *The Interpretation of Cultures*, New York: Basic Books, 1973

Gibbon, Edward, *The Decline and Fall of the Roman Empire*, 3 vols., New York: Modern Library, N.D.

Hadas, Moses, ed. and trans. *A History of Rome: From Its Origins to 529 A.D. as Told by the Roman Historians*, New York: Doubleday Anchor Books, 1956

Harnack, Adolf von, *The Mission and Expansion of Christianity*, 2 vols., trans. and ed. James Moffatt, New York: G.P. Putnam's Sons, 1908

Hocking, William Ernest, *The Coming World Civilization*, London: George Allen & Unwin, 1958

Rethinking Missions, New York: Harper & Brothers, 1932

Hodgson, Marshall G.S., 'The Interrelations of Societies in History' in *Comparative Studies in Society and History*, 1962–63, 227–250

Hourani, Albert, *Europe and the Middle East*, Berkeley and Los Angeles: University of California Press, 1980

Johnson, Aubrey R., *The One and the Many in the Israelite Conception of God*, Cardiff: University of Wales Press, 1961

Kaufman, Gordon D., 'Theological Method and Indigenization: Six Theses' in *A Vision for Man: Essays on Faith, Theology and Society*, ed. Samuel Amirtham, Madras: Christian Literature Society, 1978

Kraemer, Hendrick, *The Christian Message in a Non-Christian World*, London: Edinburgh House Press, 1938

Latourette, Kenneth Scott, *A History of the Expansion of Christianity* 7 vols., New York: Harper & Brothers, 1937

Leach, Edmund, *A Runaway World?* BBC Reith Lectures of 1967, London: BBC Publictions, 1968

Minamiki, George, *The Chinese Rites Controversy: From Its Beginning to Modern Times*, Chicago: Loyola University Press, 1985

Newbigin, Lesslie, *Foolishness to the Greeks: The Gospel and Western Culture*, Geneva: World Council of Churches, Grand Rapids Mich.: Wm. B. Eerdmans, 1986

The Open Secret, Grand Rapids, Mich.: Wm. B. Eerdmans, 1978, 1981

Nida, Eugene A. and William D. Reyburn, *Meaning Across Cultures*, Maryknoll, N.Y.: Orbis Books, 1981

Niebuhr, H. Richard, *Christ and Culture*, New York: Harper Colophon Books, 1951, 1975

Radical Monotheism and Western Culture, The Montgomery Lectures, 1957, New York: Harper & Brothers, 1960

O'Connor, Flannery, *The Habit of Being*, New York: Farrar, Straus, Giroux, 1979

Pannenberg, Wolfhart, ed. *Revelation as History*, New York: Macmillan, 1969

Plato, *The Laws* in *The Collected Dialogues*, eds. Edith Hamilton and Huntington Cairns, New York: Pantheon Books for Bollingen Foundation, 1961

The Republic in *The Collected Dialogues*, eds. Edith Hamilton and

Huntington Cairns, New York: Pantheon Books for Bollingen Foundation, 1961

Radice, Betty, ed. and trans., *The Letters of Pliny the Younger*, New York: Penguin Books, 1969, 1985

Sanneh, Lamin, 'Christian Missions and the Western Guilt Complex' in *The Christian Century*. April 8, 1987

Scriptures of the World, London, New York, and Stuttgart: United Bible Societies, 1984

Smith, Robert C. and John Lounibos, eds., *Pagan and Christian Anxiety: A Response to E.R. Dodds*, Lanham, Md.: University Press of America, 1984

Smith, Wilfred Cantwell, 'Philosophia, as One of the Religious Traditions of Humankind: The Greek Legacy in Western Civilization Viewed by a Comparativist' in *Différences valeurs hierarchie: textes offerts à Louis Dumont*, ed. Jean-Claude Galey, Paris: École des Hautes Études en Sciences Sociales, 1984

Staniforth, Maxwell, trans. and ed., *Early Christian Writings: The Apostolic Fathers*, New York: Penguin Books, 1968, 1982

Steinmetz, Paul B., *Pipe, Bible and Peyote Among the Ogala Lakota*, Stockholm Studies in Comparative Religion, Stockholm: University of Stockholm, 1980

Stine, Philip C., ed., *Bible Translation and the Spread of the Church: The Last 200 Years*, Leiden, New York, Copenhagen, and Cologne: E.J. Brill, 1990

Takenaka, Masao, *God is Rice: Asian Culture and Christian Faith*, Geneva: World Council of Churches Risk Book Series, 1986

4

Donovan, Vincent, *Christianity Rediscovered*, Maryknoll, N.Y.: Orbis Books, 1978

Kenyatta, Jomo, *Facing Mount Kenya*, New York: Vintage Books, 1938, 1953, 1962

Murray, Jocelyn, 'The Kikuyu Spirit Churches', *Journal of Religion in Africa* vol. 5, no. 3, 1974, 198–234

Newbigin, Lesslie, *Foolishness to the Greeks: The Gospel and Western Culture*, Geneva: World Council of Churches, Grand Rapids Mich.: Wm. B. Eerdmans, 1986

The Gospel in a Pluralist Society, Geneva: World Council of Churches, Grand Rapids, Mich.: Wm. B. Eerdmans, 1989

The Open Secret, Grand Rapids, Mich.: Wm. B. Eerdmans, 1978, 1981

Saitoti, Tepilit Ole and Carol Beckwith, *Maasai*, New York: Abradale Press of Harry N. Abrams, Inc., Times Mirror Publishers, 1980

Toynbee, Arnold J., *Christianity Among the Religions of the World*, New York: Charles Scribner's Sons, 1957

Civilization on Trial, New York: Oxford University Press, 1948
An Historian's Approach to Religion, London and New York: Oxford University Press, 1956
Trimingham, J. Spencer, *Christianity Among the Arabs in Pre-Islamic Times*, London: Longman; Beirut: Librairie du Liban, 1979
Troeltsch, Ernst, *The Absoluteness of Christianity and the History of Religions*. Trans. David Reid. Richmond: John Knox Press, 1971
Wallace-Hadrill, John Michael, *The Frankish Church*, Oxford: Clarendon Press, 1983
Ywahoo, Dhyani, *Voices of Our Ancestors: Cherokee Teachings from the Wisdom Fire*, Boston and London: Shambhala Publications, 1987

5

Ahlstrom, Sydney E., *A Religious History of the American People*, New Haven: Yale University Press, 1972
Ahmed, Akbar, *Discovering Islam: Making Sense of Muslim History and Society*, London: Routledge, 1988
'The Threat of the Western Media to Traditional Society: The Case of Islam', Unpublished manuscript based on Akbar Ahmed and Ernest Gellner's *Post-modernism and Islam*, London: Routledge, 1992
Barker, Ernest, *Principles of Social and Political Theory*, Oxford: Clarendon Press, 1951
Board of Social Ministry, Lutheran Church of America, *Religious Liberty*, New York: Board of Social Ministry, Lutheran Church of America, 1968
Brentano, Robert, ed., *The Early Middle Ages: 500–1000* in series *Sources in Western Civilization*, New York: The Free Press, London: Collier Macmillan, 1964
Brunner, Emil, *The Word and the World*, 2nd ed., London, 1932
Cochrane, Charles Norris, *Christianity and Classical Culture: A Study of Thought and Action from Augustus to Augustine*, London, Oxford, and New York: Oxford Univesity Press, 1957
Cox, Harvey, *Religion in the Secular City*, New York: Simon and Schuster, 1984
The Silencing of Leonardo Boff, Oak Park, Il.: Meyer-Stone Books, 1988
Cragg, Kenneth, *The Call of the Minaret*, Maryknoll, N.Y.: Orbis Books, 1985
Dennis, James S, *Christian Missions and Social Progress* 2 vols., New York: Revell, 1897
Eco, Umberto, *Foucault's Pendulum*, New York: Ballantine Books, 1990
Evola, Julius, *Il Mistero del Graal*, Rome: Edizioni Mediterranee, 1993
Fischer, Michael M.J. and Mehdi Abedi, *Debating Muslims: Cultural Dialogues in Postmodernity and Tradition*, Madison, Wis.: University of Wisconsin Press, 1990

Friedman, Lawrence, *The Republic of Choice: Law, Authority, and Culture*, Cambridge, Mass.: Harvard University Press, 1990

Gellner, Ernest, 'Post-Traditional Forms in Islam: The Turf and Trade, and Voices and Peanuts' in *Muslim Society*, Cambridge: Cambridge Universtiy Press, 1983, 99–113

Goldman, Ari L., 'More People Are Staying at Home to Worship' in *The New York Times*, Dec. 1, 1991, 1,44

Goodpasture, H. McKennie, ed. *Cross and Sword: An Eyewitness History of Christianity in Latin America*, Maryknoll, N.Y.: Orbis Books, 1989

Hastings, Adrian, *A History of English Christianity: 1920–1985*, London: Fount Paperbacks, 1986

Hocking, William Ernest, Chairman, Commission of Appraisal, *Re-thinking Missions: A Laymen's Inquiry after one hundred years*, New York: Harper & Brothers, 1932

Hutchison, R.C., 'Islam and Christianity' in *The Atlantic*, November, 1926

'Can I Give My Life to Christian Missions?' in *International Review of Missions*, vol. 16, January, 1927

Kabbani, Rana, *Letter to Christendom*, London: Virago Press, 1989

Landis, Benson Y., *The Third American Revolution*, New York: Association Press, 1933

Lasch, Christopher, *The Culture of Narcissism: American Life in an Age of Diminishing Expectations*, New York: Norton, 1978

Leuchtenburg, William E., *Franklin D. Roosevelt and the New Deal: 1932–1940*, New York: Harper & Row, 1963

Levenson, Jon D., 'The God of Abraham and the Enemies of Eurocentrism' in *First Things*, Oct. 1991, 15–21

McAfee, Joseph E., *The Crisis of Missionary Method*, New York: 1911

Machen, J. Gresham, *Christianity and Liberalism*, New York: Macmillan, 1923

McGavran, Donald, ed., *The Conciliar-Evangelical Debate: The Crucial Documents, 1964–76*, Pasadena, Calif.: William Carey Library

MacKenzie, W. Douglas, *Christian Ethics in the World War*, 1918

Martin, B.G., 'A Muslim Political Tract from Northern Nigeria: Muhammad Bello's Usúl al-Siyása' in *Aspects of West African Islam*, vol. 5, eds. Daniel F. McCall and Norman R. Bennett, Boston: Boston University Press, 1971

Mensch, Betty and Alan Freeman, 'Religion in the Schools: Should We Celebrate Church-State Separation?' in *Tikkun*, a bimonthly Jewish critique of politics, culture, and society, March/April 1992, 31–36

Newbigin, Lesslie, *Honest Religion for Secular Man*, London: SCM Press, 1966

Northrop, F.S.C., *The Meeting of East and West: An Inquiry Concerning World Understanding*, New York: Collier Books, London: Collier-Macmillan, 1960, repr. Woodbridge, Ct. 1975

O'Brien, Conor Cruise, 'Innocent nation, wicked world' in *Harper's*, April, 1980

Pettifer, Julian and Richard Bradley, *Missionaries*, London: BBC Books, 1990

Pirenne, Henri, *Mohammed and Charlemagne*, London: Unwin University Books, 1968

Randall, Robert L., 'Ministers and Churches at Risk' in *The Christian Century* vol. 108, no. 34, Nov. 20–27, 1991, 1093–95

Rauschenbusch, Walter, *A Theology for the Social Gospel*, New York: Macmillan, 1918

Searle, Hugh, 'Choice Between restoration and rebirth' in *Church Times*, 10 July, 1992

Showalter, Nathan, *The End of a Crusade: The Student Volunteer Movement For Foreign Missions and the Great War*, unpublished Th.D. dissertation, Cambridge, MA.: Harvard Divinity School, 1990

'Sodomy Law Opposed' in *The Christian Century* vol. 108, no. 24, Aug. 21–28, 1992, 769–770

Speer, Robert E., *Are Foreign Missions Done For?* New York: Board of Foreign Missions in the Presbyterian Church, U.S.A., 1928

Tuveson, Ernest, *Redeemer Nation: The Idea of America's Millennial Role*, Chicago: University of Chicago Press, 1968

Twain, Mark, 'Mark Twain on American Imperialism' in *The Atlantic*. Vol. 269, No. 4, April 1992, 49–65

Van Buren, Paul, *Discerning the Way*, New York: 1980

General Bibliography

Aagaard, Anna Marie and Lesslie Newbigin, 'Mission in the 1990s: Two Views' in *International Bulletin of Missionary Research* 13:3 (July 1989): 98–102

Adams, James Truslow, *History of the United States*

Ahlstrom, Sydney, E., *A Religious History of the American People*, New Haven: Yale University Press, 1972

Ahmed, Akbar, *Discovering Islam: Making Sense of Muslim History and Society*, London: Routledge, 1988

'The Threat of the Western Media to Traditional Society: The Case of Islam', Unpublished manuscript based on Akbar Ahmed, *Postmodernism and Islam: Predicament and Promise*, London & New York: Routledge, 1992

Alexander, Jeffrey C. and Steven Seidman, eds., *Culture and Society: Contemporary Debates*, Cambridge: Cambridge University Press, 1990

Allen, Frederick Lewis, 1931, *Only Yesterday*, repr. New York: Bantam Books, 1959

Amegatcher, Andrew W., 'Akropong: 150 Years Old' in *West Africa*, July 14, 1986

'Ancient Letter Discovered: The Seminary Crisis at Nicopolis' in *The Christian Century*, Feb. 5–12, 1992, 116–17

Aristotle, Nicomachean Ethics, in *Introduction to Aristotle*, ed. Richard McKeon, New York: The Modern Library of Random House, 1947

Arnold, Matthew, 'Culture and Anarchy' in *Selected Prose*, ed. P.J. Keating, London: Penguin Classics, 1987

Augustine, *City of God*, New York: Penguin Books, 1972

Confessions, New York: Image Book of Doubleday & Anchor, 1960

Austen, Ralph, 'Africans Speak; Colonialism Writes: The Transcription and Translation of Oral Literature Before World War II', Boston University Discussion Paper, *AH Number 8*, 1990

Averroës, *The Incoherence of the Incoherence* (Taháfut al- Taháfut) 2 vols, ed. and trans. Simon van de Bergh, London: Luzac & Co., 1954

Bacon, Francis, *Advancement of Learning*, 1605, ed. G.W. Kitchin, London: J.M. Dent & Sons, 1915

The Masculine Birth of Time, 1603 in *The Philosophy of Francis Bacon*, trans. and ed. B. Farrington, Chicago: University of Chicago Press, 1964

New Atlantis in *The Works of Francis Bacon*, vol. III. eds. J. Spedding, R.L. Ellis and D.D. Heath, London, 1857

Barish, Evelyn, *Emerson: The Roots of Prophecy*, Princeton: Princeton University Press, 1989

Barker, Ernest, *Principles of Social and Political Theory*, Oxford: Clarendon Press, 1951

Barrett, David B., *World Christian Encyclopaedia*, Nairobi: Oxford University Press, 1982

Barth, Fredrik, 'Are Values Real? The Enigma of Naturalism in the Anthropological Imputation of Values' in M. Hechter, Lynn Nadel and R. Michod, eds., *The Origin of Values*, 1993

Beaver, R. Pierce, 'Nationalism and Missions' in *Church History* 26:1 (March 1957): 22–42

Beker, J. Christian, *Paul the Apostle: The Triumph of God in Life and Thought*, Philadelphia: Fortress Press, 1980

Bellah, Robert, Richard Marsden, William M. Sullivan, Ann Swidler & Steven M. Tipton, *Habits of the Heart: Individualism and Commitment in American Life*, Berkeley: University of California Press, 1985, repr. New York: Harper and Row, 1986

Belloc, Hilaire, *Cranmer, Archbishop of Canterbury, 1533–1556*, Philadelphia: J.P. Lippincott & Co., 1931

Benedict, Ruth, *Patterns of Culture*, Boston: Houghton Mifflin Co., 1934, 1961, 1989

Benjamin, Walter, 'The Task of the Translator' in *Illuminations*, ed. Hannah Arendt, trans. Harry Zohn, New York: Schocken Books, 1969

Bent, Ans J. van der, 'Christianity and Culture: An Analytical Survey of Some Theological Approaches' in *Ecumenical Review* 39:2 (April 1987) 222–227

Bidney, David, 'The Concept of Value in Modern Anthropology' in *Anthropology Today: An Encyclopedic Inventory*, Chicago: University of Chicago Press, 1953, 682–99

Black, Matthew, 'The Biblical Languages' in *The Cambridge History of the Bible vol. i, From the Beginnings to Jerome*, eds. P.R. Ackroyd and C.F. Evans, Cambridge: Cambridge Unversity Press, 1970, 1988, 1–29

Board of Social Ministry, Lutheran Church of America, *Religious Liberty*, New York: Board of Social Ministry, Lutheran Church of America, 1968

Bohm, David, *Wholeness and the Implicate Order*, London: Ark Paperbacks of Routledge & Kegan Paul, 1983

Borgman, Albert, 'Christianity and the Cultural Center of Gravity' in *Listening: Journal of Religion and Culture*, 18:2 (Spring 1983) 93–102

Bradley, Henry, *The Making of English*, New York and London: Macmillan, 1904

Brauer, Jerald C., ed., *Impact of the Church Upon Its Culture: Reappraisals of the History of Christianity*, Chicago: University of Chicago Press, 1968

Brentano, Robert, ed., *The Early Middle Ages: 500–1000* in series *Sources in Western Civilization*, New York: The Free Press, London: Collier-Macmillan, 1964

Bujo, Bénézet, 'The Understanding of Conscience in African Ethics' in *Studies in Interreligious Dialogue*, vol. 2, no. 1, 1992

Bury, J.B., *A History of Freedom of Thought*, New York: Henry Holt & Co., 1913

Bushmann, Walter, 'Christianity and Culture' in *Lutheran Quarterly* 9:3 (August 1957) 260–265

Butler, Joseph, *Sermons*, London: 1862

Butterfield, Herbert, *The Origins of Modern Science*, London: G. Bell, 1949

Carey, John, *The Intellectuals and the Masses: Pride & Prejudice among the Literary Intelligentsia, 1880–1938*, London: Faber, 1992

Carino, Feliciano V., 'The Willowbank Report: A Critical Response' in *South East Asia Journal of Theology* 19:2 (1978) 38–49

Carman, John, B., 'Missions and the Translatable Gospel' in *Christian Century*, Aug. 30–Sept. 6, 1989

Carr, E.H., *What Is History?* New York: Alfred A. Knopf, 1962, 1964

Carrier, Herve, *Gospel Message and Human Cultures: From Leo XIII to John Paul II*, trans. John Drury, Pittsburgh: Duquesne University Press, 1989

Chesterton, G.K., *All Things Considered*, Philadelphia: Dufour Editions, 1908, 1969

The Everlasting Man, London: Hodder & Stoughton, 1925

'The Priest of Spring' in *Stories, Essays and Poems*, London: Everyman's Library (no. 913), 1935, 1965

Chittick, William, *Ibn al-ʿArabi's Metaphysics of Imagination: The Súfí Path of Knowledge* Albany: State University of New York Press, 1989

Cho, Kiyoko Takeda, 'Weeds and the Wheat: An Inquiry into Indigenous Cultural Energies in Asia' in *Ecumenical Review* 27:3 (July 1975): 220–229

Christaller, J.G., *Dictionary of the Asante and Fante Language: Called Twi*, 1881, 2nd edition, Basel: Basel Evangelical Missionary Society, 1933

Cochrane, Charles Norris, *Christianity and Classical Culture: A Study of Thought and Action from Augustus to Augustine*, London and New York: Oxford University Press, 1957

Colenso, John W., *Bringing Forth Light: Five Tracts on Bishop Colenso's Zulu Mission*, Pietermaritzburg: University of Natal; Durban: Killie Campbell Africana Library, 1982

Collingwood, R.G., *An Essay on Metaphysics*, Oxford: Oxford University Press. Reprinted, Lanham, Md.: University Press of America, 1972

The Idea of History, London and New York: Oxford University Press, 1946, 1966

Comaroff, Jean and John, *Of Revelation and Revolution: Christianity, Colonialism and Consciousness in South Africa*, Chicago: University of Chicago Press, 1991

Coote, Robert T. and John Stott, eds., *Down to Earth: Studies in Christianity and Culture: The Papers of the Lausanne Consultation on Gospel and Culture*, Grand Rapids, Mich.: Wm. B. Eerdmans Publishing, 1980

Coulon, Christian, *Les Musulmans et le Pouvoir en Afrique Noire: Religion et Contre-culture*, Paris: Editions Karthala, 1983

Cox, Harvey, *Religion in the Secular City*, New York: Simon and Schuster, 1984

The Silencing of Leonardo Boff, Oak Park, Il.: Meyer-Stone Books, 1988

Cragg, Kenneth, *The Call of the Minaret*, Maryknoll, N.Y.: Orbis Books, 1985 and London: William Collins

The Christ and the Faiths: Theology in Cross-reference, London: SPCK, Philadelphia: Westminster, 1987

Crollius, Ary Roest and Theoneste Nkeramihigo, *What Is So New About Inculturation?* Rome: Centre 'Cultures and Religions', Pontifical Gregorian University, 1984

Cronin, Vincent, *A Pearl to India: The Life of Robert de Nobili*, London: Rupert Hart Davis, 1959

Daneel, Marthinus L., 'The Encounter Between Christianity and Traditional African Culture: Accommodation or Transformation?' in *Theologia Evangelica* 22:3 (September 1989) 36–51

Danquah, J.B., *The Akan Doctrine of God*, London: Lutterworth Press, 1944

Davis, Asa J., 'The Orthodoxy of the Ethiopian Church' in *Tarikh* vol. 2, No. 1

Dawson, Christopher, *Beyond Politics*, 1939

Religion and the Rise of Western Culture, London: Sheed and Ward, 1950

Debrunner, Hans W., *A History of Christianity in Ghana*, Accra, Ghana: Waterville Publishing House, 1967

Deissmann, Adolf, *The New Testament in the Light of Modern Research*, The Haskell Lectures. New York: Doubleday, Doran & Co., 1929

Derrida, Jacques, *Of Grammatology*, trans. Gayatri C. Spivak, Baltimore: Johns Hopkins University Press, 1976

'Structure, Sign, and Play in the Discourse of the Human Sciences', in *Writing and Difference*, trans. Alan Bass, Chicago: University of Chicago Press, 1978.

D'Espagnat, Bernard, *Reality and the Physicist: Knowledge, Duration and the Quantum World*, Cambridge: Cambridge University Press, 1989

Dietrich, Wendell S., *Cohen and Troeltsch: Ethical Monotheistic Religion and Theory of Culture*, Atlanta: Scholars Press, 1986

Divarkar, Parmananda R., 'Encounter of the Gospel with Culture: Reflections on the Problem of Inculturation' in *Zeitschrift für Missionswissenschaft und Religionswissenschaft* 61:3 (1977):

214–220

Dodd, C.H., *The Meaning of Paul for Today*, London: Fontana Books, 1964

Dodds, Eric R., *Pagan and Christian in an Age of Anxiety*, New York: W.W. Norton, 1970

Doke, Clement M., *The Phonetics of the Zulu Language*, a special publication of *Bantu Studies*, a journal devoted to the scientific study of Bantu, Hottentot, and Bushmen, vol. II, July 1926, Johannesburg: University of Witwatersrand Press

'Scripture Translation into Bantu Languages' in *Contributions to the History of Bantu Linguistics*, eds. C.M. Doke and D.T. Cole, Johannesburg: University of Witwatersrand Press, 1961

Donovan, Vincent, *Christianity Rediscovered*, Maryknoll, N.Y.: Orbis Books, 1978

'Response to Reflections on *Christianity Rediscovered*' in *Missiology: An International Review* 18:3 (July 1990): 277–278

Drohan, Michael, 'Christianity, Culture, and the Meaning of Mission' in *International Review of Missions*, 75:299 (July 1986): 285–303

Dryness, William A., 'Beyond Niebuhr: The Gospel and Culture' in *The Reformed Journal* 38:2 (February 1988): 11–13

Dvornik, Francis, *Byzantine Missions Among the Slavs: SS. Constantine-Cyril and Methodius*, New Brunswick, N.J.: Rutgers University Press, 1970

Eco, Umberto, *Foucault's Pendulum*, New York: Ballantine Books, 1990

Eliot, T.S., *Christianity and Culture: The Idea of a Christian Society and Notes Towards the Definition of Culture*, New York and London: Harcourt Brace Jovanovich, 1968

Elshtain, Jean Bethke, 'The American Battlefield' in *First Things* No. 23, May 1992, 69–72

Elton, G.R., *Reformation Europe: 1517–1559*, Cleveland, Ohio: Meridian Histories of Modern Europe, 1964

Emerson, Ralph Waldo, 'The American Scholar' in *Selections from Ralph Waldo Emerson*, ed. Stephen E. Whicher, Boston: Houghton Mifflin Co., 1960

Encyclopaedia of Religion and Ethics, Article on 'Culture' vol. IV, ed. James Hastings, Edinburgh: T. & T. Clark; New York: Charles Scribner's Sons, 1981

Erasmus, Desiderius, *Christian Humanism and the Reformation: Selected Writing* (with the life of Erasmus by Beatus Rhenanus), ed. John C. Olin, New York: Harper Torchbooks, 1965

Evans-Pritchard, Sir Edward, *A History of Anthropological Thought*, ed. André Singer, New York: Basic Books, 1981

Nuer Religion, New York: Oxford University Press, 1956

Theories of Primitive Religion, Oxford: Clarendon Press, 1965

Witchcraft, Oracles and Magic Among the Azande, Oxford: Clarendon Press, 1937; revised abridged edition, New York: Oxford University Press, 1976

Evola, Julius, *Il Mistero del Graal*, Rome: Edizioni Mediterranee, 1983

Fabian, Johannes, *Language and Colonial Power: The Appropriation of Swahili in the Former Belgian Congo, 1880–1938*, Cambridge: Cambridge University Press, 1986

Fenn, Eric, 'The Bible and the Missionary' in *The Cambridge History of the Bible: vol. iii, The West from the Reformation to the Present Day*, ed. S.L. Greenslade, Cambridge: Cambridge University Press, 1963, 1988

Fischer, Michael M. J. and Mehdi Abedi, *Debating Muslims: Cultural Dialogues in Postmodernity and Tradition*, Madison, Wis.: University of Wisconsin Press, 1990.

Fitzpatrick, Joseph P., *One Church, Many Cultures: Challenge of Diversity*, Kansas City, Mo.: Sheed and Ward, 1987.

Fleming, Daniel Johnson, 'Different Cultural Mentalities' in *Religion in Life* 24:1 (Winter 1954–1955): 56–65

Forell, George W., *The Proclamation of the Gospel in a Pluralistic World: Essays on Christianity and Culture*, Philadelphia: Fortress Press, 1973

Frazer, James, *The Golden Bough: Part IV, Adonis, Attis, Osiris: Studies in the History of Oriental Religion*, 3rd edition London: Macmillan & Co., 1914

Frend, W.H., *The Rise of Christianity*, Philadelphia: Fortress Press, 1984

Freud, Sigmund, *The Future of an Illusion*, ed. & trans. James Strachey, New York: W.W. Norton, 1961

Introductory Lectures on Psycho-analysis. 4th edition, trans. Joan Riviere, London, 1933

Friedman, Lawrence, *The Republic of Choice: Law, Authority, and Culture*, Cambridge, Mass.: Harvard University Press, 1990

Fuze, Magema M., *The Black People: And Whence They Came*, Pietermaritzburg: University of Natal Press; Durban: Killie Campbell Africana Library, 1922, 1979

Garrett, John, *To Live Among the Stars*, Suva: University of South Pacific, 1982

Geertz, Clifford, *The Interpretation of Cultures*, New York: Basic Books, 1973

'Anti antirelativism' in *American Anthropologist* 1984, 263–278

Gellner, Ernest, 'Post-Traditional Forms in Islam: The Turf and Trade, and Voices and Peanuts' in *Muslim Society*, Cambridge: Cambridge University Press, 1983. 99–113

Postmodernism, Reason and Religion, London & New York: Routledge, 1992

Gérard, Albert S., *Four African Literatures: Xhosa, Sotho, Zulu, Amharic*, Berkeley and Los Angeles: University of California Press, 1971

Gibbon, Edward, *The Decline and Fall of the Roman Empire* 3 vols., New York: Modern Library, N.D.

Gilkey, Langdon Brown, *Society and the Sacred: Toward a Theology of Culture in Decline*, New York: Crossroad, 1981

Gillman, Peter and Leni, *Collar the Lot! How Britain Intervened and Expelled Wartime Refugees*, London and New York: Quartet Books, 1980

Glover, T.R., *The Conflict of Religions in the Early Roman Empire*, 3rd edition, London: Methuen, 1909. Reprinted, New York: Cooper Square Publishers, 1975

Goldman, Ari L., 'More People Are Staying at Home to Worship' in *The New York Times*, Dec. 1, 1991, 1,44

'Gospel and Culture: The Working Statement Developed at Riano Consultation' in *International Review of Missions* 74:294 (April 1985): 264–267

Gration, John A., 'Conversion in Cultural Context' in *International Bulletin of Missionary Research* 7:4 (October 1983): 157–158, 160–162

Gray, Richard, *Black Christian, White Missionaries*, New Haven: Yale University Press, 1991

Gremillion, Joseph, ed., *The Church and Culture Since Vatican II: The Experience of North and Latin America*, Notre Dame, Ind.: University of Notre Dame, 1985

Grubb, Kenneth, review article, 'The Relations of Church and State' in *International Review of Missions*, vol. 36, no. 142, April, 1947

Gunton, Colin, 'Knowledge and Culture: Towards an epistemology of the concrete' in Hugh Montefiore, ed. *The Gospel and Contemporary Culture*, London: Mowbray, 1992

Guy, Jeff, *The Heretic: A Study of the Life of John William Colenso: 1814–1883*, Johannesburg: Ravan Press; Pietermaritzburg: University of Natal Press, 1983

Hadas, Moses, ed. and trans. *A History of Rome: From Its Origins to A.D. 529 as Told by the Roman Historians*, New York: Doubleday Anchor Books, 1956

Haile, Getatchew, 'A Christ for the Gentiles: The Case of the za-Krestos of Ethiopia' in *Journal of Religion in Africa*, vol. 15, no. 2

Hampson, Norman, *The Enlightenment*, Harmondsworth, Middx.: Penguin University Books, 1968, 1976

Hartman, Geoffrey H., 'Art and Consensus in the Era of Progressive Politics' in *The Yale Review*, vol. 80, no. 4, 1992

Harnack, Adolf von, *The Mission and Expansion of Christianity* 2 vols, trans. and ed. James Moffatt, New York: G.P. Putnam's Sons, 1908

Hastings, Adrian, *A History of English Christianity: 1920–1985*, London & Glasgow: Collins, Fount Paperbacks, 1987

Havel, Vaclav, *Living in Truth*, ed. Jan Vladislav, London: Faber & Faber, 1986

Hazard, Paul, *The European Mind: 1680–1715*, Harmondsworth: Penguin University Books, 1973

Hechter, Michael, Lyn Nadel & Richard E. Michod, eds.: *The Origin of Values*, Hawthorne, N.Y.: Aldine de Gruyter, 1993

Herskovits, Melville, *Man and His Works*, New York: Alfred A. Knopf, 1948

Hick, John and Paul F. Knitter, eds., *The Myth of Christian Uniqueness*, Maryknoll, N.Y.: Orbis Books, 1987

Problems of Religious Pluralism, New York: St Martin's Press, 1985

God and the Universe of Faiths, London: Macmillan, 1973

Hiebert, Paul G., 'Culture and Cross-Cultural Differences' in Ralph D. Winter & Steven C. Hawthorne, eds.: *Perspectives on the World Christian Movement: A Reader*, Pasadena: Wm. Carey Library, 1981, 367–375

Hocking, William Ernest, *The Coming World Civilization*, London: George Allen & Unwin, 1956

Hocking, William Ernest, Chairman, Commission of Appraisal, *Re-Thinking Missions: A Laymen's Inquiry after one hundred years*, New York: Harper & Brothers, 1932

Hodgson, Marshall G.S., 'The Interrelations of Societies in History' in *Comparative Studies in Society and History*, 1962–63. 227–250

Holmes, Oliver Wendell, *Autocrat of the Breakfast Table*, 1858

Hourani, Albert, *Europe and the Middle East*, Berkeley and Los Angeles: University of California Press, 1980

Hutchison, R.C., 'Islam and Christianity' in *The Atlantic*, November, 1926

'Can I Give My Life to Christian Missions?' in *International Review of Missions*, vol. 16, January, 1927

Hutchison, William R., 'Christianity, Culture, and Complications: Protestant Attitudes Toward Missions' in *Pushing the Faith: Proselytism and Civility in a Pluralistic World*, eds. Martin E. Marty and Frederick E. Greenspahn, New York: Crossroad, 78–92

Inch, Morris A., *Doing Theology Across Cultures*, Grand Rapids, Mich.: Baker Book House, 1982

The Influence of the English Bible upon the English Language and upon English and American Literatures, New York: American Bible Society, 1947

Johnson, Aubrey R., *The One and the Many in the Israelite Conception of God*, Cardiff: University of Wales Press, 1961

Johnson, Paul, review article, 'Eliminate the negative . . . ' in *The Sunday Times Book Review*, 12 July, 1982

Johnson, Samuel, *The History of the Yorubas*, London: Routledge & Kegan Paul, 1921, 1969

Kabbani, Rana, *Letter to Christendom*, London: Virago Press, 1989

Kant, Immanuel, *Critique of Judgement*, trans. J. H. Bernard, New York: Hafner Press of Macmillan Publishing Co., 1951

Critique of Pure Reason, 1781, trans. N. Kemp Smith, London: Macmillan, 1929

Kaplan, Steven, 'The Africanization of Missionary Christianity: History and Typology' in *Journal of Religion in Africa* 16:3 (October 1986): 166–186

Katoke, Israel K., 'Christianity and Culture: An African Experience' in *Transformation: An International Dialogue on Evangelical Social Ethics* 1:4 (October-December 1984): 7–10

Kaufman, Gordon D., 'Theological Method and Indigenization: Six Theses' in *A Vision for Man: Essays on Faith, Theology and Society*, ed. Samuel Amirtham, Madras: Christian Literature Society, 1978

Kenyatta, Jomo, *Facing Mount Kenya*, New York: Vintage Books, 1938, 1953, 1962

Ker, Ian, *John Henry Newman: A Biography*, Oxford: Oxford University Press, 1990

Klaaren, Eugene M., *Religious Origins of Modern Science: Belief in Creation in Seventeenth Century Thought*, Lanham, Md.: University Press of America, 1985

Kraemer, Hendrick, *The Christian Message in a Non-Christian World*, London: Edinburgh House Press, 1938

World Cultures and World Religions: The Coming Dialogue, London: Lutterworth Press, 1960

Lamb, Charles and Mary, *Tales from Shakespeare*, New York: Grosset & Dunlap, N.D.

Landis, Benson, Y., *The Third American Revolution*, New York: Association Press, 1933

Lasch, Christopher, *The Culture of Narcissism: American Life in an Age of Diminishing Expectations*, New York: Norton, 1978

Latourette, Kenneth Scott, *The Gospel, the Church, and the World*, vol. 3. New York: Harper and Brothers, 1946

A History of Christianity, 2 vols, Revised edition, New York: Harper & Row, 1953, 1975

A History of the Expansion of Christianity, 7 vols, New York: Harper & Brothers, 1937

Lawday, David, 'My Country, Right . . . or What?' *The Atlantic*, vol. 268, no. 1

Leach, Edmund, *A Runaway World?* BBC Reith Lectures of 1967, London: BBC Publications, 1968

Lefevere, André, *Translating Literature: The German Tradition: From Luther to Rosenzweig*, Assen/Amsterdam: Van Gorcum, 1977

Leuchtenburg, William E., *Franklin D. Roosevelt and the New Deal: 1932–1940*, New York: Harper & Row, 1963

Levenson, Jon D., 'The God of Abraham and the Enemies of "Eurocentrism"' in *First Things*, Oct. 15–21, 1991

Lévi-Strauss, Claude, *The Scope of Anthropology*, trans. Sherry Ortner Paul & Robert A. Paul, London: Jonathan Cape, 1967

Lewis, C.S., *Christian Reflections*, Grand Rapids, Mich.: Wm. B. Eerdmans, 1967, and London: Fount Paperbacks

A Grief Observed, London: Faber & Faber, 1961

Miracles: A Preliminary Study, London and Glasgow: Fontana Books, 1963

'New Learning and New Ignorance' in *Oxford History of English Literature: English Literature in the Sixteenth Century*, London and

New York: Oxford University Press, 1954
'The Vision of John Bunyan' in *Selected Literary Essays*, Cambridge: Cambridge University Press, 1979. 146–53
Lienhardt, Godfrey, 'Modes of Thought' in *The Institutions of Primitive Society*, Oxford: Blackwell, 1961
Lipner, Julius, 'Being One, Let Me Be Many: Facets of the Relationship Between the Gospel and Culture' in *International Review of Mission* 74:294 (April 1985): 158–168
Little, David, John Kelsay and Abdulaziz A. Sachedina, *Human Rights and the Conflict of Cultures: Western and Islamic Perspectives on Religious Liberty*, Columbia, S.C.: University of South Carolina Press, 1988
Livingstone, David, *Missionary Researches and Travels in South Africa*, London: John Murray, 1857
Livingstone, David and Charles, *Narrative of an Expedition to the Zambesi and Its Tributaries and of the Discovery of the Lakes Shirwa and Nyassa: 1858–1864*, New York: Harper & Brothers, 1866
Locke, John, *The Reasonableness of Christianity*, ed. & abridged I.T. Ramsey, Stanford: Stanford University Press, 1958
Loewen, Jacob Abram, *Culture and Human Values: Christian Intervention in Anthropological Perspective: Selections from the Writings of Jacob A. Loewen*, ed. William A. Smalley, South Pasadena, Calif.: William Carey Library, 1975
Luzbetak, Louis J., *The Church and Cultures: New Perspectives in Missiological Anthropology*, Maryknoll, N.Y.: Orbis Books, 1988

McAfee, Joseph, E., *The Crisis of Missionary Method*, New York, 1911
McGavran, Donald, ed., *The Conciliar-Evangelical Debate: The Crucial Documents, 1964–76*, Pasadena, Calif.: William Carey Library
Machen, J. Gresham, *Christianity and Liberalism*, New York: Macmillan, 1923
Mackay, John Alexander, *The Other Spanish Christ: A Study in the Spiritual History of Spain and South America*, New York: Macmillan, 1932
MacKenzie, W. Douglas, *Christian Ethics in the World War*, 1918
Malinowski, B.,'The Rationalisation of Anthropology & Administration' in *Africa*, vol. 3, no. 4, 1930
Martey, Emmanuel, *African Theology: Inculturation and Liberation*, Maryknoll, N.Y.: Orbis, 1993
Martin, B.G., 'A Muslim Political Tract from Northern Nigeria: Muhammad Bello's Usúl al-Siyása' in *Aspects of West African Islam*, vol. 5, eds. Daniel F. McCall and Norman R. Bennett, Boston: Boston University Press, 1971
Mayers, Marvin Keene, *Christianity Confronts Culture*, Grand Rapids, Mich.: Zondervan, 1974
Mazrui, Ali A., 'Religion and Political Culture in Africa' in *Journal of the American Academy of Religion* 53:4 (December 1985): 817–839
Mbiti, John, 'African Indigenous Culture in Relation to Evangelism and Church Development' in *The Gospel and Frontier Peoples: A Report*

of a Consultation, December 1972, South Pasadena, Calif.: William Carey Library, 1973. 79–95

'Christianity and Culture in Africa' in *Facing the New Challenges: The Message of PACLA*, Kisumu, Kenya: Evangel Publishing House, 1978. 272–284

Confessing Christ in Different Cultures: Report on Colloquium Held at the WCC Ecumenical Institute, Bossey, Switzerland: Ecumenical Institute, 1977

Medawar, Sir P., 'On the Effecting of All Things Possible' in *The Listener*, lxxxii

Mensch, Betty and Alan Freeman, 'Religion in the Schools: Should We Celebrate Church-State Separation?' in *Tikkun*, a bimonthly Jewish critique of politics, culture, and society, March/April 1992. 31–36

Metropolitan Dorotheos, 1985, 'The Influence of the Moravian Mission on the Orthodox Church in Czechoslovakia' in *International Review of Mission*, vol. 74, no. 294 (April)

Meyer, Ernest H., *Elizabethan Chamber Music: The History of a Great Art from the Middle Ages to Purcell*, London: Lawrence & Wishart, 1946

Mill, John Stuart, *Journals and Debating Speeches: Collected Works of John Stuart Mill*, vol. xxvii, London: Routledge; Toronto: University of Toronto Press, 1988

Minamiki, George, *The Chinese Rites Controversy: From Its Beginning to Modern Times*, Chicago: Loyola University Press, 1985

Montefiore, Hugh, ed., *The Gospel and Contemporary Culture*, London: Mowbray, 1992

Morgan, John H., ed., *Understanding Religion and Culture: Anthropological and Theological Perspectives*, Washington: University Press of America, 1979

Mosala, Jerry, 'African Traditional Beliefs and Christianity' in *Journal of Theology for Southern Africa* 43 (June 1983): 15–24

Moyo, Ambrose Mavingire, 'The Quest for African Christian Theology and the Problem of the Relationship Between Faith and Culture: The Hermeneutical Perspective' in *Africa Theological Journal* 12:2 (1983): 95–108

Mudimbe, V., *The Invention of Africa*, Bloomington, Ind.: Indiana University Press, 1989

Murray, Jocelyn, 'The Kikuyu Spirit Churches' in *Journal of Religion in Africa*, vol. 5, no. 3. 1974

Newbigin, Lesslie, 'Christ and the Cultures' in *Scottish Journal of Theology* 31:1 (1978) 1-22

The Relevance of Trinitarian Doctrine for Today's Mission, London: Edinburgh House Press, 1963

Honest Religion for Secular Man, London: SCM Press, 1966

The Other Side of 1984, London: BCC, 1983

Foolishness to the Greeks: The Gospel and Western Culture, Geneva: World Council of Churches; Grand Rapids Mich.: Wm. B. Eerdmans, 1986

The Gospel in a Pluralist Society, Geneva: World Council of Churches; Grand Rapids, Mich.: Wm. B. Eerdmans, 1989

Mission and the Crisis of Western Culture, ed. Jock Stein, Edinburgh: Handsel Press, 1989

The Open Secret, Grand Rapids, Mich.: Wm. B Eerdmans, 1978, 1981

Nida, Eugene Albert, *Message and Mission: The Communication of the Christian Faith*, South Pasadena, Calif.: William Carey Library, 1975

Religion Across Cultures, New York: Harper & Row, 1968

Customs and Cultures, 1954, repr. Pasadena: Wm. Carey Library, 1986

'Communication and Social Structure' in Ralph D. Winter & Steven C. Hawthorne, eds.: *Perspectives on the World Christian Movement: A Reader*, Pasadena: Wm. Carey Library, 1981, 428–443

and William D. Reyburn, *Meaning Across Cultures*, Maryknoll, N.Y.: Orbis Books, 1981

Niebuhr, H. Richard, *Christ and Culture*, New York: Harper Colophon Books, 1951, 1975

Radical Monotheism and Western Culture, The Montgomery Lectures, 1957. New York: Harper & Brothers, 1960

Niranjana, Tejaswini, *Siting Translation: History, Post-Structuralism, and the Colonial Context*, Berkeley & Los Angeles: University of California Press, 1992

Northrop, F.S.C., *The Meeting of East and West: An Inquiry Concerning World Understanding*, New York: Collier Books; London: Collier-Macmillan, 1960. Repr. Woodbridge, Ct.: Ox Bow Press, 1979

Nthamburi, Zablon, 'Toward Indigenization of Christianity in Africa: A Missiological Task' in *International Bulletin of Missionary Research* 13:3 (July 1989): 112–118

Nyembezi, C.L. Sibusiso, *A Review of Zulu Literature*, Pietermaritzburg: University of Natal Press, 1961

O'Brien, Conor Cruise, 'Innocent nation, wicked world' in *Harper's*, April, 1980

O'Connor, Flannery, *The Habit of Being*, New York: Farrar, Straus, Giroux, 1979

Ogletree, Thomas, *The Use of the Bible in Christian Ethics*, Philadelphia: Fortress Press, 1987

Oman, John, *The Natural and the Supernatural*, Cambridge: Cambridge University Press, 1931

Onoge, Obafume F., 'The Counterrevolutionary Tradition in African Studies: The Case of Applied Anthropology' in Gerrit Huizer & Bruce Mannheim, eds. *The Politics of Anthropology*, The Hague: Mouton, 1979

Orwell, George, *A Collection of Essays*, New York: Harcourt Brace Jovanovich, 1953

Padilla, C. Rene, 'The Contextualization of the Gospel' in *Journal of Theology for Southern Africa* 24 (September 1978): 12–30

Pan, James Ying-kau, *Cultural Presuppositions in the Religious Thought of Arnold J. Toynbee, Hendrik Kraemer and H. Richard Niebuhr: With Reference to the Encounter of Christian Faith and Other Faiths*, Edinburgh: University of Edinburgh, unpublished Ph.D. thesis, 1970 (microfilm copy of abstract of thesis)

Pannenberg, Wolfhart, ed., *Revelation as History*, New York: Macmillan, 1969

Pascal, Blaise, *Pensées*, New York: Penguin Books, 1987

Paz, Octavio, 'Edith Piaf Among the Pygmies' in *New York Times Book Review*, Sept. 6, 1987

Pedersen, Holger, *The Discovery of Language: Linguistic Science in the Nineteenth Century*, trans. John Webster Spargo, Bloomington, Ind.: Indiana University Press, 1959, 1962

Pettifer, Julian and Richard Bradley, *Missionaries*, London: BBC Books, 1990

Phillips, James M., *From the Rising of the Sun: Christians and Society in Contemporary Japan*, Maryknoll, N.Y.: Orbis Books, 1981

Pirenne, Henri, *Mohammed and Charlemagne*, London: Unwin University Books, 1968

Plato, *The Laws* in *The Collected Dialogues*, eds. Edith Hamilton and Huntington Cairns, New York: Pantheon Books for Bollingen Foundation, 1961

The Republic in *The Collected Dialogues*, eds. Edith Hamiton and Huntington Cairns, New York: Pantheon Books for Bollingen Foundation, 1961

Poggi, Vincenzo and Patrick J. Ryan, *Islam and Culture*, Rome: Centre 'Cultures and Religions', Pontifical Gregorian University, 1984

Polanyi, Michael, *Personal Knowledge*, Chicago: University of Chicago Press, 1958

The Tacit Dimension, London, 1966

Powles, Cyril H., 'Christianity in the Third World: How Do We Study Its History?' in *Studies in Religion/Sciences Réligieuses* 13:2 (1984): 131–144

Presler, Titus, '*Christianity Rediscovered*: A Reflection on Vincent Donovan's Contribution to Missiology' in *Missiology: An International Review* 18:3 (July 1990): 267–276

Quiller-Couch, Arthur, *On the Art of Reading: Lectures Delivered in the University of Cambridge*, Cambridge: Cambridge University Press, 1920

Radice, Betty, ed. and trans., *The Letters of Pliny the Younger*, New York: Penguin Books, 1969, 1985

Randall, Robert L., 'Ministers and Churches at Risk' in *The Christian Century*, vol. 108, no. 34. Nov. 20–27, 1991. 1093–95

Rauschenbusch, Walter, *A Theology for the Social Gospel*, New York: Macmillan, 1918

Reichley, A. James, *Religion in American Public Life*, Washington, DC: Brookings Institution, 1985

Reindorf, Carl Christian, *The History of the Gold Coast and Asante*, Basel, 1889

Richardson, Don, 'Do Missionaries Destroy Cultures?' in Ralph D. Winter & Steven C. Hawthorne, eds.: *Perspectives on the World Christian Movement: A Reader*, Pasadena, Calif.: Wm. Carey Library, 1981, 482–493

Roberts, Julian, *Walter Benjamin*, Atlantic Highlands, N.J.: Humanities Press, 1983

Robertson, A.T., *A Short Grammar of the Greek New Testament*

Rolleston, Thomas William, *Life of Gotthold Ephraim Lessing*, London, 1889

Roof, Wade Clark, ed., *World Order and Religion*, Albany: State University of New York Press, 1991

Rouner, Leroy S., *To Be At Home: Christianity, Civil Religion, and World Community*, Boston: Beacon Press, 1991

Rupp, George, *Commitment and Community*, Minneapolis: Fortress Press, 1989

Rushdie, Salman, *The Satanic Verses*, London and New York: Viking Penguin, 1988

Ruskin, John, *The Art Criticism of John Ruskin*, ed. and abridged Robert L. Herbert, New York: Da Capo Press, 1964

Russell, Bertrand, *Autobiography*, London: Unwin Paperbacks, 1975, repr. 1989

Ryle, Gilbert, *The Concept of Mind*, London: Hutchinson, 1949, repr. Penguin Books, 1980

Saitoti, Tepilit Ole and Carol Beckwith, *Maasai*, New York: Abradale Press of Harry N. Abrams, Inc., Times Mirror Publishers, 1980

Salehi, M.M., *Insurgency Through Culture and Religion: The Islamic Revolution of Iran*, New York: Praeger, 1988

Sanneh, Lamin, 'Christian Mission in the Pluralist Milieu: The African Experience' in *International Review of Mission* 74:294 (April 1985): 199–211

'Source and Influence: Towards a Comparative Study of Religion and Culture in Africa' in Merry I. White and Susan Pollak, eds., *The Cultural Transition*, London: Routledge & Kegan Paul, 1986

'Pluralism and the Plausibility of Faith' in *The Christian Century*, January 31, 1990

'American Ideals and Muslim Faith in the Gulf Conflict' in *The Christian Century*, January 2–9, 1991

'Religion and Politics: Third World Perspectives on a Comparative Religious Theme' in *Daedalus*, Journal of the American Academy of Arts and Sciences, Summer, 1991

'Modern Education among Freetown Muslims and the Christian Stimulus' in Richard Gray, E. Fashole-Luke, Adrian Hastings & Goodwin Tasie, eds., *Christianity in Independent Africa*, London: Rex Collins, Bloomington, Ind.: Indiana University Press, 1978

'Christian Missions and the Western Guilt Complex' in *The Christian Century*, April 8, 1987

Translating the Message: The Missionary Impact on Culture, Maryknoll, N.Y.: Orbis Books, 1989, 1990

West African Christianity: The Religious Impact, Maryknoll, N.Y.: Orbis Books, 1983, 1990

'The Yogi and the Commissar: Christian Missions and the African Response' in *International Bulletin of Missionary Research*, January 1991

Saunders, George R., ed., *Culture and Christianity: The Dialectics of Transformation*, New York: Greenwood Press, 1988

Schilder, Klaas, *Christ and Culture*, trans. G. van Rongen and W. Helder, Winnipeg:Premier, 1977

Schiller, Friedrich, *Über naive und sentimentalische Dichtung*, 1796

Schlesinger, Arthur Jr., *The Disuniting of America: Reflections on a Multicultural Society*, New York: W.W. Norton & Co., 1992

'The Opening of the American Mind' in *The New York Times Book Review*, July 23, 1989

Schopenhauer, Arthur, *The World as Will and Representation*, 2 vols. trans. E. F. J. Payne, New York: Dover, 1958, 1969

Scriptures of the World, London, New York, and Stuttgart: United Bible Societies, 1984

Scriven, Charles, *The Transformation of Culture: Christian Social Ethics After H. Richard Niebuhr*, Scottsdale, Pa.: Herald Press, 1988

Searle, Hugh, 'Choice Between restoration and rebirth' in *Church Times*, 10 July, 1992

Shorter, Aylward, *Toward a Theology of Inculturation*, Maryknoll, N.Y.: Obis Books, 1988

Showalter, Nathan, *The End of a Crusade: The Student Volunteer Movement For Foreign Missions and the Great War*, unpublished Th.D. dissertation, Cambridge, MA.: Harvard Divinity School, 1990

Simmel, Georg, *Schopenhauer and Nietzsche*, trans. Helmut Loiskandl, Deena Weinstein & Michael Weinstein, Urbana: University of Illinois Press, 1991

Smart, Ninian and Steven Konstantine, *Systematic Theology in a World Context*, London: HarperCollins, 1991

Smith, Edwin W., *The Golden Stool: Some Aspects of the Conflict of Cultures in Modern Africa*, London: Holborn Publishing House, 1926

In the Mother Tongue, London: British and Foreign Bible Society, 1930

The Life and Times of Daniel Lindley (1801–80), London: The Epworth Press, 1949

Robert Moffat, One of God's Gardeners, London: Student Christian Movement, 1925

Smith, Robert C. and John Lounibos, eds., *Pagan and Christian Anxiety: A Response to E.R. Dodds*, Lanham, Md.: University Press of America, 1984

Smith, Wilfred Cantwell, 'Philosophia, as One of the Religious Traditions of Humankind: The Greek Legacy in Western Civilization Viewed by a Comparativist' in *Différences valeurs hiérarchie: textes offerts à Louis Dumont*, ed. Jean-Claude Galey, Paris: École des Hautes Études en Sciences Sociales, 1984

Towards a World Theology: Faith and the Comparative History of Religion, Maryknoll, N.Y.: Orbis Books, 1989

'Sodomy Law Opposed' in *The Christian Century*, vol. 108, no. 24. Aug. 21–28, 1992. 769–770

Stackhouse, Max L., *Creeds, Society and Human Rights*, Grand Rapids: Wm. B. Eerdmans, 1984

Stamoolis, James J., *Eastern Orthodox Mission Theology Today*, Maryknoll, N.Y.: Orbis Books, 1986

Staniforth, Maxwell, trans. and ed., *Early Christian Writings: The Apostolic Fathers*, New York: Penguin Books, 1968, 1982

Steiner, George, *Real Presences: The Leslie Stephen Memorial Lecture*, Cambridge: Cambridge University Press, 1986. Published as a book London: Faber & Faber, 1989

Language and Silence: Essays on Language, Literature and the Inhuman, New York: Atheneum, 1970

Steiner, T.R., *English Translation Theory: 1650–1800*, Assen/Amsterdam; Van Gorcum, 1975

Steinmetz, Paul B., *Pipe, Bible and Peyote Among the Ogala Lakota*, Stockholm Studies in Comparative Religion, Stockholm: University of Stockholm, 1980

Stine, Philip C., ed. *Bible Translation and the Spread of the Church: The Last 200 Years*, Leiden, New York, Copenhagen, and Cologne: E.J. Brill, 1990

Stirner, Max, *The Ego and His Own*, 1845

Strachey, Lytton, *Eminent Victorians*, New York: Modern Library, 1918

Takenaka, Masao, *God is Rice: Asian Culture and Christian Faith*, Geneva: World Council of Churches Risk Book Series, 1986

Talbi, Mohamed, 'Possibilities and Conditions for a Better Understanding Between Islam and the West' in *Journal of Ecumenical Studies*, 25:2 (Spring 1988): 161–193

Tamney, Joseph B., *Resilience of Christianity in the Modern World*, Albany: State University of New York Press, 1992

Tamrat, Taddesse, *Church and State in Ethiopia: 1270–1527*, Oxford: Clarendon Press, 1972

Tawney, R.H., *The Radical Tradition: Twelve Essays on Politics, Education & Literature*, London: Penguin Books, 1966

Thomas, Keith, *Religion and the Decline of Magic*, New York: Charles Scribner's Sons, 1971

Tillich, Paul, *Theology of Culture*, New York: Oxford Galaxy Book, 1959, 1969

Toniolo, Elias and Richard Hill, eds., *The Opening of the Nile Basin: Writings by Members of the Catholic Mission to Central Africa on the Geography and Ethnography of the Sudan: 1842–1881*, London: Christopher Hurst & Co., 1974

Toumlin, S.E. and J. Goodfield, *The Fabric of the Heavens*, London:

Hutchinson, 1961
Toynbee, Arnold J., *Christianity Among the Religions of the World*, New York: Charles Scribner's Sons, 1957
Christianity and Civilisation, London: Student Christian Movement Press, 1940
Civilization on Trial, New York: Oxford University Press, 1948
An Historian's Approach to Religion, London and New York: Oxford University Press, 1956
Trevor-Roper, Hugh, 'The Paracelsian Movement' in *Renaissance Essays*, Chicago: Chicago University Press, 1985
Religion, the Reformation, and Social Change, London: Macmillan, 1967
Trimingham, J. Spencer, *Christianity Among the Arabs in Pre-Islamic Times*, London: Longman; Beirut: Libraire du Liban, 1979
Troeltsch, Ernst, *The Absoluteness of Christianity and the History of Religions*, trans. David Reid, Richmond: John Knox Press, 1971
Religion in History, Minneapolis, Minn.: Fortress Press, 1991
Turgenev, Ivan, *Fathers and Children*, 1861
Tuveson, Ernest, *Redeemer Nation: The Idea of America's Millennial Role*, Chicago: University of Chicago Press, 1968
Twain, Mark, 'Mark Twain on American Imperialism' in *The Atlantic*, vol. 269, no. 4, April 1992. 49–65

Ullendorf, Edward, *Ethiopia and the Bible*, London: Oxford University Press, 1988
Uzukwu, Elochukwu E., ed., *Religion and African Culture*, Enugu: Spiritan Publications, 1988

van Buren, Paul, *Discerning the Way*, New York, Seabury Press, 1980
Vilakazi, Absalom, *Zulu Transformations: A Study of the Dynamics of Social Change*, Pietermaritzburg: University of Natal Press, 1962

Waldenfels, Hans, 'On the Hermeneutics of Intercultural Encounter: Christianity and Chinese Thought: A Case Study' in *Studies in Interreligious Dialogue*, vol. 2, no. 1, 1992
Walhout, Donald, 'The Culturally Conditioned Christian' in *Religion in Life* 30:2 (Spring 1961): 279–284
Walker, D.P., *Spiritual and Demonic Magic: From Ficino to Campanella*, London: The Warburg Institute, University of London, 1958
Wallace-Hadrill, John Michael, *The Frankish Church*, Oxford: Clarendon Press, 1983
Walls, Andrew F., 'Culture and Coherence in Christian History' in *Evangelical Review of Theology* 9:3 (July 1985): 214–225
'The Gospel as the Prisoner and Liberator of Culture' in *Faith and Thought* 108, nos. 1–2, 1981
'The Legacy of David Livingstone' in *International Bulletin of Missionary Research*, July, 1987
Walsh, Brian J., 'The Transformation of Culture: A Review Essay' in *Conrad Grebel Review* 7:3 (Fall 1989): 253–267

Weltin, E. G. *Athens and Jerusalem: An Interpretative Essay on Christianity and Classical Culture*, Atlanta: Scholars Press, 1987.

Wendon, John, 'Christianity, History, and Mr. Toynbee' in *Journal of Religion* 36:3 (1956): 139–149

Westermann, Diedrich, 'The Place and Function of the Vernacular in African Education' in *International Review of Mission*, January 1925

Whitehead, Raymond L., 'Christ and Cultural Imperialism' in *Justice as Mission: An Agenda for the Church*, eds. Christopher Lind and Terry Brown, Burlington, Ontario, Canada: Trinity Press, 1985. 24–34

Wightman, W.P.D., *Science in a Renaissance Society*, London: Hutchinson University Library, 1972

Williams, Bernard, *Ethics and the Limits of Philosophy*, Cambridge, Mass.: Harvard University Press, 1985

Williams, John, *A Narrative of Missionary Enterprises in the South Sea Islands*, New York: D. Appleton & Co., 1838

Wilson, F. Paul, Letter to the editor in *New York Times Book Review*, Aug. 13, 1989

Winckelmann, *Werke*, Dresden, 1808–25

Wolff, Kurt, ed. and trans., *The Sociology of Georg Simmel*, New York: The Free Press; London: Collier-Macmillan, 1950; paperback, 1964

Wright, Robert, 'Quest for the Mother Tongue: Is the Search for an Ancestor of All Modern Languages Sober Science or Simple Romanticism?' in *The Atlantic*, April 1991, 39–68

Yannoulatos, Anastasios, 'Culture and Gospel: Some Observations From the Orthodox Tradition and Experience' in *International Review of Mission* 74:294 (Spring 1985): 185–198

Ywahoo, Dhyani, *Voices of Our Ancestors: Cherokee Teachings from the Wisdom Fire*, Boston and London: Shambhala Publications, 1987

Index